THE GROUP PROBLEM SOLVING PROCESS

Studies of a Valence Model

L. Richard Hoffman

PRAEGER

PRAEGER SPECIAL STUDIES • PRAEGER SCIENTIFIC

Library of Congress Cataloging in Publication Data
Main entry under title:

The Group problem solving process.

Bibliography: p.
Includes index.
1. Problem solving, Group--Addresses, essays, lectures. I. Hoffman, L. Richard, 1930-
HM133.G75 301.18'5 79-12518
ISBN 0-03-047636-4

To

Norman R. F. Maier

PRAEGER PUBLISHERS
PRAEGER SPECIAL STUDIES
383 Madison Avenue, New York, N.Y. 10017, U.S.A.

Published in the United States of America in 1979
by Praeger Publishers,
A Division of Holt, Rinehart and Winston, CBS, Inc.

9 038 98765432

Printed in the United States of America

PREFACE

This book is dedicated to the late Dr. Norman R. F. Maier for reasons that go well beyond the subject matter of the book. More than any other psychologist Norm shaped the positive aspects of my professional life. His own career as a psychologist was a model of unstinting dedication to the discovery of psychological principles through empirical observation. This reliance on the data led him to challenge the dominant theories in such diverse areas as brain functioning, learning theory, and psychopathology. Even in his promotion of participative management in organizations (Maier 1952; 1963), he deviated from the mainstream by emphasizing the need for developing skills in group leadership if participation is to work effectively. His courageous willingness to stand alone in these deviant positions was personally costly, and we can only be grateful that he failed to succumb to the rewards of conformity. His contributions to psychology are just beginning to be appreciated, and the quality of his work makes even his early research relevant today in many instances.

The extensive references to his work in this book reflect the particular intellectual debt I owe Norm Maier for his pioneering work on group problem solving. His insights and inventiveness in developing techniques for improving the effectiveness of problem-solving groups were unique. I feel privileged in having had the opportunity to collaborate with him and to share those insights. The basic concepts of the valence model stem directly from that collaboration, even though he was very dubious about our initial forays into the morass of process observation required to operationalize the concept. Although I believe that this work owes its origins to Norm Maier, whatever failings there are in either concept or implementation are, of course, my own.

There are a number of other people whose contributions to this work can only partly be recognized by their coauthorships or mention in footnotes. For the past four years Dr. Kenneth Friend has been helping me hone my thinking about valence and has provided encouragement, statistical insight, and computer sophistication without which most of the work on the Personnel Selection Problem would never have been accomplished. Dr. Gary Bond, too, has been an able, insightful, and patient collaborator during these past few years. My students over the years, at both Michigan and Chicago, have been indispensable sources of stimulation and gratification. The stimulation has come typically from an initial doubt and suspicion about the validity of the valence model, and the gratification from their ultimate conversion and enthusiasm for it. Several of the articles in this volume originated that way. I am very grateful to all of them for taking the risk of investing in the valence model and learning the valence coding method, when its general acceptance has been so problematic. Most recently Karyl Kinsey and Richard Pearse have started down that path, and were instrumental in the analyses of the data in several of these articles. Both are also collaborating with me on extensions of the model to new phenomena.

There is a standard joke in academic circles that a good secretary is worth two research assistants. In the case of my secretary, Mary Woolridge, it is no joke—and the number of equivalent research assistants is closer to five. Her outstanding efforts in bringing this book to fruition are the culmination of many years of performing miracles to save my professional life, for which I can never thank her enough. Thank you, thank you, thank you, Mary.

My daughter, Elizabeth, rose to the occasion by organizing the references and by recruiting her friends to help in the data analysis.

Finally, I want to thank the many friends who offered me encouragement and help during this period and who tolerated my abandonment of them during the total immersion of the final months of completion.

ACKNOWLEDGMENTS

The following publishers have generously given me permission to reprint articles I have previously published in their journals:

Journal Press:

L. R. Hoffman. "Conditions for Creative Problem Solving," Journal of Psychology 52 (1961): 429-44.

American Psychological Association:

L. R. Hoffman and Norman R. F. Maier, "Valence in the Adoption of Solutions by Problem-Solving Groups: Concept, Method, and Results," Journal of Abnormal and Social Psychology 69 (1964): 264-71.

______, "Valence in the Adoption of Solutions by Problem-Solving Groups: II. Quality and Acceptance as Goals of Leaders and Members," Journal of Personality and Social Psychology 6 (1967): 175-82.

Psychological Reports:

Reprinted with permission of publisher from
L. R. Hoffman, R. J. Burke, and N. R. F. Maier, "Participation, Influence, and Satisfaction Among Members of Problem-Solving Groups," Psychological Reports 16 (1965): 661-67.

Permission to reproduce the Change of Work Procedures Problem was granted by John Wiley and Sons.

Support for the early stages of this research came from U.S. Public Health Service Grant no. MH-02704 to Norman Maier. Later studies have benefited from small grants from the University of Chicago Graduate School of Business and Social Science Division research committees.

CONTENTS

LIST OF TABLES

LIST OF FIGURES

INTRODUCTION

The studies reported here are focused on a single issue: the process by which groups adopt solutions to problems. In that sense they are narrowly conceived, since they ignore many other aspects of problem solving in groups. I justify their presentation in this form on several grounds.

While there have been many attempts to provide a systematic theory of the group problem-solving process (such as Bales and Strodtbeck 1951; Maier 1963; Davis 1973; Fisher 1974), these have been inadequate for a variety of reasons. The model of R. F. Bales and F. L. Strodtbeck offered an innovative derivation from Bales's equilibrium process (1953), but ignored the content of the problem-solving discussion. N. R. F. Maier probed most deeply into the process, gave us many insights into the interrelationships between task and maintenance functions in groups, and focused our attention on the skills that leaders and members need to function effectively on both dimensions. However, his principles (see Maier 1963, chap. 9) of effective group problem solving were never organized into a coherent theory. B. A. Fisher, too, has formulated some descriptive dimensions of problem-solving groups, which are closest in form to the intent of the valence model presented here. However, he neither theoretically nor empirically helps us understand why groups function as they do.

Therefore, the principal justification for these studies is that they illuminate an aspect of the problem-solving process that has never been studied directly and systematically before. Inferences about the process from traditional input-outcome experiments are imprecise (Maier 1963), often limited for use in effecting interventions into the process (Hollander 1978), and possibly even inaccurate in depicting the process as it really occurs (Davis 1973).

Another advantage of the approach derived from the studies to be presented here is the precision with which it identifies movement in the problem-solving process. Both the stability of and the regular variations in the solution valence-adoption process provide a basis for extending our understanding of the concomitants and precursors of that process. Just as the regularity of the participation structure in groups has permitted the study of variations in status structures (Berger, Cohen, and Zelditch 1972), so leadership, decision rules, and other matters may be studied in their impact on the solution valence-adoption process. Third, the solution-valence phenomena can best be appreciated when the studies are seen together, rather than in the single-article form in which several have already appeared. Only by comparing the results of one study with those of the next can one appreciate both the consistency of the findings and the predictable effects that different experimental variations have on the valence-indexed process. By presenting the studies from their origins in the theoretical paper, "Conditions for Creative Problem Solving," and following their evolution through the answers to a number of questions raised by each succeeding study, readers will become aware of the far-reaching import of the phenomena, identify the limits, and, it is hoped, be stimulated to explore related issues.

The book starts with the original theoretical presentation of the valence concept, adapted from Kurt Lewin (1935) to the problem-solving process. While that article was written to provide the theoretical underpinnings for a dialectical model of the creative uses of conflict, the first empirical tests of the model revealed very little conflict in most groups, as conflict was defined in that model. Rather, as shown repeatedly, in groups with leaders and in leaderless groups working on various problems, a solution valence-adoption process appeared rather regularly. Those studies are reported in Part II. Since there has been some confusion among the readers of written and the hearers of oral presentations concerning the solution-valence concept—mostly about its relationship to mere discussion of the solutions—there is a note in Part II that attempts to differentiate between valence and mere discussion.

The studies in Part III are concerned with the effects of the solution-valence process on members' commitment to their group's decisions. While the solution-adoption process seems to be an emergent group phenomenon, commitment to the decision has a strong individual character. However, this may be an artifact of the laboratory situation, as suggested by M. W. Block's study of cohesiveness as a determinant of commitment. How much influence members exercise over the decision is also distinguished from their mere participation in the discussion, in order to reveal an important difference between these two aspects of members' activities in the group.

Finally, extensions of the solution valence-adoption process have been begun in studies of normative conflict and decision rules. The results of those studies, in combination with the earlier ones, suggest a more elaborate model than the one presented originally, with theoretical and methodological implications for studies of group problem solving.

It is hoped that the many questions raised by reading these chapters will stimulate other investigators to help clarify the process further. For that reason I have included the methods used in our studies as appendixes.

PART I

THE INITIAL VALENCE MODEL

1

CONDITIONS FOR CREATIVE PROBLEM SOLVING

L. Richard Hoffman

PURPOSE

Duncan (1959) concluded his review of recent research on problem solving by pointing to some major gaps in the area. One of the gaps is a lack of adequate theory due to "unanalyzed and nondimensionalized variables" and to the "great variety of tasks to provide problems" for research. These are certainly justifiable complaints. Little progress has been made in problem-solving theory since John Dewey's description of the creative process: (1) the feeling of unease or dissatisfaction, (2) identification of the problem, (3) establishing hypotheses, (4) logical or empirical verification, (5) acceptance of the conclusion. This description offers a systematic approach to the creative process, but it lacks an explanation of when unease is felt, for example, or how hypotheses are generated; and thus tells us little about how creative problem solving might be encouraged.

The present paper is an attempt to fill part of the theoretical gap in problem solving with respect to a limited set of tasks. The

---

Received in the editorial office on July 31, 1961, and published immediately at Provincetown, Massachusetts. Copyright by The Journal Press.

This paper was written as part of a project supported by U.S. Public Health Service research grant M-2704 from the National Institute of Mental Health, Public Health Service. The author expresses grateful appreciation to Norman R. F. Maier and Helen Peak for their constructive comments on the paper.

framework to be used rests heavily on the creative thinking and research of Maier (1930; 1931; 1932), Duncker (1945), and Wertheimer (1945) in this area. Limiting the discussion to particular types of problems precludes any attempt to integrate all the various studies that have been called problem solving. Further, there are certainly conditions under which creative problem solving will occur other than those to be stated.

The purpose of the article is to present a framework capable of explaining the results of a number of studies, of suggesting next steps for research on the problem-solving process, and of pointing to the types of techniques that should be developed to enhance creative problem solving. The theory appears applicable equally to individual and group problem solving and even, possibly, to problem solving at the societal level.

The paper will present the conditions for creative problem solving and illustrate their usefulness in explaining the results of some selected studies.

CREATIVE PROBLEM SOLVING: A DEFINITION

Before stating the conditions for creative problem solving, a definition of the term is needed. Following Wertheimer (1945) and Maier (1933), creative problem solving is the process of forming a solution pattern that is a combination of previously dissociated experiences. These experiences may have been thought of previously as incompatible or irrelevant, or they may never have been considered together prior to the problem-solving situation. The new solution pattern is more than merely an abstraction from the elements of the "experiences," but is in fact a new organization of them, an organization that combines the elements of the experiences in a new and different way. In most cases the elements of the creative solution will bear different relations to each other than they did in their presolution organization. For example, Newton's gravitational principles put apples and cannonballs in a relation to each other they had never had before.

Despite the importance society attaches to creativity, the progress of research appears to require that the product of creative problem solving be evaluated presently only with reference to the person or group doing the problem solving. It is creative when it is new for the individual, regardless of how new it is for society. Anderson (1959, p. 261) has termed this type of definition "internal locus of evaluation," as distinct from "external evaluation." Bartlett's definition of thinking is also consistent with the present one: "the use of any contributory sources of evidence that are available to reach a terminal point which is treated as if it had not been achieved before . . . (1958, p. 74).

Although these definitions of creative problem solving combine societal inventions with childhood discoveries, they seem fruitful in helping us learn about creativity in as many situations as possible, after which we might apply this knowledge to situations that are potentially societally creative. The definition also implies that everyone is creative or potentially so. And this is probably true, although we shall see from the conditions to be stated why most of us are not creative.

CONDITIONS FOR CREATIVE PROBLEM SOLVING

The following conditions appear to be necessary for creative problem solving, as defined above.

Condition 1. Differing, but comparable, cognitions must coexist. The general term "cognition" is used here to indicate any type of ideation, such as the definition of a problem, the "direction" or approach to solving the problem, a solution to the problem, or even a fact or an interpretation of a fact. The cognitions should be comparable with respect to the aspect of the problem for which they are relevant, such as the definition of the problem or the interpretation of facts. Thus, while two different proposed solutions to a problem satisfy condition 1, a solution to a problem and a definition of the problem do not. The former condition may result in a creative solution, but the latter will not unless an additional and different solution to, or definition of, the problem emerges. In this way the incongruity concept of Osgood, Suci, and Tannenbaum (1957) is appropriate for defining "differing cognitions," as are similar concepts like Festinger's "dissonance" (1957) and Peak's "disparity" (1955; 1958), although at a somewhat more molecular level than is usually considered in problem-solving research. In terms of the above definition of problem solving, these differing cognitions would be the "previously dissociated experiences."

In a group setting, satisfaction of condition 1 would entail at least two contributions concerning a problem, ordinarily from different group members. Such contributions commonly take the form of potential solutions. For example, a department head might be concerned that the department was not turning out production as fast as the demand for the product warranted. At a meeting of the staff, the head might suggest the elimination of certain of the more expensive parts of the production operation in favor of a faster rate. A junior member of the staff might counter with the suggestion that quality should be maintained at all costs, and that, since quality takes time, the production rate will have to be sacrificed for quality considerations. Here are two differing cognitions, different solutions to a problem.

Condition 1 may be diagrammed, as shown below, by two opposing arrows to indicate the differences between two ideas.

The representation of these two ideas by opposing lines foretells the concept of the valence of a cognition,* which must be introduced before going on to condition 2. Valence is used here, analogously to Lewin's usage with respect to the attraction of goals (1935), to represent the degree of acceptability a cognition may have for a problem-solving unit, that is, the likelihood that it will be accepted by the unit, be it individual or group. Positive valence would indicate an acceptable cognition, and negative valence an unacceptable cognition. A cognition may acquire positive valence from a variety of sources, and the effects of these sources may be presumed to accumulate to increase the valence of the cognition.

A cognition may have positive valence for an individual as a function of the amount of past learning about the subject, the frequency of past experience with the cognition, the number of facts perceived to support the cognition, the degree to which the cognition fits in with other knowledge or attitudes held, the extent to which one "needs" to hold this cognition as a function of personal motive structure, and so on.

At the group level, the concept of valence may be translated to mean the degree to which a suggestion by a group member is acceptable to all members of the group. Although a solution will have different valence for each group member at any point in the discussion—even, presumably, at the time of final decision—since a group usually is asked for and produces a single solution, it is useful to think of the valence of any solution for the group as a whole. Group valence may turn out empirically to be merely some combination of individual valences, but this does not destroy the utility of considering it as a concept at the group level.

---

*Originally this concept was called "potency," to represent the positive force an idea usually exerts on a group. The seemingly identical properties of "potency" and Lewin's valence concept have caused the author to adopt the valence terminology in the interest of saving psychology one more idiosyncratic term.

Substituting the word "group" for "individual" in the above listing of sources of positive valence, these sources also act at the group level. In addition, the following sources of positive valence in a group setting come to mind: the persuasiveness of the person presenting an idea, the total power of the person making the suggestion in the group, the enthusiasm with which the suggestion is made, the degree of support for the suggestion in the group, and so on. For example, in the above illustration, the department head's suggestion has positive valence by virtue of his formal position in the organization. We may assume that the subordinate's suggestion would thereby have less positive valence. The department head's suggestion may acquire further positive valence if the rest of the subordinates are a group of "yes men," or if the head seems to be enthusiastic about his suggestion, or if the head was particularly persuasive in presenting his idea. If the valence of the department head's idea were based on all of these sources, it would then be so great as to overwhelm the countersuggestion of the subordinate and the group would decide to eliminate the unnecessary operations. This situation is diagrammed below.

Department Head Subordinate

On the other hand, if the department head's suggestion were seen as a threat by the group, the resulting defensiveness might focus their support for the countersuggestion, or the subordinate might have been extremely persuasive, or facts might be marshaled to support the subordinate's proposal in opposition to the initial one. The force picture would thereby be changed, and the group would decide to maintain the present form of operation, as shown below.

Department Head Subordinate

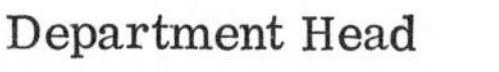

In other words, the valence of an idea acts as a force and, as in Lewin's model of conflict resolution (1935), the idea with the greatest positive valence is adopted. Of course, the valence of an idea is not a fixed value and may change during the problem-solving process, either increasing as new facts are offered to support the proposition or enthusiasm is generated for it, or decreasing as the support of the group moves to other alternatives.

If the valence of all alternatives remains small—nobody is particularly enthusiastic about any of the ideas—apathy may result and no decision may be reached. The existence of such conditions necessitates a minimum threshold concept, such that at least one alternative must acquire valence beyond this minimum for a group to arrive at any decision. When all alternatives have low valence, the mere suggestion "Let's do 'A' so we take some kind of action" will give "A" enough positive valence for the group to agree to take that action. It is probable, however, that the type of acceptance, that is, willingness and enthusiasm to carry out the decision, usually posited to accompany the process of group decision (as in Maier 1952; Coch and French 1948) can be achieved only when the valence of the alternative finally agreed upon is considerably greater than the minimum threshold level, and/or the solution has substantially higher than minimum valence for all the group members. Such a high value would reflect the group's identification with and enthusiasm and support for the agreed-upon decision.

The elaboration of the valence concept and the description of its mode of operation are essential as a prelude to the second condition necessary for creative problem solving.

Condition 2. At least two differing cognitions must acquire greater positive valence than the minimum threshold value (but less than some maximum value, which will be discussed in condition 3) and must be approximately equal in value, so that none of the alternatives can be accepted and an impasse is reached. The rationale for the desirability of an impasse between cognitions rests on the assumption that if two cognitions are equally desirable, yet neither is acceptable, there are advantages and disadvantages regarding, or facts supporting, each. The creative solution to such a problem would exploit the advantages of both alternatives and minimize the disadvantages, or would incorporate the seemingly incompatible facts supporting the several alternatives. To achieve such a solution would require the type of restructuring that Wertheimer has discussed (1945).

Simpson (1960) has provided us with an example of such a creative solution in the realm of evolutionary theory. He points to neo-Darwinism, the natural selection process, and mutationism as the current fact-supported theories of evolution. The two theories, however, have been offered as contradictory explanations of the process of evolution. Neo-Darwinism proposes that evolution is an adaptive selective process, while mutationism suggests that adaptive changes occur randomly, with the nonadaptive mutants dying off. Simpson concludes that "Mutationism is not an alternative to Neo-Darwinism but a supplement of it . . . if the actual course of evolution is to a large extent adaptive, then some additional factor or process must frequently intervene between the occurrence of mutations and the incorporation of some of them into evolving populations. . . . Natural selection is just a process, and . . . is in large part a synthesis of selection theory and mutation theory."

Thus, opposing fact-supported theories are reconciled into a single, more elaborate theory that encompasses both sets of facts.

Impasses, however, have been known to cause breakdowns in problem-solving conferences. Precontract negotiation conferences between labor and management frequently result in impasses, followed by collapse of negotiations and strikes.

The three problem-solving situations described above—the single prepotent cognition, the apathetic, and the impasse—are diagrammed in Figure 1.1 with their probable outcomes. Two possible outcomes are indicated for the impasse condition, no solution or a creative solution. A third possibility is for the situation to regress to the single prepotent cognition state. To account for the emergence of a creative solution rather than a breakdown of problem solving in the impasse situation, a third condition is necessary.

FIGURE 1.1

Problem-Solving Situations and Their Outcomes

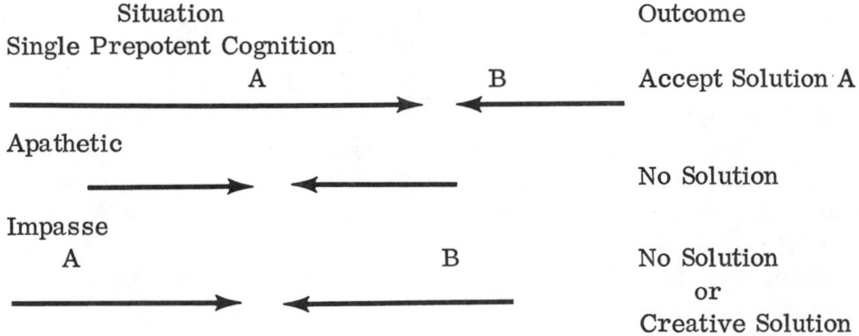

Source: Compiled by the author.

Condition 3. Problem solving must occur in a situation in which the problem-solving unit is required to arrive at the best possible decision.

This requirement may be achieved either through externally imposed requirements, such as by a company president's demand for the best solution from subordinates, or from the needs of the group members themselves, such as to show everyone how bright they are. The requirement to arrive at the best possible decision may be considered as a boundary condition for the problem-solving unit and must therefore be more powerful than the valence of any of the ideas offered. Diagrammatically, Lewin's life space model may be borrowed again to represent this boundary around the problem-solving situation (see below). This boundary must be of sufficient strength to prevent the problem-solving unit from "leaving the field." Condition 3 does not permit the unit to "agree to disagree."

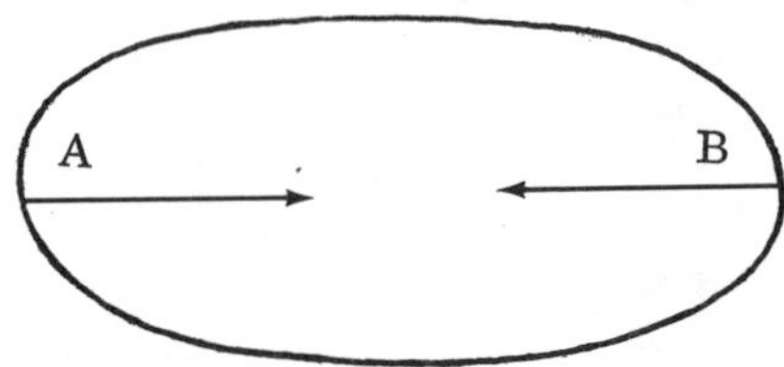

The presence of a requirement to make the best decision may also help to satisfy conditions 1 and 2. Motivation for the best solution should encourage the production of ideas and prevent the premature acceptance of any early suggestions before other possibilities have been explored. Failure to satisfy condition 3 has probably been the source of many people's failure to solve problems adequately. Having arrived at a possible solution to the problem, they do not explore the ramifications of the solution to determine its inadequacies. Or, discovering certain flaws in the solution, they rationalize their acceptance of the inadequate solution by some phrase like "Well, nothing in this world is perfect."

Many breakdowns in labor-management negotiation can probably be traced to a lack of need on the part of one or the other of the parties to arrive at a high-quality solution to the problem. For example, management may feel it is able to tolerate a strike since it has stockpiled sufficient inventory to supply the needs of its customers for a considerable period. Or labor may recognize that seasonal layoffs are about to occur anyway and they have nothing to lose by striking.

The postulation in condition 3 of the existence of a force field toward arriving at a best solution places an upper limit on the valence of any of the alternatives being considered. Where the valence of any of the alternatives exceeds this upper bound, it must be reduced if a creative solution is to emerge. Otherwise this highly valent solution will be accepted before the creative solution is discovered. Often, in practical group situations, such high valence reflects extreme emotional identification with the idea on the part of one of the parties, for example, defensive behavior. If the emotional support for such a proposal is reduced, for example, by the two-column method (Maier, Solem, and Maier 1957), a balance of valences frequently can be achieved at a manageable level—that is, in the range between the minimum threshold level and the level of the force toward solution. The problem can then be restructured and a creative solution developed. The need to arrive at a best decision may help a group member to recognize that his/her own first suggestion may not always be the best one.

For example, in the hypothetical situation offered previously, where the department head suggested a speeding up of operations and one of the subordinates insisted on maintaining quality, the discussion may have progressed to the point where each of these suggestions had equal valence. The department head should then have reidentified the problem as "how to achieve a higher rate of production while maintaining an adequate level of quality." The solution to such a problem would probably result in the elimination of certain parts of the present production process as well as suggestions for its reorganization. It might be possible in this way to achieve the desired level of production while maintaining the same standards of quality.

The ability of the department head so to rephrase the conflicting alternatives illustrates a fourth condition desirable for creative problem solving.

Condition 4. The cognitive components of the valence of each of the conflicting alternatives should be abstracted and their points of conflict recognized. Although Maier (1931) has shown that a subject need not be able to report the basis for a solution in order to achieve it, awareness of the conflict to be resolved is probably helpful in arriving at a solution. By becoming aware of the conflicting elements of the problem, the subject can adopt a fruitful direction for solving the problem and is in a position to search for variations in these elements that are appropriate for the solution (cf. Wertheimer's "recentering" 1945).

The inability to define the cognitive basis of an impasse situation often defeats the search for a creative solution. In groups, opposing solutions may become inseparable from personal dislike between the people suggesting the solutions, so that a real cognitive conflict is lost by its being seen only as an emotional conflict. Such a situation may deteriorate to the point where the motivation to arrive at a best solution is superseded by motivation to resolve the conflict in the easiest way and leads to the adoption of an inferior solution. Individuals, too, may become discouraged by their inability to determine just what relationship two ideas have to each other and, therefore, accept one alternative in order to escape an uncomfortable situation.

In summary, if the first three conditions of this paper are satisfied, the stage appears to be set for creative problem solving to occur. The problem-solving situation at that point has the following characteristics.

At least two alternative cognitions (such as solutions) have approximately equal positive valence that is sufficient to make either one acceptable. Because their valences are equal, however, neither can be accepted in preference to the other. The problem-solving unit (individual or group) has sufficient need to produce the best possible solution so that it will neither withdraw from the problem nor accept one of the alternatives for the sake of expediency (or for some other reason). Beyond the satisfaction of conditions 1 through 3, a fourth condition has been postulated as desirable, although not necessary for achieving a creative solution. Condition 4 states that when the problem solver is in the situation just described—where conditions 1, 2, and 3 have been satisfied—he/she will be more likely to achieve a creative solution if he/she is able to identify the conflicting cognitions present.

THE RESEARCH EVIDENCE

Some examples from the research literature will illustrate the usefulness of viewing problem solving in terms of these conditions. Unfortunately for the purpose of the review, problem-solving research has been concerned mostly with conditions that prevent successful problem solving, and little with conditions that increase problem-solving effectiveness. Thus, much evidence could be marshaled to show that failure to satisfy the postulated conditions will interfere with creative problem solving, but little evidence is available to substantiate the productive effects of satisfying the conditions. Also, most of the tasks used in these studies do not completely satisfy the definition of creative problem solving being used here, since satisfaction of conditions 1 and 2 is often sufficient for the subjects to attain the solution. Even in these tasks, however, failure to solve the problem or to arrive at the best solution may be due to poor motivation of the subjects in the problem situation, thus not satisfying condition 3.

Luchins' series of Einstellung experiments (1942) using water-bottle problems are interesting in light of the stated conditions. He showed that past experience with a particular method for solving problems caused subjects to use that method in solving problems that could have been solved using a simpler method, and reduced their ability to solve similar problems for which the method was inappropriate. The past experience seemingly blinded subjects to the existence of an alternative method, thus failing to satisfy condition 1 (differing cognitions), and the Einstellung method has sufficient positive valence to be accepted, thus failing to satisfy condition 2 (two equally valent alternatives). Furthermore, most subjects interpreted the experimenter's instructions to find the "best solution" to mean an accurate answer, not necessarily the simplest or most direct answer. Thus condition 3 was not satisfied in most of the experiments. When subjects were given the problems untimed, instructed to look over their work, told to find "a more sensible and more direct solution to the problem," and given experience with a problem having another method for solution, thus presumably satisfying the first three conditions of this paper, recovery from the Einstellung effect was "very good" (Luchins 1942, p. 59, experiment 5).

Duncker's (1945) classic studies of "functional fixedness" illustrate a more specific Einstellung situation that fails to satisfy the conditions. The valence of the object's most common function, especially in the "preutilization conditions," is so great that it surpasses the lower threshold value and is accepted as the sole use of the object. The valence of other functions of the object is presumably below threshold, so the problem cannot be solved.

Flavell, Cooper, and Loiselle's report (1958) shows that the valence of functions other than the "fixed" one can be increased by giving subjects a variety of "non-specialized" preutilization experiences with the object. Their findings suggest that condition 1, at least, was satisfied and resulted in a higher than ordinary proportion of successful problem solutions.

Studies by Rokeach (1960) and Milton (1958), showing that subjects' attitudes may interfere with effective problem solving, may be interpreted as evidence that certain attitudes interfere with the emergence of differing perceptions or orientations to problems, thus failing to satisfy condition 1. Carey's (1958) ability to improve women's problem-solving success, merely by changing their attitudes toward problem solving, tends to support this interpretation.

Hoffman's (1959) and Hoffman and Maier's (1961a) studies of the effects of personality homogeneity and heterogeneity on group problem solving explicitly attempted to satisfy condition 1 in groups. They assumed that people with dissimilar personalities would have a greater variety of perspectives on problems than would people with similar personalities and, therefore, have greater problem-solving success. The consistent problem-solving superiority of the heterogeneous groups confirmed this hypothesis. The fact that none of the other conditions of this paper was controlled in these studies, however, probably accounts for the small differences obtained.

Studies by Torrance (1955), Riecken (1958), and Maier and Solem (1952) show how formal status, "talkativeness," and majority opinion, respectively, may contribute to the valence of incorrect solutions and prevent the acceptance of correct answers—failure to satisfy condition 2.

Torrance showed that in Air Force crews solving Maier's Horse Trading Problem, the status hierarchy was related directly both to the degree to which groups accepted the correct solution held by one of the members, and to the amount of talking by each of the group members. Solutions suggested by low-ranking members rarely acquired enough valence to be accepted by the group.

Riecken's (1958) study of "talkativeness" parallels Torrance's findings in showing that the most talkative group member, regardless of the adequacy of his/her information, exerts considerable influence over the group's decision. Riecken compared the effect of giving a hint concerning the "elegant" (creative) solution to the most talkative versus the least talkative member of groups. The hint was much more often accepted from the most talkative member. Furthermore, Riecken's data suggest that "success in gaining acceptance for the elegant solution (for both high and low talkers) seems to depend, not on amount of opposition aroused, but on amount of support the hint-holder musters," thus offering direct support for the present valence analysis.

Maier and Solem (1952) have shown that a discussion leader may aid in overcoming majority influence. In most of the unled groups, the initial solution held by the majority was retained after group discussion and, where the majority was initially incorrect, few members changed to the correct answer as a result of the discussion. The effect of the discussion leader in helping the group arrive at the correct answer was most marked in those groups where the majority initially had the wrong answer. Maier and Solem interpreted their findings as revealing the discussion leader's effective use of minority opinions (raising their valence) to overcome the influence of the majority.

Another series of studies may be interpreted to show that satisfaction of the first three conditions yields creative problem solutions. These studies used a role-playing problem in which two alternative solutions are favored by people differing in status position and authority. Maier and Hoffman (1960b) showed that groups that solved the problem twice produced a higher proportion of integrative (creative) solutions the second time than the first. Hoffman, Price, and Maier (unpublished data) later showed that this effect was produced in part by an increase in the influence of the low-status group members over the second solution. Presumably the valence of the alternative favored by the low-status members was increased the second time, more nearly equaled the valence of the other alternative, and caused the group to develop a creative solution. Even where the valence of each alternative was high originally, the second problem-solving session permitted other solutions to acquire greater valence as the group was forced to reexamine the problem situation. In a later study using the same problem, Hoffman, Harburg, and Maier (1962) experimentally increased the valence of the low-status members' favored alternative and produced a high proportion of integrative solutions. When conflicting solutions that had approximately equal valence were put into opposition, groups searched for new solutions that incorporated the advantages of each of the original solutions.

Finally, two studies may be cited to show very different reasons why condition 3 (need to arrive at a best decision) may not be satisfied. Typical of the experimental—and probably practical—effects of time pressure is to make "the best decision" a less desirable goal and to allow the subject to be satisfied with a less adequate, sometimes inadequate, solution. In one variation of his Einstellung experiments, Luchins (1942) showed that, when he made the problems a "speed test," the Einstellung effect was greater than in the general study; many subjects submitted the Einstellung solution to the "critical" problem (for which it was inappropriate), and a number of subjects gave up.

However, the need postulated in condition 3 may be unsatisfied, not only because of stronger conflicting needs but also because the situation is not conducive to such motivation. The studies of business decision making by Cyert, Dill, and March (1958) show how the presence of "organizational slack"—a surplus of resources—allowed certain decisions to be accepted without adequate criticism, consideration of other alternatives, or even a definition of the problem to be solved. Motivation to produce a "best decision" (condition 3) was low due to the feeling that the costs of a poor decision could be absorbed by the surplus resources available. Thus failures to satisfy condition 3 caused failures of conditions 1 and 2 and resulted in poor decisions.

IMPLICATIONS AND CONCLUSIONS

Although the evidence presented is certainly not conclusive, these formulations of the necessary conditions seem useful for understanding the results of a variety of studies of problem solving, by both individuals and groups. If satisfaction of these conditions is conducive to creative problem solving, we can now look for behaviors and attitudes that will tend to satisfy the conditions.

Techniques need to be developed to promote these conditions for both individuals and groups. A few successful attempts have been made in this direction. Maier (1933) increased the proportion of successful problem solutions by lecturing subjects to seek for various problem difficulties and to "keep your mind open for new meanings (and) . . . for new combinations." Maltzman and his associates (Maltzman, Brooks, Bogartz, and Summers 1958; Maltzman, Bogartz, and Breger 1958; Maltzman, Simon, Raskin, and Licht 1960) have been orienting subjects toward the same objectives by forcing them to generate unusual (low-valence) associations to common stimuli. These methods appear conducive to establishing condition 1.

Shaw's (1960) results suggest that subjects' motivation to achieve a high-quality product (condition 3) may be increased by increasing their share of responsibility for the group output.

Maier's human relations training course includes various functions a group discussion leader may perform to help assure the satisfaction of these conditions (Maier 1952; 1958). Among these functions are (a) "respect minority opinions"—promotes condition 1 by revealing differing viewpoints; (b) separate the idea-getting process from the idea-evaluating process—promotes condition 2 by allowing all ideas initially to achieve more than minimum positive valence without revealing their possible negative valence; (c) "state the problem in such a manner that there is mutual interest"—promotes condition 3 by assuring that a good solution to the problem is desired by all members of the group.

Research is now under way to operationalize the concepts defining the conditions set forth in this paper and to test the adequacy of the formulations of the conditions. The evidence cited suggests that such effort may be rewarded in giving psychologists greater understanding of the problem-solving process and greater success in producing more creative solutions to problems.

2

VALENCE IN THE ADOPTION OF SOLUTIONS BY PROBLEM-SOLVING GROUPS: CONCEPT, METHOD, AND RESULTS

L. Richard Hoffman
Norman R. F. Maier

In Chapter 1, Hoffman applied Lewin's (1935) concept of valence to the attractiveness of cognitions arising in the solving of problems by groups. He assumed that group members become emotionally attached to or repelled by the several ideas that are offered in the course of discussion, and that the solution finally adopted reflects this emotional attachment by the group as a whole.

The present paper is a report of a fairly successful attempt to operationalize the concept of valence by means of a coding system for observing the problem-solving process in groups. This first attempt at operationalization has been limited to the valence of possible solutions, although theoretically the concept may be applied to cognitions at any stage of the problem-solving process, for example, definitions of the problem.

VALENCE CONCEPT

Briefly, the following are properties of valence as applied to problem solutions, according to Hoffman's postulations in Chapter 1.

1. Valence is the degree of acceptability a solution has for a group or an individual. Positive valence indicates an acceptable solution and negative valence, an unacceptable one. The valence

---

The research reported here was conducted in conjunction with grant M-2704 from the National Institutes of Health, U.S. Public Health Service.

of any solution may vary in sign and magnitude among the several group members, regardless of the valence that the solution has for the group as a whole. Similarly, different solutions may have different valences for the group.

2. A solution, to be adopted by a group, must acquire more positive valence than some minimum value. (a) If no solution acquires more valence than the minimum value, the group will fail to adopt a solution. (b) If only one solution acquires more than the minimum amount of positive valence, it will be adopted. (c) If more than one solution acquires more than the minimum amount of positive valence, either the solution with the highest positive valence will be adopted or a conflict situation occurs that may or may not be resolved. The conditions under which each of these alternatives might occur cannot be specified at this time.

3. Member acceptance of the solution, that is, satisfaction with the solution, will be high only if the member's individual valence for the solution is substantially above the minimum threshold value.

METHOD

Observational System

In this first attempt to operationalize the valence concept, a system was developed for coding members' statements about possible solutions to one particular problem during the discussion. Previous systems for observing group process (for example, Bales 1950; Chapple 1940; Heyns and Lippitt 1954) have coded general types of behaviors without regard to their relevance to the specific problem under discussion. For example, Bales's category "Asks Question" includes questions about any topic whatever, whereas we were concerned with questions about specific solutions to a problem. The inadequacy of these prior systems for our purposes led us to develop a new observational system that would relate the acts of the group members directly to the solution finally adopted by the group.

Problem

The Parasol Assembly Problem (Maier 1952) was adapted from its role-playing form to a problem without roles. The problem involves a seven-man group who assemble carburetors in a series of sequential operations. An instance of inadequate production is described and the problem consists of discovering the best means of achieving maximum productivity.

Coding Grid

The observational system used a series of large (11 x 13 inches) coding sheets on which the most frequently discussed solutions were listed in a column down the left-hand side of each page and space was left for the coder to write in additional solutions. Each solution defines a row on the sheet, and the various members' acts relevant to that solution and a number corresponding to the person who spoke are recorded on that row. Vertical lines divide the page to enable the coder to record these acts as they occur in sequence.

Where a combination of the categorized solutions, for example, group competition with incentives, was being discussed, the coders were instructed to bracket the two solutions and code along one row. In the analysis the acts coded following a bracket were assigned to both solutions, on the grounds that they were contributing valence to both solutions. The procedure implies that while one part of the combination may be rejected by the group, the other part may retain its accumulated valence. For example, certain group members might reject the incentive scheme but approve of the competition between groups. Thus, the total number of acts recorded by a coder often exceeded the actual number of statements made.

Definition of an Act

An act is defined as a statement or a consecutive series of statements pertaining to a particular solution that can be classified according to one of the behavior categories defined in the next section. A new act was recorded if another person started to talk, another solution was referred to, or the same person made a statement referring to the same solution that could be coded in a different category. The last criterion will become clearer when the behavior categories have been described.

No act was recorded if the statements made did not refer to any particular solution, so that all the interaction that occurred in the group was not recorded. This condition adds a fourth criterion for recording an act, namely, when a codable act followed an uncodable one.

Behavior Categories

Acts were coded into the following seven categories:*

S—Statement of the solution: complete and partial descriptions of solutions

J—Justification: arguments supporting the solution

A—Agreement: expression of agreement that the solution is a good one, without justification

V—Vote: attempts to elicit support for the solution

R—Reconnaissance: questions seeking detail about the solution

Q—Questions: interrogative statements implying doubt or criticism about the solution†

C—Criticism: statements criticizing the solution†

Questionnaire

After the group had adopted a solution, the members were asked individually, "How satisfied are you with the solution reached by your group?" Responses to this question were made to a six-point scale: very dissatisfied, somewhat dissatisfied, neither satisfied nor dissatisfied, fairly satisfied, quite satisfied, very satisfied. The question was designed to measure the members' acceptance of the solution and has been shown in other studies (for example, Hoffman, Harburg, and Maier 1962; Hoffman and Maier 1959) to reflect the character of the problem-solving process. These data are used to test the proposition that satisfaction with the solution is related to high measured valence.

Subjects and Administration

Seventy-five male subjects, recruited from an introductory psychology class, solved the problem in fifteen four-person groups

---

*A more detailed description of the coding system appears in Appendix B.1. R has been eliminated and C has been expanded into four categories of negative valence.

†The Q and C categories represent negatively valent acts. In this first attempt to operationalize valence, such acts were coded in only two categories, since we were not sure of our ability to code more than seven behavior categories.

and five three-person groups.* Three coders† observed the groups, but rotated their assignments so that all groups were not observed by the same pair of coders. At least two coders were present for all but one group.

Reliability of the Coding System

Examinations of the total number of acts coded revealed consistent differences among the three coders. The *t* tests of the differences in the total number of acts recorded by each pair of coders on the groups they coded together yielded values of 12.71 ($p < .01$), 2.35 ($p < .05$), and .16. One coder tended to record substantially more acts than the two others, who were in closer agreement on the average. The size of the differences in number of acts coded varied from group to group, but suggests that a fair degree of disagreement existed about the definition of a codable act. A small and unsystematic sample of comparisons between the tape-recorded interactions and the code sheets suggests that errors of commission as well as omission occurred.

While this difference in the total number of acts coded was discouraging, the data were analyzed further to determine the character of the discrepancy among coders. First, the data for each coder were tabulated by solution-act categories within each group, for example, the number of J acts coded for the solution, put slow workers first, summed across all group members.‡

The data in this form were then used to answer the question "How well did the coders agree in their relative assignment of acts?"

---

*The three-person groups occurred because one person assigned to each of these groups did not appear for the experimental session.

†Paul Kimmel and Bruce Springborn gave excellent assistance in developing the coding system, serving as coders, and analyzing the data. Johann Aamodt was very helpful in analyzing the reliability data.

‡Before performing the reliability analysis, the protocols for each coder were examined for instances where they had written in the solution being discussed. Where, in the judgment of the analyst, such a solution could be assigned to one of the 24 principal solution categories, that was done. This procedure seemed justified on the grounds that the coder had written the solution down and therefore it was part of the raw data.

Correlations between coders were computed for the number of acts assigned by each coder to each solution-act cell. Such a correlation permits the maximum amount of discrepancy between coders to be revealed, since examination of the coding records revealed almost no error in assigning acts to people.

The resulting correlations, corrected for double-length by the Spearman-Brown prophecy formula, were, with few exceptions, quite respectable. The median correlation was .95 and 76 percent of the 25 correlations were above .80. This analysis revealed that disagreements between raters occurred principally in assigning acts to solution, rather than behavior, categories and in groups with large numbers of solution-act categories. It should be mentioned also that these correlations may be somewhat spuriously high due to a tendency for the acts to cluster in a small number of solution-act cells for both coders.

The generally high levels of intercoder agreement shown by this analysis seemed to justify use of the data to test for the hypothesized relationships of valence, as measured by the coded behaviors, to the adoption of solutions. To permit the best possible testing of the hypotheses, the coded data were edited again slightly to correct certain discrepancies between the observers. By referring to the tape recordings of the problem-solving discussion, disagreements about the assignments of act sequences to solution categories were reconciled. The entire editing process was done without knowledge of the results of the discussion or of the way in which the changes made affected the tests of the hypotheses.

RESULTS

Two general types of analysis were conducted. In the first analysis the data summed over the entire process were examined for relationships between the valence indexes and the adoption of and satisfaction with solutions. In the second analysis the problem-solving process was studied sequentially to determine how the relationships found in the first analysis developed at successive stages of discussion in the groups.

Two possible measures of valence were examined: the algebraic sum of positive (S, J, A, V) acts minus negative (Q, C) acts, and the algebraic sum of S acts plus J acts minus C acts (S + J - C), which were the three most frequently coded types of acts. In addition, to check on the possibility that merely talking about a solution, whether favorably or unfavorably, leads to its adoption, the total number of acts associated with a solution was also related to the adoption or rejection of solutions. The last is not considered as a possible valence index, since it cannot take on negative values to indicate a member's negative feelings about a solution.

Analysis of Cumulative Valence Indexes and Solution Adoption

Both potential measures of valence satisfied the first set of properties postulated earlier. Individual members varied considerably in their measured support for each solution discussed, especially for the solutions that received most of the coded acts, and even for the solution adopted by the group. Furthermore, the solutions discussed by a group varied considerably also, ranging from negative valence indexes of as low as -20 to positive values as high as 96.

Since all groups arrived at some solution to the problem, we may assume that the minimum value a solution must acquire to be adopted is less than or approximately equal to the lowest value attained by any principal adopted solution.* The smallest positive-minus-negative value for any principal adopted solution was 14 and the smallest S + J - C value was 9, both occurring for the same solution in the same group. Only 22 acts were coded for that solution, which was the smallest number coded for a principal adopted solution. Thus, the minimum positive values would appear to be about 14 for the positive-minus-negative index and 9 for the S + J - C index.

Using the values of 14 and 9 to represent the minimum valence values for the positive-minus-negative and S + J - C indexes, respectively, each group's solution was identified with the type of outcome predicted in the earlier section, Valence Concept. On the positive-minus-negative index, six groups adopted the only solution whose valence exceeded the minimum (outcome 2b), ten groups adopted the solution with the highest valence of two or more that exceeded the minimum (first part of outcome 2c), one group adopted a combination of two that exceeded the minimum (second part of out-

---

*Each group was asked to submit the single solution the members thought would best solve the problem. Despite this instruction, groups frequently reported solutions that represented combinations of several solution categories listed on the observation sheets. A judgment was made, therefore, for each such report as to which was the principal solution offered. The other solutions were then termed subordinate. In one report no distinction could be made, so both are considered principal solutions.

come 2c), and two groups failed to fit the predictions. For the S + J - C index, five groups fit outcome 2b; twelve groups, first part of outcome 2c; two groups, second part of outcome 2c; and only one group failed to fit the predictions.

Thus, as shown in Table 2.1, the solution with the highest positive valence was adopted as the principal solution in 17 of the 20 groups, according to the positive-minus-negative index, and by 18 of the 20 groups, according to the S + J - C index. Since these two values exceed only slightly the 16 of 20 groups in which the adopted solution had the highest number of all types of acts, discussion of a solution could be considered to have resulted in its adoption. It is clear from more refined analyses, however, that the valence of the acts was critical in determining the adoption of solutions. A solution was adopted when the number of positive acts exceeded substantially the number of negative acts.

TABLE 2.1

Number of Times Adopted Solution Had Highest Value in 20 Groups

Index	Positive-Minus-Negative Acts	S + J - C	Total Acts
Number of solutions adopted	17	18	16

Source: Compiled by the authors.

Of interest at this point was whether there was some relationship between the valence value of a solution and the probability of its being adopted by a group. The valence values and the total number of acts for each solution discussed, regardless of the group that produced it, were cross-tabulated with whether the solution was adopted as the principal solution, as a subordinate solution, or discussed but not adopted. These relationships are shown in Table 2.2, with the index values grouped to produce stable cell entries.

For all three measures the proportion of principal adopted solutions increases consistently for successively higher index values. The two valence indexes were approximately equal in identifying the principal adopted solutions without risk of misidentifying solutions that were not adopted. Thus, the results suggest that a quantitative

TABLE 2.2

Relationships between Index Values and Adoption of Solutions

Index Value	Adopted Solutions		Solutions Discussed	Total
	Principal*	Subordinate	But Not Adopted	
Positive-minus-negative acts				
40 or higher	10	0	1	11
30-39	7	1	3	11
20-29	1	3	5	9
10-19	3	4	11	18
1-9	0	3	111	114
0 or less	0	0	83	83
S + J - C				
30 or higher	11	0	1	12
20-29	6	4	6	16
10-19	3	4	13	20
1-9	1	3	109	113
0 or less	0	0	85	85
Total acts				
50 or higher	17	1	10	28
30-49	3	5	15	23
20-39	1	1	16	18
10-19	0	4	42	46
1-9	0	0	131	131

*One of the 20 groups produced two principal solutions.

Source: Compiled by the authors.

relationship exists between the valence value finally achieved by a solution and the probability of its adoption by a group.

Sequential Analysis of Valence Indexes and Solution Adoption

Having shown that the proposed valence measures, when summed across the entire group process, were strongly related to the adoption of solutions, the question may be raised whether the accumulation of valence causes the adoption of a solution or whether the high valence values are a product of the decision. If the adopted solution can be identified early in the group process by means of the valence index, the causal hypothesis would receive strong support.

Toward this end the two valence indexes and the total number of acts for each solution were examined at several points in the history of each group. The observational records were divided into approximately equal segments containing from about 45 to 70 acts, identifiable on each coder's record at clearly comparable points. The valence values and total number of acts for each solution were calculated for each segment and then plotted on a graph with segments on the abscissa and index values on the ordinate. A cursory examination of these plots revealed that in most cases the principal adopted solution became clearly differentiated from the others at a rather early stage of the discussion, sometimes as early as the first segment. Typically, the principal adopted solution exhibited a sudden, sharp rise in valence in a single segment, even though it frequently was not the solution discussed most often in that segment. Figure 2.1 shows the plots of the S + J - C values for the five most discussed solutions of two groups that illustrate this phenomenon. The numbers next to the lines represent the code numbers of the solutions. All the solutions plotted had more than 5 percent of the total acts coded, and in both groups a solution other than the one adopted had more than 50 acts.

The examination of these plots suggested that a value of the valence indexes might be found that, when first surpassed, would predict the adoption of that solution. Since the minimum threshold values for the two proposed valence indexes had been identified earlier as being about 14 for the positive-minus-negative index and 9 for the S + J - C index, values starting from 10 for each index were examined for such predictive properties.

In each group the solution that first acquired the specified valence value during the problem-solving process was predicted to be the principal adopted solution. Table 2.3 shows the percentage of times the prediction was correct for increasing values beyond the minimum threshold value. From the high proportion of correct predictions achieved, it appears that once a solution acquired more than some specified amount of valence, about 15 for both indexes, the likelihood of some alternative solution being adopted was reduced considerably. Furthermore, the results of a comparable analysis using the total number of acts indicate that a lot of early discussion of a solution was substantially less predictive of its adoption than was either of the valence measures.

FIGURE 2.1

Accumulation of Valence (S + J - C Index) for Solutions in Two Groups

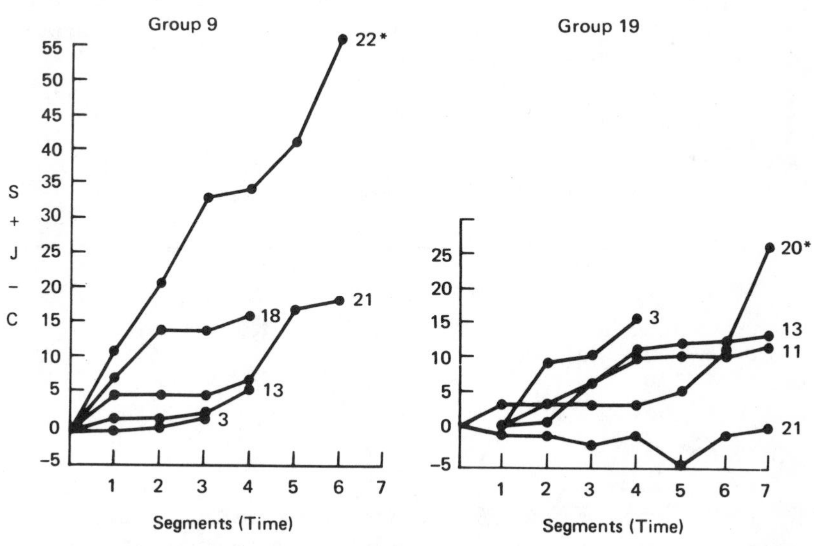

Notes: Numbers identify the solutions discussed.
The asterisks indicate the principal adopted solution.
Source: Compiled by the authors.

Cumulative Valence and Member Satisfaction with the Solution

The valence model also predicted that members would be satisfied with the solution adopted to the extent that the solution surpassed the minimum threshold value. Since all groups adopted a solution, it is assumed that all solutions surpassed the minimum threshold value. Therefore the 75 members' rated satisfaction with the solution was correlated with their individual valence values for the solutions adopted.* The correlations were .59 for the positive-minus-negative index and .46 for the S + J - C index, both of which are significantly different from zero, thus supporting the hypothesis.

TABLE 2.3

Percentage of Solutions Adopted Whose Index Values First Attained Value Indicated

S + J - C		Positive-Minus-Negative Acts		Total Acts	
Index Value	Percent Adopted	Index Value	Percent Adopted	Index Value	Percent Adopted
10	65.0	10	65.0	15	50.0
12	70.0	12	65.0	20	45.0
15*	80.0	14	80.0	25	45.0
		16*	85.0	30	45.0
				34*	55.0

*Values higher than these for each index are not included, since no solution in one or more groups exceeded that value.

Source: Compiled by the authors.

DISCUSSION

While the coding system developed for operationalizing valence in group problem solving has many obvious weaknesses, there appears to be sufficient agreement between observers to justify its further refinement. That the relationships between the derived valence indexes and adoption of, and satisfaction with, the solutions were consistent with expectations from the valence model supports the basic validity of the operations. The degree of emotional

*Since the members did not distinguish in their reported solutions between the principal and subordinate solutions, for this analysis the valence of the adopted solution has been taken as the algebraic sum of the valences for the principal and subordinate solutions.

attachment of the members for a solution appears to be represented in quantitative terms by the two valence indexes, that is, the algebraic difference between the number of supporting comments minus the number of critical comments. Not only were the valence values for the solutions adopted almost invariably the highest of the solutions discussed in each group, but the chances of a solution being adopted increased regularly as its valence value increased. Almost all solutions with positive-minus-negative values of 40 or more or S + J - C values of 30 or more were adopted. Similarly, a valence value of 15 was shown to be some type of threshold point for the adoption of solutions, since, in most groups, the first solution that achieved that value on either index was adopted. Such relationships and values must, of course, be cross-validated on other leaderless groups and on other problems before they can be accepted. However, if they are validated, they provide one of the few measures of social-psychological variables with ratio scale properties (Stevens 1951) so far discovered.

Assuming the validity of the relationships obtained in this study, certain interesting conclusions about the problem-solving process in groups may be drawn. First, the solution finally produced by a group does not reflect, necessarily, a total group effort. High valence for a single solution frequently occurred because one or two members of a group argued strongly and frequently in its favor, either over the objections of the other members or without their participation. Furthermore, the nonparticipating members were occasionally quite satisfied with such a solution, even though their individual valence for that solution was low. However, the positive correlation between individual valence and satisfaction with the solution suggests that many favorable comments for a solution by all members are desirable for obtaining acceptance for a solution, even if they are not needed to have the solution adopted.

Second, the fact that in 80 percent or more of the groups, the solution that first achieved a valence value of 15 was the one adopted suggests that the decision point for a group's solution may occur relatively early in a meeting, despite the fact that alternative possibilities are still discussed after that point. This fact would seem to have negative implications for the creative potential of groups, since objectively good solutions that are offered after the decision point have very little chance of being adopted. It should be noted that the vast majority of solutions offered to this problem were of poor quality, so that the facts were not important in determining which solutions were adopted. Rather, the tendency for groups to adopt a solution without truly considering other alternatives supports Maier's (1958) contention that people tend to be "solution-minded" rather than "problem-minded." The value of trying to bring forth all solution possibilities before any are evaluated, thus delaying solution adoption, would appear to be consistent with these results (Maier and Solem 1962).

Third, satisfaction with the solution, as suggested in earlier articles (Hoffman and Maier 1959; 1961a), seems to reflect the character of the problem-solving process more than it does the quality of the solution produced. The more the members contributed to the valence of the solution adopted, the more satisfied they were with it. It is also clear, however, that occasionally members who did not contribute were satisfied with the solution if the other members contributed sufficient valence. Thus, the frequent attempts by one member to promote the adoption of a solution seem not only to increase his/her emotional attachment to it substantially, but also to increase slightly the emotional attachment to it of the members who hear him/her.

The success of this observational system in the present instance as an operational measure of valence opens up new possibilities for research on small problem-solving groups. The act categories seem applicable to every problem in which separate solution possibilities are identifiable. The possibility arises of measuring quantitatively the influence of different types of leaders, of members with different personalities, of groups of different sizes, and so on, in terms of changes in the valence values needed to gain the adoption of solutions. Furthermore, more refined tests of the conditions hypothesized to enhance creativity in problem solving (see Chapter 1) become possible through experimental manipulation of the determinants of the valence values.

PART II

VALENCE AND THE ADOPTION OF SOLUTIONS

3

VALENCE IN THE ADOPTION OF SOLUTIONS BY PROBLEM-SOLVING GROUPS: II. QUALITY AND ACCEPTANCE AS GOALS OF LEADERS AND MEMBERS

L. Richard Hoffman
Norman R. F. Maier

The present study was designed to extend our understanding of the relationship between the valence of solutions—their attractiveness or unattractiveness for the members—and their adoption by the group (see Chapter 1). In a prior study with leaderless groups (see Chapter 2), the valence of a solution, measured from a system of process observation, was shown to be positively correlated with the probability of its adoption by a group. Furthermore, the solution adopted by about 80 percent of the groups had the highest valence of all the solutions they discussed, and the adoption of this solution could be predicted at a relatively early stage of the problem-solving discussion. The use of this observational system in the present study permitted us to test the stability of these relationships and to examine possible variations of them in groups with leaders. In addition, the leaders and members in different groups, as a result of separate instructions, sought the same or different goals concerning the group's solution to the problem given them.

Two types of goals were used, consistent with N. R. F. Maier's (1952) distinction between the quality and acceptance of group solutions to a problem. Quality refers to the adequacy of the solution in terms of the objective facts of the problem. Acceptance refers to the members' motivation to carry out the decision. Therefore, in half the groups the leaders were given the objective of a high-quality solution (a monetary reward was promised), while the other leaders' objective was to gain the members' acceptance,

The research reported here was supported by grant MH-02704 from the U.S. Public Health Service.

measured by their rated satisfaction (Maier and Hoffman 1960b). Similarly, the members of half the groups received the high-quality goal, while the goal of the members of the remaining groups was the leader's acceptance. By instructing leaders and members separately, four combinations of leader's and members' goals were established. The principal question to be examined by this design was whether the acceptance orientation would reduce the tendency, especially among the leaders, for people concerned with solution quality to attempt unduly to influence the final decision. If merely changing the reward conditions could so influence these untrained leaders' behavior, the elaborate training programs in leadership skills (Maier 1952) could be eliminated.

METHOD

Problem

The Parasol Assembly Problem (Maier 1952) was adapted from its role-playing form to a problem without roles. The problem involves a group of seven men who assemble carburetors in a series of sequential operations. An instance of inadequate production is described and the problem is to recommend the best means of achieving maximum productivity. A great variety of solutions are offered, but only about 10 percent of college-student groups usually develop the best solution. It should be noted that the problem appears to be intrinsically challenging to subjects, and they usually spend the full 40 minutes available in trying to solve it.

Experimental Procedure

When the group members had convened, one person, preselected randomly, was told that he was the leader and was responsible for reporting the group's solution. The others were told that they were the members. A problem statement was given to each subject and then read aloud to them by the experimenter. The leader was then taken into the hall by the experimenter's assistant*

---

*Bruce Springborn or L. R. Hoffman served as experimenter in all groups, and two undergraduates, James Ardis and Sheldon Shrieberg, served as assistants in giving instructions to the leaders and in coding the group process.

and told that he would receive $1.50 if he achieved the goal set for him. For half the leaders the goal was a group solution of the highest quality (LQ condition), while the other half sought the members' satisfaction with the group's solution (LMs condition). At the same time the experimenter informed the members of their goal and of the reward of $1.50 each would receive if they achieved it.* The members of half of the groups had a group solution of highest quality as their goal (MQ condition), while members of the other half of the groups had as their goal the leader's satisfaction with the group's solution (MLs condition). In each group all members had the same goal. All subjects were told not to reveal their goals to the others in the group or they would forfeit the possible reward. No subject ever violated this instruction either directly or by implication.

Following the instructions the leader was returned to the group and the entire group was told to recommend the single best action to be taken to maximize productivity in the situation described. This instruction obviously complicated the task for the subjects with satisfaction orientations, since they had to appear to be working toward the quality objective in order to keep their instructions secret, while at the same time trying to gain their counterparts' satisfaction with the solution.

After the problem had been solved, each subject rated his satisfaction with the solution on a six-point scale from "very dissatisfied" (1) to "very satisfied" (6).

Combinations of the two leader and member variations provided four experimental conditions: LQ-MQ, both leader and members have solution quality as their goal; LQ-MLs, leader seeks solution quality while members try for his satisfaction with the solution; LMs-MQ, leader seeks members' satisfaction with the solution, while members strive for solution quality; LMs-MLs, leader's goal is the members' satisfaction and the members seek his satisfaction with the solution.

---

*The experimenter's assistant instructed the leaders while the experimenter instructed the members regarding the goals. It was found that when the experimenter's assistant instructed the members, subjects tended to regard the offer of reward as a psychological trick. As a result of this skepticism, it was necessary to discard 13 groups. The problem did not arise when the experimenter instructed the members and the experimenter's assistant instructed the discussion leaders. The authors are quite disturbed about the image introductory psychology students have of the use of deception in psychological experiments.

Groups were assigned at random to the four conditions in a balanced order. Nine three-man groups and ten four-man groups were assigned to each condition, a total of 76 groups.

Subjects

The 268 male subjects were obtained from the introductory psychology course as part of their class requirement and assigned as their schedules permitted to experimental groups. They were mostly freshmen and sophomores with only a vague acquaintance with the industrial scene.

The Observational System and the Measurement of Valence

The system used for recording the problem-solving statements is described in detail in Appendix B.1, and was modified only slightly in the present study. The observer records, for each statement subject makes about a particular solution, a number corresponding to the person and a letter indicating the category of statement made. There are five categories that indicate support for the solution (positive valence) and five corresponding categories of rejection (negative valence). Since each statement is recorded in the order it is made, a chronological record of the problem-solving process is obtained. No estimate of the length of each statement is made.

The valence of a solution for each individual in the group is measured by taking the algebraic sum of the number of positively valent statements he makes about a solution minus the number of negative statements he makes about it. The group valence measure is the algebraic sum of the individual valences for that solution.

Analysis Designs

The effects of the leaders' and members' orientations and of group size have been examined, for the most part, by either of two types of statistical techniques: analysis of variance or partition of chi-square. All metric data were subjected to the three-factor analysis of variance shown in Table 3.1, on the assumption that all variables were fixed. To conserve space, the tabular presentation of results will indicate only those sources of variance that were significant at the .10 level. The p value will be shown in parentheses, for example, leader goal (.05). Frequency data were tested by partitions of chi-square that will be shown in the relevant tables.

TABLE 3.1

Analysis-of-Variance Design

Source	df
Leader goal (L)	1
Member goal (M)	1
Group size (S)	1
L x M	1
L x S	1
M x S	1
L x M x S	1
Error within cells*	68

*Used as error for all F tests.
Source: Compiled by the authors.

RESULTS

Comparison with Study of Leaderless Groups

The principal objective of this experiment was to test the generality of the basic propositions of the valence model of group problem solving (see Chapter 1) for groups with formal leaders under the various experimental conditions. What effects, if any, did the experimental conditions have on the various relationships found in Chapter 2 between valence indexes (see "Method" section for a description of the valence index) and the adoption of solutions by leaderless groups?

The first question to be raised is the issue of a minimum valence threshold for adoption, which was found to be about 14 in the leaderless groups. As in the previous study, none of the groups in this study failed to submit a solution, but the lowest valence for a principal adopted solution was 8. It is not clear just how meaningful this number is, since the next lowest valence value for an adopted solution was 17. Certainly sampling variability around this threshold and the unreliability remaining in the coding system could produce a variation as large as this.

More meaningful, perhaps, is the fact that the mean valence value attained by the principal adopted solutions in these 76 groups (48.8) was insignificantly different from that value in the 20 leaderless groups (51.4). Furthermore, although the range of mean valence values across conditions was from 39.6 in the LMs-MQ three-man groups to 55.5 in the LQ-MLs four-man groups, there was sufficient variability within conditions to produce no significant sources of variance when these were analyzed in the three-factor analysis-of-variance design (see Table 3.2). The valence value of the principal adopted solution in each group seems to have been peculiar to the unique character of the process in that group.

TABLE 3.2

Mean Valence Indexes for Principal Adopted Solutions

Group Size	LQ-MQ	LQ-MLs	LMs-MQ	LMs-MLs	Total
3-man	41.8	55.1	39.6	44.0	45.1
4-man	55.0	55.5	52.3	45.4	52.0
Total	48.7	55.3	46.3	44.7	48.8

Note: No significant sources of variance.
Source: Compiled by the authors.

A second question concerns the frequency with which the groups adopted that solution, among the several discussed, which had the highest positive valence.* The principal adopted solution had the highest valence of all solutions discussed in 69 (90.8 percent) of the 76 groups and one of the subordinate adopted solutions had the highest valence in three additional groups. The 90.8 percent adoption rate in these groups is only slightly, and not significantly, higher than the 85.0 percent rate obtained in the 20 leaderless groups in the earlier study. Furthermore, the variation across

*Despite the instructions to all groups to submit a single action step for their solution, a number of groups proposed two or three steps as a single package. Prior to the analysis, the major part of such a package was identified as the principal adopted solution and the others were termed subordinate adopted solutions.

conditions in the percentages of adoptions of the highest valent solutions—83 percent to 100 percent—was not significant. Thus the appointment of a leader and goal instructions had little effect on the tendency to adopt the solution with the highest valence.

The relationship between the valence level achieved by solutions and whether they were adopted as principal or subordinate solutions or not adopted at all was also tabulated. Table 3.3 shows these relationships for each of the four conditions, for the two group sizes, and, for purposes of comparison, the same relationship from the study of the leaderless groups. The similarity in the relationships is striking. The higher the valence value achieved by a solution, the greater was its probability of being adopted as the principal solution, regardless of goals, group size, or whether the groups had leaders or not. Chi-square comparisons across conditions and group size, and between groups with and without leaders, showed the valence level by adoption comparison to be the only significant one ($p < .001$).

Another finding from the earlier study was the location of an adoption threshold point with a valence value of about 15. In 88 percent of those leaderless groups, the first solution whose valence equaled 15 was adopted as the principal solution. This analysis in the present study showed that 73 percent of the groups adopted the first solution whose valence equaled 15 (see Table 3.4). In another 4 percent of the groups the solution that first passed this threshold point was one of the subordinate adopted solutions. Although this percentage is less than in the leaderless groups, the difference is not statistically significant. Also, chi-square analysis showed no significant variations due to experimental conditions or to group size. Thus, the tendency was confirmed for a large proportion of groups to adopt the first solution for which the number of positive comments exceeded the number of negative comments by 15.

Finally, the earlier study revealed a correlation ($r = .59$, $p < .01$) between an individual's valence for the solution(s) adopted by his group and his rated satisfaction with the solution. The same correlation in the present study, over all 268 subjects, was .32 ($p < .01$), which is significantly lower ($p < .01$) than in the leaderless groups. Whether this reduced correlation is a function, at least in part, of the varied goals of leaders and members could not be determined from the data. The two goals may have provided different bases for determining satisfaction.

The correlations between individual valence for and satisfaction with adopted solutions are shown for various sets of leaders and members in Table 3.5. In general, the correlations are all positive and of similar magnitude and, overall, about the same for leaders and members. Why they are generally smaller for the

TABLE 3.3

Relationship between Final Valence Index and Adoption

Valence	LQ-MQ			LQ-MLs			LMs-MQ			LMs-MLs			3-Man (N = 36 groups)			4-Man (N = 20 groups)			Leaderless Groups (N = 20 groups)		
Index	P[a]	S[b]	DNA[c]	P	S	DNA	P	S	DNA	P	S	DNA	P	S	DNA	P	S	DNA	P	S	DNA
40	11	0	0	14	2	0	11	2	2	11	0	1	19	0	2	28	4	1	10	0	1
30-39	6	1	2	4	1	2	5	1	3	4	0	0	8	2	5	11	1	2	7	1	3
20-29	0	3	4	1	2	4	3	1	1	3	2	4	7	5	5	0	3	8	1	3	5
10-19	2	6	8	1	3	14	1	0	12	1	2	14	3	5	23	2	6	25	3	4	11
1-9	0	0	103	0	1	90	0	1	90	1	1	94	0	2	172	1	1	205	0	3	111
0	0	0	72	0	1	53	0	0	68	0	0	45	0	0	96	0	1	142	0	0	83

[a]Adopted as principal solution.

[b]Adopted as subordinate solution.

[c]Solution discussed but not adopted.

Source: Compiled by the authors.

TABLE 3.4

Adoptions of First Solutions with Valence Equal to 15

Group Size	No. Groups per Condition	LQ-MQ		LQ-MLs		LMs-MQ		LMs-MLs		Total	
		N	%	N	%	N	%	N	%	N	%
3-man	9	5	62.5*	7	77.8	7	77.8	6	66.7	25	71.4
4-man	10	8	80.0	6	60.0	8	80.0	7	77.8*	29	74.4
Total	19	13	72.2	13	68.4	15	78.9	13	72.2	54	73.0

*One group in this condition had no solution with valence greater than or equal to 15. The percentage is based on the reduced N, as are totals that include the condition.

Note: No significant comparisons by chi-square analysis.

Source: Compiled by the authors.

TABLE 3.5

Correlations between Individual Valence for Adopted Solutions and Satisfaction with the Solutions

	LQ-MQ	LQ-MLs	LMs-MQ	LMs-MLs	3-Man	4-Man	Total
Leaders	.51** (19)	.24 (19)	.32 (19)	.35 (19)	.23 (36)	.46***(40)	.36***(76)
Members	.27 (48)	.34** (48)	.37** (48)	.19 (48)	.16 (72)	.38***(120)	.28***(192)
Total	.35***(67)	.32***(67)	.39***(67)	.24**(67)	.20**(180)	.42***(160)	.32***(268)

**$p < .05$.

***$p < .01$.

Note: Numbers in parentheses are N's for correlations.

Source: Compiled by the authors.

three-man groups is not clear, but suggests that the problem-solving process may have been somewhat different in the three-man and four-man groups. However, the variability among conditions may be due to the above-noted differences in goals.

Leaders' and Members' Contributions to the Valence of Adopted Solutions

Although it has been shown in Table 3.2 that the mean group valence index for the principal adopted solutions did not vary across conditions, one may still ask whether the leaders' and members' contributions to valence differed.

The data relevant to this question are presented in Table 3.6, where the leaders' and members' mean valence indexes for the solutions adopted by their groups are shown. The leader's valence for the adopted solution was affected not only by his own goal orientation but also by the members' orientation. The LQ-MLs leaders had the highest mean valence, while LQ-MQ leaders had the lowest. The LMs leaders were not significantly different from each other, although the means of those with quality-oriented members tended to be slightly higher. Thus the LMs leaders were no less likely to influence the final group decision than were the LQ leaders.

TABLE 3.6

Mean Valence Indexes for Principal Adopted Solutions

Group Size	LQ-MQ	LQ-MLs	LMs-MQ	LMs-MLs	Total
Leaders[a]					
3-man	17.3	21.6	19.3	17.3	18.9
4-man	13.3	27.0	18.6	15.1	18.5
Total	15.2	24.4	18.9	16.2	18.7
Members[b]					
3-man	24.4	33.6	20.2	26.7	26.2
4-man	41.7	28.5	33.7	30.3	33.6
Total	33.5	30.9	27.3	28.6	30.1

[a]Significant effect: leader goal x member goal interaction (.05).

[b]Significant effects: member goal x group size interaction (.05), group size (.10).

Source: Compiled by the authors.

The only significant source of variation for the members' valence was an interaction between the members' goal and group size. While in the four-man groups members with quality orientations were more influential than members with the goal of leader's satisfaction, the reverse was true for the three-man groups. There was no effect on the members of their leaders' orientations.

The data also permit us to look at the leader's contribution to the valence of the adopted solution in comparison with the average member's contribution. Was the acceptance goal effective in reducing the leader's tendency to dominate the discussion, thus equalizing the influence relationship between him and the members? For this analysis the mean valence index of the members was subtracted from the leader's valence index in each group. The mean differences are reported in Table 3.7. In general, the leaders had significantly higher valence indexes, thus more influence (cf. Hoffman, Burke, and Maier 1965), than did the average member by about seven valence points (55 percent). When the data are examined by individuals (Table 3.8), we find that 52.0 percent of the leaders had the highest valence index in their group, as compared to a chance expectancy of 28.9 percent ($p < .001$). Thus the leaders, on the average, not only had more influence than the average member, but often had more influence than any of the other members.

TABLE 3.7

Leader's Minus Average Member's Valence Indexes for the Principal Adopted Solution

Group Size	LQ-MQ	LQ-MLs	LMs-MQ	LMs-MLs	Total
3-man	5.0	4.7	9.2	4.2	5.8
4-man	-0.5	17.5	7.3	4.9	7.3
Total	2.1	11.4	8.2	4.6	6.6***

***$p < .01$, by t test.

Note: Significant effects: leader goal x member goal interaction (.05), member goal x group size interaction (.10).

Source: Compiled by the author.

The results in Tables 3.7 and 3.8 demonstrate also, however, some sharp distinctions among the four conditions (leader goal x member goal interaction, $p < .05$). LQ-MLs leaders were the most influential relative to the average member (by about 11 valence points), and most often (74 percent had the highest valence for the

TABLE 3.8

Leaders with Highest Valence for Principal Adopted Solutions

Group Size	No. Groups per Condition	LQ-MQ		LQ-MLs		LMs-MQ		LMs-MLs		Total	
		N	%	N	%	N	%	N	%	N	%
3-man	9	3	33.3	6	66.7	6	66.7	4.5[a]	50.0	19.5	54.2**
4-man	10	3	30.0	8	80.0	4	40.0	5	50.0	20	50.0***
Total	19	6	31.6	14	73.7***	10	52.6*	9.5	50.0**	39.5	52.0***

Summary of Chi-Square Analysis (comparing leader highest and leader not highest)

Comparison	df	x^2
Leader goal (L) x highest valence (V)	1	0.01
Member goal (M) x V	1	2.97*
Group size (S) x V	1	0.13
L x M x V	1	3.81**
L x S x V	1	0.63
M x S x V	1	0.87
L x M x S x V	1	0.06
Total	7	8.48

[a]Leader was tied with another member for highest valence.

*$p < .10$.

**$p < .05$.

***$p < .01$.

Source: Compiled by the authors.

adopted solutions. LQ-MQ leaders had about the same influence as the average member and were most influential with only about chance frequency (32 percent).

The most surprising result is the influence of the LMs leaders. In both LMs-MQ and LMs-MLs groups the leaders had higher valence indexes than the average member ($p < .01$) and had, significantly more often than chance, a higher valence than any member of their groups ($p < .05$). It would appear that in trying to achieve a solution satisfactory to all members, these leaders most often tried to persuade the members to adopt a solution that the leaders favored, rather than letting the members resolve their disagreements among themselves.

This is not to say that the members had no influence over the solution. A comparison of the grand means in Table 3.6 shows that the sums of the members' valence for the principal adopted solutions generally exceeded the leader's valence by about 11 valence points ($p < .01$). The members' totals exceeded the leaders' valence in all conditions, but especially in the four-man LQ-MQ groups (mean difference = 28.4).

Thus, while groups in the various conditions did not differ generally in the valence they contributed to their principal adopted solutions, there were substantial differences in the leaders' and members' contributions to the valence. Where the leader's goal was quality and the members' goal was his satisfaction, the leader tended to contribute more valence and thus dominate the discussion. The leaders whose goal was members' satisfaction also tended to dominate their meetings, although not quite to the extent of the LQ-MLs leaders. Only in the LQ-MQ condition were the leaders generally undifferentiated from the members in their influence over the solution. In fact, in the four-man LQ-MQ groups the leaders' preference was often overridden by the combined efforts of several members.

DISCUSSION

The data are striking in the consistency of the relationships between the valence index and the adoption of solutions both between these groups with leaders and the leaderless groups reported on in Chapter 2 and across the experimental conditions, despite the substantial behavioral differences among leaders and members in the different conditions. Three such sets of consistent relationships were found:

1. The mean valence for the adopted solutions did not vary significantly across conditions or between these groups and the leaderless groups.

2. The positive relationship between the valence index and the probability of solution adoption did not vary across conditions or between these groups and the leaderless groups.

3. The percentage of adopted solutions that first reached a valence of 15 (73 percent), while slightly lower than the comparable percentage for leaderless groups, was not significantly lower, nor did it vary across conditions.

These relationships, when considered together, suggest (a) that a mechanism exists by which the group members "decide" that a solution that achieves a certain amount of support has been adopted, (b) that when this level of support has been achieved, resistance to that solution disappears or becomes relatively negligible, (c) that the discussion then focuses on providing further justification for adopting that solution, and (d) that the search for or the thorough discussion of additional alternatives is inhibited. Furthermore, the present evidence suggests that the level of support needed to activate this mechanism may be provided by either leaders or members, but that, once achieved, the leader takes an active role in directing the production of further positive valence for the solution.

To the extent that the leader is able to evoke positively valent comments from the members for the adopted solution, he may increase their satisfaction with it, as suggested by the positive correlation between the individual valence and satisfaction. However, the tendency among these leaders to provide their own justification for such solutions would seem to be reflected in their higher levels of satisfaction as compared to the members (leaders' mean satisfaction, 5.1; members' satisfaction, 4.7; $\underline{p}$ difference $<.01$). Leaders should be trained, then, in the skills of eliciting members' reactions to solution proposals if the latter's acceptance of adopted solutions is to be achieved.

The objective of gaining high-quality decisions also appears to run the risk of being defeated by this model problem-solving process. Since this process did not vary across conditions, the chance that a high-quality solution will be the first to surpass the adoption threshold would appear to be almost a matter of happenstance. Thus, one of the more important leadership functions, which must be developed through training, should be the prevention of solutions achieving this threshold before a sufficient number of solution possibilities have been brought forth for consideration by the group (cf. Maier and Solem 1962).

In general, with respect to the effects of the different goals on the leaders' behaviors, these were largely overshadowed by their general tendency to dominate and control the discussion. Leaders exercised more influence on the adopted solution than did the average member of their group and, in more than half the groups, more than any other member, even though the leaders were assigned randomly. This finding contrasts with the oft-reported relationship between personality characteristics and emergent leadership in leaderless groups (Mann 1959; 1961; Hoffman 1965). Thus, the goal of attaining members' satisfaction with the solution was insufficient to modify the behavior associated with the stereotyped role of the leader as one who dominates and controls the problem-solving discussion. Merely providing a reward for gaining the members' satisfaction is an inadequate substitute for training such relatively naive college students in the techniques for attaining this goal (Maier 1963). Faced with the responsibility for producing a group solution and with the conflicting suggestions of the group members, these untrained leaders lacked the skills for resolving the conflict and chose, instead, to influence the group to adopt their (the leaders') preferred solutions.

4

PROBLEM DIFFERENCES AND THE PROCESS OF ADOPTING GROUP SOLUTIONS

L. Richard Hoffman
Kenneth E. Friend
Gary R. Bond

Hoffman's (1965) review of the group problem-solving literature concluded that one of the barriers to progress in this field has been the lack of understanding of the parameters of the various tasks used by different investigators. He suggested that identifying the nature of such parameters and their impact on the problem-solving process would be a worthwhile enterprise. Since then work by Hackman (1975), Hackman and Morris (1978), Davis (1973), and Steiner (1972) has demonstrated the substantial importance of task variations for the nature of the group's process. Hackman and Morris, in particular, have emphasized the interaction between the task characteristics and the group process for understanding the effectiveness of group performance.

The present study examines the import of one important task characteristic for the process by which groups solve problems. The principal comparison we will draw is between a generative problem and a choice task. A generative problem is one for which the group must invent possible solutions before choosing one of them. Examples of this type of problem include how do we increase production in the plant? what type of marketing approach should we adopt this year? where should we go on vacation? A choice problem is one in which a single solution must be chosen from a given, but exhaustive, set of mutually exclusive alternatives. Decisions regarding the hiring or promotion of personnel or determining the guilt or innocence of a suspect are examples of choices often made by groups.

One principal difference between the generative and choice problems would appear to arise from the more limited set of options available to a group for resolving disagreements on the choice task. The members may not generate a new alternative, since the set is exhaustive, nor may they compromise or create a new solution by combining the best parts of two or more options. These methods were available to, and often used by, groups to solve the generative problem.

The question we ask in the present study is whether and in what ways the differences between these types of problems affect groups' methods for arriving at a decision. We shall attempt to answer this question in two ways. Our first concern is whether the valence model of problem solving (see Chapter 1) would apply to the choice problem as it had to the generative one (see Chapters 2, 3). The valence model was designed to describe the ongoing process by which groups move from the initial presentation of a problem to the adoption of a solution. The model posits that groups adopt a solution by generating positive valence for it sufficient to exceed both an adoption threshold (initially) and the valence for all other solutions (ultimately). The operational measures of the valence concept have supported this description of the process on the generative problem. Therefore, we shall apply valence analysis to compare the problem-solving processes on the generative and choice problems. That comparison will be followed by a more detailed analysis of the unique features of the choice problem.

A second approach to this question derives from an extension to the work on individual decision making by Bruner (1957), Newell and Simon (1972), and Wright and Barbour (1977). They have shown that individuals reduce the "cognitive complexity" of choice tasks by initially reviewing all the alternatives given, then discarding the unacceptable ones, and, finally, selecting from among the reduced set of possible solutions. If groups also follow this "decision-tree" approach, a two-stage process should be identifiable for the choice problem. In the first stage the group would focus on rejecting unacceptable alternatives, and in the second on adopting one as the final solution. Such a process was not apparent in solving the generative problem.

METHOD

Subjects and Procedure

The data for the generative problem had been collected at an earlier time from 44 three-, four-, and five-person groups recruited from introductory psychology classes, and have been reported in part in Chapters 2 and 3. Neither tape recordings nor transcripts of these group discussions are available at this time. Only the valence and numbers of acts in different segments have been retained. Data for the choice problem were collected from 43 groups of three, four, and five persons during their class sessions in an MBA program. (Fifteen of these were middle-management students in an executive program.) There were no consistent or substantial differences among groups of different sizes on either problem, so they have been combined for all analyses. Each group was observed by two coders trained in valence analysis. Transcripts were made of 28 of the latter 43 groups, from which valence was coded and verbal comments were taken. Valence in all other groups was coded while the groups solved the problem. Although slight differences in the results were attributable to whether valence was coded in situ or from transcripts, they were too small to affect the results described herein.

Problems

The Assembly Problem (the generative problem) describes a case of industrial underproduction and asks the group to suggest the best remedy. The typical group mentions about 12 possible solutions, but over 50 different solutions to the problem have been identified during the course of the research. The Personnel Selection Task (choice problem) presents five mythical résumés of candidates for a hypothetical job, and asks the group to select the best one. The résumés were created for the present study (Block unpublished) and were designed to vary along several dimensions considered relevant to the task. Each mythical candidate was either high or low on job experience, job mobility, age, and education. These variables were incorporated in the résumés on the basis of pretests to prevent any candidate from being particularly favored. Thus, each of the candidates was adopted by some groups. The patterns of results bore no relationship to the particular candidate adopted by the groups.

Valence Coding System

Described briefly, the valence system involves the tabulation of all comments identifiable with a particular solution to the problem. Each comment is coded as favorable (+) or unfavorable (-) to the solution. The valence index for any solution is the algebraic sum of the number of positive and negative comments for that solution. The valence index has shown strong correlations with the adoption of, and satisfaction with, solutions to the generative problem (see Chapters 2, 3), as will be seen in the tables comparing those results with those for the choice problem.

RESULTS

Problem Similarities

The first question to be answered is whether the valence model (see Chapter 1) is as descriptive of the problem-solving process on the choice problem as it was on the generative problem. The valence model posited that when faced with a new problem, the group acquires, through discussion, valence for each solution proposed. Three hypotheses were derived from the model:

1. To be considered for adoption, a solution must acquire more than the minimum valence value, known as the adoption threshold.
2. Beyond that threshold, the likelihood of adoption increases with increasing valence.
3. The group adopts the solution with the highest valence.

Tests of these hypotheses yielded very comparable values for the generative and choice problems. On the generative problem the adopted solution in all 45 groups (100 percent) exceeded the valence value of 15, identified as the adoption threshold. All the adopted solutions to the choice problem also exceeded 15.

Table 4.1 shows that for both problems the percentage of times a solution was adopted increased as the valence increased beyond the adoption threshold of 15. The left-hand half of the table shows that on the generative task, 26.2 percent of the 42 solutions whose valence was between 15 and 29 were adopted as the principal solution, while successively larger percentages were adopted at higher valence levels (50.0 percent from 30 to 39, 81.8 percent for over 40). An almost identical pattern was revealed by the choice problem, as seen in the right-hand half of the table. None of the differences between the two problems in the percentage adopted at each valence level is statistically significant. Thus, once a solution had passed the adoption threshold, its chances of being adopted increased with the amount of valence it accumulated.

The final proposition—that groups would adopt the solution with the highest valence—was also supported to the same degree on both problems: on the generative problem in 80.0 percent of the groups and on the choice problem in 89.5 percent, a statistically insignificant difference.

The significance of the adoption threshold for both these problems may be seen in another empirical consistency associated with it. On both problems about two-thirds of the groups (68.9 percent on the generative problem and 67.4 percent on the choice problem)

TABLE 4.1

Valence Index and Adoption of Solutions

Valence Index	Generative Problem (N = 44 groups) Percent of Solutions: Adopted: Principal*	Adopted: Subordinate	Not Adopted	Number of Solutions	Choice Task (N = 43 groups) Percent of Solutions: Adopted	Not Adopted	Number of Solutions
≥ 40	81.8	6.1	12.1	33	80.0	20.0	35
30 to 39	50.0	16.7	33.3	12	58.3	41.7	12
15 to 29	26.2	35.7	38.1	42	36.4	63.6	22
1 to 14	0.0	2.6	97.4	302	0.0	100.0	28
-9 to 0	0.0	0.0	100.0	134	0.0	100.0	52
-10 to -19	0.0	0.0	100.0	1	0.0	100.0	51
≤ -20	0.0	0.0	100.0	0	0.0	100.0	15
				524			215

*Many groups, although asked to produce a single solution, solved the problem by combining two of our separately coded solutions as a single one, for instance, to give the workers a bonus and train the foreman. In all but one instance, one of the two solutions was described in great detail, while the other was added on, usually to satisfy a dissenting member. The detailed solution was labeled the principal adopted solution and the other, the subordinate.

Source: Compiled by the authors.

adopted the first solution whose valence passed 15. Although a second solution surpassed the adoption threshold in many of these groups, it would appear that once one solution had passed that level, it was implicitly adopted and became difficult to dislodge.

Problem Differences

Although the process of adopting the final solution seems similar for the two types of problems, further analysis of the data for the choice problem reveals a more complicated, if complementary, picture. The bottom two rows of Table 4.1 show that while only 1 (0.2 percent) of the 524 possible solutions suggested for the generative problem accumulated a negative valence of less than -10, 66 (30.7 percent) of the solutions to the choice problem were rejected so vigorously, with 15 (7.0 percent) falling below -20. The statistical significance of this difference is unquestionable, but its implications for the character of the group problem-solving process are unclear. Groups easily discarded most solutions to the generative problem by turning to a different alternative or with a few negative comments, while on the choice problem much more negative argument was required to reject a candidate. This difference in the magnitude of the negative valence generated and the opportunity to examine the decision-tree hypothesis stimulated us to a more detailed analysis of the problem-solving process on the choice problem.

Identifying a Rejection Threshold on the Choice Problem

Having observed the large negative valence values on the choice problem, we searched for a rejection threshold, analogous to the adoption threshold in its implicit rejection of a possible solution. Using several statistical criteria,* including, of course, that such solutions were never adopted, a valence value of -8 was identified tentatively as a rejection threshold. At least one solution (sometimes more) accumulated a valence index of -8 or less in 37 (86 percent) of the 43 groups. A total of 77 (37 percent) solutions dropped below -8 in these 37 groups. Only 1 of these 77 solutions

---

*Details of this analysis may be obtained from Dr. Kenneth E. Friend, School of Management, Clarkson College, Potsdam, N.Y. 13676.

was ever adopted as the final solution. Mostly, groups either stopped discussing such solutions or continued to add negative valence to them. We have used -8 as a tentative rejection threshold to identify the active rejections in the analyses of the choice problem that constitute the remainder of this report, thereby distinguishing between solutions that were actively rejected by their groups and solutions that failed to be adopted because another was preferred. Solutions that were verbally discarded were sometimes of the first type and sometimes of the second. These analyses will be based on the 41 groups for which recordings were available. *

Decision-Tree Hypothesis on the Choice Problem

Examination of the content of the choice discussions reliably identified† a two-stage process in 35 (85 percent) of the 41 groups. The first, the rejection phase, was usually ended by a comment like "We've discarded two of them" or "We only have these two left," but suggested no preferences among the retained solutions. In the second, the adoption phase, the group selected one solution from the remainder. The length of the rejection phase varied considerably from group to group. Eight (23 percent) of the groups spent three-fourths of their meeting on the rejection phase, while seven (20 percent) groups spent only the first third or less on that phase. The only necessary condition for a change in phase seemed to be the conduct of at least a cursory review of all possible candidates. However, we remind the reader that 15 percent of the groups adopted a candidate without ever formally concluding the rejection phase.

The announcement that signaled the end of the rejection phase strongly focused the rest of the group discussion. Few comments were made in the adoption phase about solutions the group had

---

*Recordings of two groups were stolen before this analysis was completed. However, since the solution valence for these groups was coded as the groups discussed, those results were included in the total valence analyses.

†Gideon Falk and Gary Bond established a set of rules for determining whether the group had reduced the set of possible solutions from the original five to two or three. Twenty-two groups (54 percent) reduced to two and 13 (32 percent) to three, while six groups (15 percent) did not explicitly separate the two phases. These judgments were made without knowledge of the valence status of the solutions.

verbally discarded by the end of the rejection phase. Solutions that were verbally discarded by the group had a mean of 35.7 comments made about them during the rejection phase (versus 30.1 for those retained), but only about 7.4 comments were made subsequently. The retained candidates received an average of 48.4 comments after the others were rejected. Of the 92 candidates verbally rejected by their groups, 49 (53 percent) of them were not discussed, or received only one comment in the adoption phase. Almost needless to say, no candidate a group declared it had discarded was subsequently adopted. Thus, as hypothesized, most of these groups attempted to reduce the "cognitive complexity" of the task by initially discarding unacceptable candidates, then by explicitly limiting their discussion to choosing one from only two or three remaining.

Relationship between Valence and Decision-Tree Analysis on the Choice Problem

The apparent discrepancy between the manifest, two-phase process and the seemingly unrelated process revealed by the valence analysis prompted an examination of the relationship between them. Four valence-adoption patterns were identified with respect to the announced separation into a rejection and an adoption phase. The cumulative valences for the solutions of one group from each type are plotted in Figures 4.1 through 4.4 to provide a better picture of the dynamics of the adoption process.* The valences have been aggregated across 50 acts for each point on the curve, and the points have been connected as if the valence accumulation were linear within segments. Figure 4.1 illustrates the six groups (15 percent) where no end of the rejection phase was announced. The asterisk shows the adopted solution. In Figures 4.2 through 4.4, the vertical line denotes the end of the rejection phase and "D" indicates the solutions discarded verbally at that point. Figure 4.2 plots one of the 11 groups (27 percent) in which only one solution had passed the adoption threshold during the rejection phase, although at least one other was retained into the adoption phase. Groups where two solutions (11 groups, 27 percent) and no solutions (13 groups, 32 percent) had passed the adoption threshold before the adoption phase are illustrated by Figures 4.3 and 4.4, respectively.

---

*Data for all 41 groups may be obtained from L. R. Hoffman, Graduate School of Business, University of Chicago, Chicago, Ill. 60637.

FIGURE 4.1

Patterns of Solution Valence Accumulations:
No Rejection Phase Announced

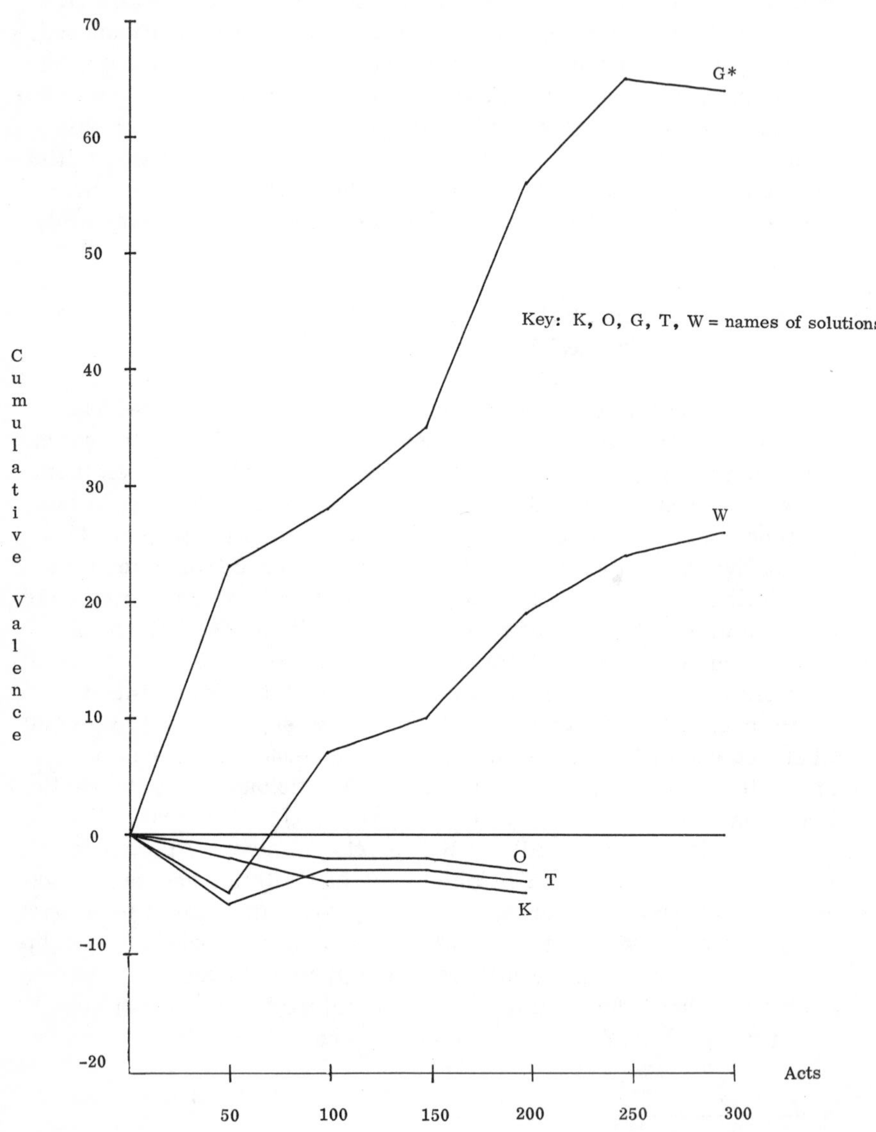

*Adopted solution.
Source: Compiled by the authors.

The group in Figure 4.1 shows a valence pattern similar to the modal one found for the generative problem (see Chapter 2). One solution passed the adoption threshold during the first 50 acts; accumulated valence more slowly during the next 100 acts, while the other candidates were being discussed; then showed a sharp rise again for the next 100 acts; and was finally adopted. Although only two solutions (G and W) were discussed during the last 100 acts, the group never announced an end to the rejection phase. This graph is also similar to the modal generative graph in that no solution dropped below the rejection threshold (-8). Unacceptable solutions were merely ignored toward the latter part of the session.

The treatment in Figure 4.2 of the ultimately adopted solution is very similar to the previous group. Solution O passed the adoption threshold in the first 50 acts; then accumulated valence very slowly for the next 150 acts, while other solutions were being discussed; and finally showed a continual sharp rise to its adoption at the end. This group differed from the first group both in announcing an explicit end to the rejection phase and in its active rejection of solutions (solutions T and G during the rejection phase and solution K during the adoption phase). Of the 11 groups in which only one solution passed the adoption threshold during the rejection phase, that solution was adopted in 8 (73 percent) of those groups.

The adoption pattern in Figure 4.3 looks like that of the first two groups, except for the displacement of the curve to the right by 100 acts. The adopted solution (K) did not pass the adoption threshold until act 127. But once past, it slowed its rate of accumulating valence for the next 200 acts, finally accumulating valence again at a rapid rate during the adoption phase to stave off the challenge of solution O. This group shows clearly that the first solution discussed is not necessarily the first to pass the adoption threshold or to be adopted. Once a solution passes the threshold, however, the characteristic adoption pattern tends to evolve. In the 11 groups of this type, all but one of the solutions that had passed the adoption threshold were retained into the adoption phase and, except for one group, were the only ones retained.

Unlike the groups in the previous two figures, the group in Figure 4.4 ended its rejection phase with no solution having passed the adoption threshold. This group spent much of its early discussion vigorously degrading solution W—accumulating a valence of -40—then announced the end of the rejection phase at act 164 without accumulating sufficient positive valence to push any of the other candidates beyond the adoption threshold by that point. The 13 (32 percent) groups typified by this two-phase pattern could be considered to be the only ones that truly followed the sequence of first discarding

FIGURE 4.2

Patterns of Solution Valence Accumulations: One Solution beyond Adoption Threshold

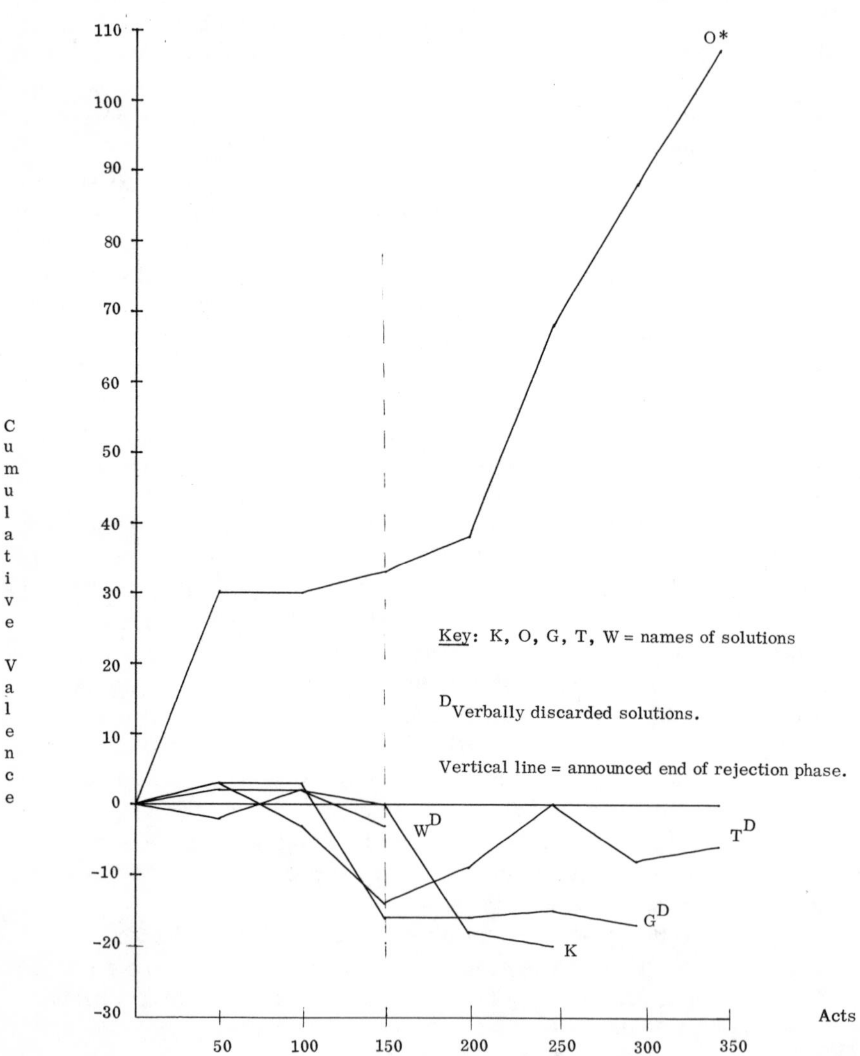

*Adopted solution.

Source: Compiled by the authors.

FIGURE 4.3

Patterns of Solution Valence Accumulations: Two Solutions beyond Adoption Threshold

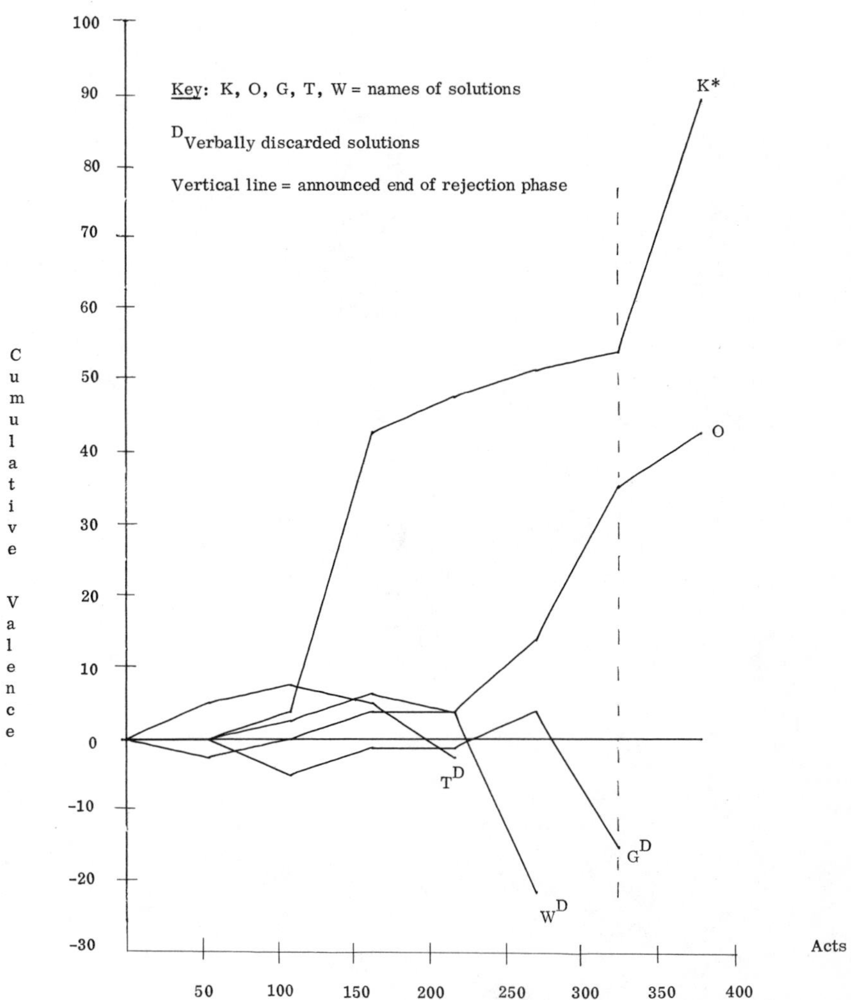

*Adopted solution.
Source: Compiled by the authors.

FIGURE 4.4

Patterns of Solution Valence Accumulations: No Solutions beyond Adoption Threshold

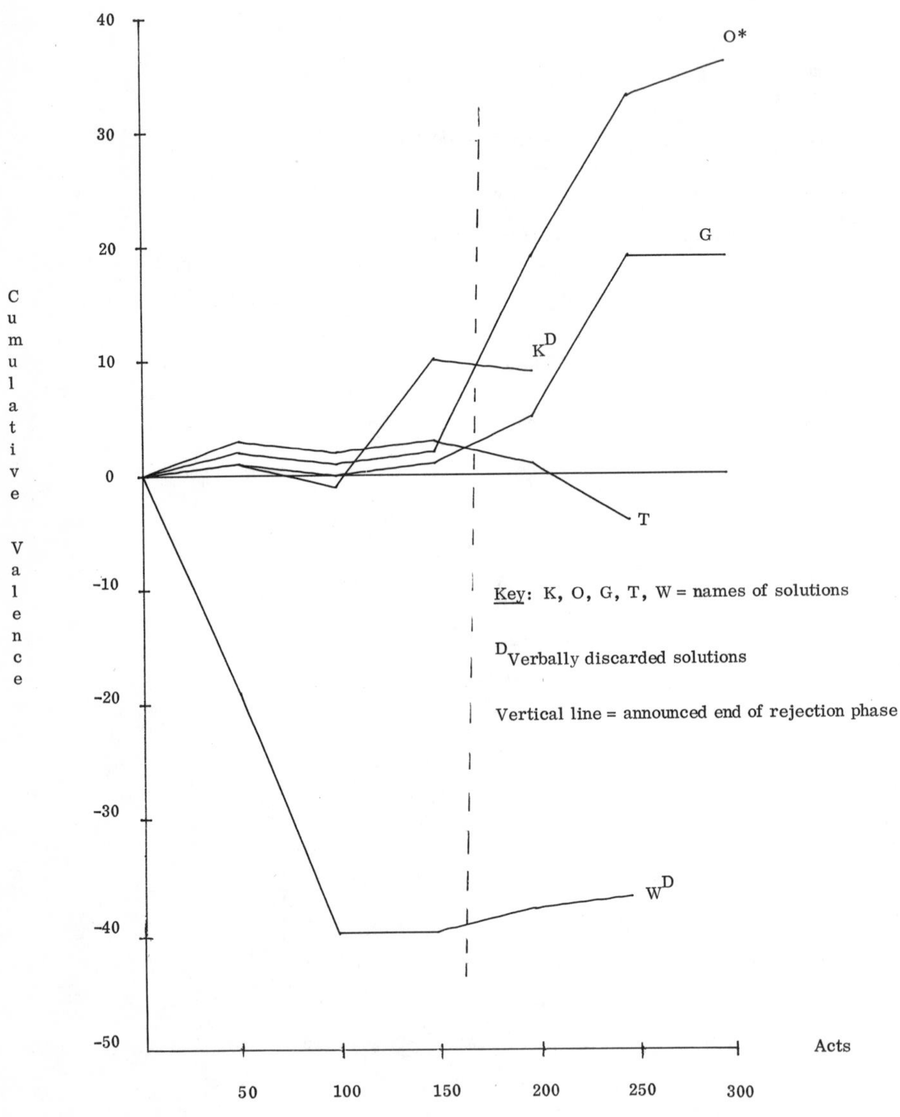

*Adopted solution.
Source: Compiled by the authors.

unacceptable alternatives, then choosing among the remainder without prejudice.

Figures 4.2, 4.3, and 4.4 are consistent with the overall effects of the two thresholds—rejection (-8) and adoption (+15)—on the disposition of solutions. Table 4.2 shows that 47 of the 48 solutions that dropped below -8 during the rejection phase (like solutions G and T in Figure 4.2) were discarded verbally by their groups. At the other extreme 33 of the 34 solutions that passed the adoption threshold during the rejection phase were retained for further discussion. Although passing the threshold was sufficient for discard or retention, it was not a necessary condition, as seen by the unpredictable disposition of solutions with valence between the two threshold values. For example, solution K in Figure 4.2 was retained with a valence of -2, while in Figure 4.4 the same solution was discarded with a valence of 10.

TABLE 4.2

Valence of Solutions at End of Rejection Phase and Group Action

	Solution Was	
Valence of Solution	Discarded	Retained
15 or more	1	33
0 to 14	16	40
-1 to -7	28	9
-8 or less	47	1

Note: Only 35 groups had both transcripts and two identifiable phases.

Source: Compiled by the authors.

The Adoption Phase

Eighty-three solutions (two or three per group) were retained into the adoption phase, but valence analysis shows that they were hardly equally probable candidates for adoption. A retained solution with valence already greater than the adoption threshold was much more likely to be adopted than were others. In the 22 groups like Figures 4.2 and 4.3, 51 solutions were retained into the adoption phase, of which 33 had passed the adoption threshold. Nineteen of the 22 adopted came from those 33 solutions ($p < .05$). Thus, even though the manifest discussion indicated no preferences among the retained solutions, valence analysis showed a distinct advantage to those with valence above the adoption threshold.

Despite the strong suggestion in these results that the groups used the adoption phase principally to confirm a decision already made implicitly, some ambiguity remains. It is clear that in those 13 groups like Figure 4.4, where no solution had passed 15, the adoption phase was used to continue to evaluate the remaining contenders before giving one solution enough valence to pass the adoption threshold and, finally, to be confirmed. Also, in groups like Figure 4.3, with two or more solutions greater than 15 at the end of the rejection phase, the adoption phase was needed to choose among the contenders.

These facts raised the possibility that when the choice problem was manifestly solved in two phases—rejection followed by adoption—the valence process operated in each stage separately, although on a reduced set of possible solutions. When the valence generated only during the adoption phase was analyzed in the 35 groups with two stages (like Figures 4.2, 4.3, 4.4), we discovered valence-adoption relationships similar to those found for the process as a whole: (1) the solution with the highest valence was adopted in 31 (88.6 percent) of the groups and (2) the probability of a solution's adoption increased with the amount of valence it accumulated (see Table 4.3). However, in seven (20 percent) groups solutions were adopted with valence accumulations of less than 15 and the entire relationship in Table 4.3 is displaced downward from that shown in Table 4.1. Thus, no clear-cut conclusion can be drawn about the functions of the adoption phase.

TABLE 4.3

Valence Index and Adoption of Retained Solutions

Valence Index	Percent of Retained Solutions: Adopted	Percent of Retained Solutions: Not Adopted	Number of Solutions
≥ 40	92.9	7.1	14
30 to 39	100.0	0.0	9
15 to 29	53.8	46.2	13
1 to 14	26.9	73.1	26
-9 to 0	0.0	100.0	16

Note: Choice task, adoption phase only.
Source: Compiled by the authors.

DISCUSSION AND CONCLUSIONS

The direct test of the generality of the valence model (see Chapter 1) showed both similarities and differences between the choice and generative problems. The similarity lies principally in the adoption mechanism. The valence-adoption relationships found on the generative problem were replicated in their aggregate form on the choice problem. Despite the clarity of the manifest two-stage decision process shown by most groups on the choice problem, the implicit process of moving the group toward adopting a solution shown by the valence index seems to have occurred quite independently of the stages. The identity of the valence-adoption relationships for the two problems—shown in Table 4.1 and in the fact that more than 80 percent of the groups adopted the highest valent solution on both problems—supports this contention. The more valence a solution accumulates, the more likely it is to be adopted. Conversely, regardless of how much a group discusses a solution, it will not be adopted unless it accumulates sufficient valence. The question of why some solutions accumulate valence while others do not is a topic for further study. It is likely that solutions that satisfy habitual definitions of the problem will receive immediate support, as would those favored by the more dominant or higher-status members of the group (Hoffman 1965; see also Chapter 3).

Equally striking was the confirmation of the valence value of 15 as the adoption threshold—the minimum value needed for a solution to be adopted by a group—and the function it plays in the problem-solving process. No adopted solution to the choice problem failed to receive at least 15 valence points. Mere discussion of a solution is not enough to ensure its adoption. Although many solutions were discussed at length (like solution T in Figure 4.4), they often failed to even achieve zero valence, and were not adopted.

Despite these similarities between the choice and generative problems in the process of adopting solutions, two principal differences between them should be noted. The process of rejecting unacceptable solution possibilities seems to have been much more difficult on the choice problem than on the generative one. On the latter, groups typically merely ignored, and ceased talking about, solutions they did not like, or rejected them with a few negative comments. Unacceptable solutions to the choice problem, on the other hand, often accumulated large negative valences (-10 to -40) before groups stopped discussing them.

This difference between the problems seems to stem from the indivisibility of the solutions to the choice problem and from the fact that each candidate had some desirable qualities. A conflict between two candidates for the job could not be resolved by selecting the best qualities of each to provide a composite "superman" for the job. On the generative problem, solutions could be combined, as when groups recommended that an incentive system be installed and that the foreman be trained, too. Being deprived of such a mechanism for resolving substantive conflict on the choice task, groups seem to have needed to muster many arguments to highlight the poor qualities of rejected candidates and deny their good ones, a form of group dissonance reduction (Festinger 1957).

The most striking characteristic of the choice problem is the manifest two-stage process used by most groups. In the first stage they systematically reviewed all five alternatives and, after rejecting two or three, announced that they would now choose among the remainder. Groups then concentrated their discussions almost exclusively on those two or three remaining candidates. Our experience with the generative problem has never suggested such an explicit separation of stages. Rather, as each solution was suggested by a group member, it was evaluated and discussed until someone either suggested another alternative or returned to a previous suggestion.

Why this difference between the tasks occurs is an open question. It is possible that the simultaneous presentation of all alternatives to the group suggests the need for a complete review. Moreover, it is easy to keep only five possible candidates in mind (Miller 1956), whereas remembering the 10 or 12 solutions offered in sequence to the generative problem would be more difficult. Perhaps these data support the need for a group memory—a blackboard or other public record—to prevent the loss of possible good solutions whose value was not recognized when they were first introduced, and were then forgotten. On the choice problem the group had all five résumés throughout the meeting.

Despite the obviousness and regularity of use of the two-stage process on the choice problem, its interplay with the underlying valence-adoption process is intriguing. On the one hand, a group's announcement that it had rejected certain candidates and had to choose between or among the others had the normative force to focus the group's discussion only on the approved candidates. On the other hand, the valence analysis revealed that the "choice" had already been made implicitly. This interplay between what the group says it is doing and what it seems to be doing according to the valence analysis deserves further study.

Another example is revealed in the graphs of the process in Figures 4.1-4.4. All four graphs show the strong impact that the first solution to pass the adoption threshold has on the remainder of the process. When that first solution passes the adoption threshold, it seems to act as a barrier to other solutions also passing it in sufficient time to be contenders. Two-thirds of the groups ultimately adopted the first solution to pass the threshold, even though they discussed the other candidates at length—for 250 more acts in the case of Figure 4.1.

Group members show no verbal awareness of the dominance of the single suprathreshold solution. For example, the group in Figure 4.2, in which the ultimately adopted solution passed the adoption threshold in the first 50 acts, ended its rejection phase at act 150 with the statement, "Well, we're down to two candidates which both have . . . not excellent characteristics, but very good." The valence of the first candidate was 32 at that point, while the second candidate had -2, indicating it had practically no chance for adoption. But the group continued the meeting for almost 200 more acts, ostensibly trying to decide between the two candidates. Thus, the group's decision is determined by an implicit process over which the members seem to have little control.

The valence-adoption process, as displayed in the graphs of Figure 4.1, also reveals the inadequacy of input-outcome experiments for describing the group problem-solving process. To assume, as Davis (1973) does, for example, that the members' initial preference distributions among alternatives are reflected directly and equally in the process of arriving at a decision is naive at best and misleading at worst. Even on this choice problem, where all the alternatives were presented at the beginning of the discussion, the early accumulation of valence, as in Figure 4.1, inhibits the full consideration of other alternatives. On generative problems, ideas may not receive sufficient valence to pass the adoption threshold and be considered seriously. Or ideas suggested after one solution has passed the adoption threshold may be compared quickly against that one and fail to be discussed thoroughly. In either case, creative ideas may be lost to the group due to the timing of their entrance into the discussion, having nothing to do with the members' initial preferences or the formal decision process used.

The ability to measure the group's movement toward adopting solutions through the valence method, while already useful for refining our understanding of that process, also raises many new questions for study. What causes one solution to acquire valence rapidly, like G in Figure 4.1, while the same solution is rejected vigorously in another group (Figure 4.3)? Can groups be trained to delay the too-early accumulation of valence for a single solution through techniques like brainstorming, or can they learn to overcome the inhibiting effects of the threshold? We believe the answers lie in the interplay between the implicit solution valence-adoption process and the values and norms of the group.

5

THE PROCESS OF SOLVING REASONING AND VALUE PROBLEMS

L. Richard Hoffman
Rory O'Day

Studies reported in the preceding chapters have used problems with two characteristics of potential importance for a group's problem-solving process: (1) the character of the solutions and (2) the prior exposure of members to the problem. On both the Assembly (generative) Problem and the Personnel Selection (choice) Problem, the groups assumed that some solution would be considered by the experimenters as better than others. For example, a solution that increased productivity would be better for the Assembly Problem than one that did not (see Chapter 3). The best candidate for the managerial position on the Personnel Selection Problem would presumably improve the sales picture for the company (see Chapter 4). However, on both problems the criteria for the best solution were not obvious to the group. The question of whether the solution adopted was truly the best could not be determined by the group itself from the data available to it.

The adequacy of solutions to certain problems that groups face is internally verifiable, however. Thompson and Tuden (1959) have indicated that where both the goal of the group and the method of achieving the goal are agreed upon, the group's decision strategy is merely computational. Determining whether investment in one product or another would have the greater payback for a firm would be of this type. Once the managerial group decides to limit its choice to those two investments and to its assumptions about such parameters as the payback period, the decision rests only on the calculations from the applicable equations. The problem raised by arithmetic reasoning problems, which are analogs of the payback problem, is usually to identify the correct method of calculation. The arithmetic operations are then quite straightforward, usually well within the competence of all group members. The group itself can then verify the correctness of a solution it is considering by determining whether they have followed the correct method in arriving at it.

Groups also often face problems that have no "objectively" correct solution, that is, where the group itself must decide what its goal is before it can decide what actions might accomplish that goal. Family groups must agree on where they want to take their vacation or on what type of behavior is acceptable in their house (Strodtbeck 1951). Compensation awards in personal injury cases are often based on what the jury thinks may be fair redress for the injury sustained. Thompson and Tuden (1959) suggested that such problems in organizational management require a compromise strategy for their resolution. The members must decide whether they can agree on a value premise before they choose an action.

The principal question in the present study is whether groups solve these two types of problems in the same way as problems they perceive to have correct but unverifiable answers. More specifically, with respect to the principal concerns of this volume, do the valence-adoption relationships previously found on the generative and choice problems hold as well for problems of arithmetic reasoning and value judgments, and equally for both?

The arithmetic reasoning problems were both of the "Eureka" type, requiring a minimum of arithmetic ability, and clearly internally verifiable. The value problems created moral dilemmas, which manifestly had no "correct" resolution and about which people were likely to have strong feelings. Both types of problems were chosen as potential threats to the generality of the earlier findings. Since the reasoning problems could be verified by simple arithmetic procedures, one might expect that the nature of the comments made, and not their frequency, would be most important in determining which solution would be adopted. In contrast, to the extent that the value problems evoked strong feelings in the members, the members might react (Brehm 1966) to any attempts to convince them to abandon their positions, thus disconfirming the earlier results and even preventing the group from reaching a decision at all (cf. Chapter 1 for a discussion of boundary conditions on conflict).

Two other aspects of the present design varied substantially from the earlier studies, but were common to both types of problems. Each problem was solved individually prior to the group discussion. Since the model assumes that such work produces prediscussion valence for all solution alternatives considered (especially positive valence for the member's preferred solution), we expected some effects to appear on the valence values generated in the group discussion and on the resulting valence-adoption relationships. If all the members agreed initially on the same solution, thus making prediscussion valence large for one solution, discussion-generated valence could be expected to be small. Little more would be required of the group than that the members verify the acceptability of that solution. Conversely, strong prediscussion valence for two or more solutions might produce sharp conflict in the discussion.

Similarly, the effects of a shorter time limit (8 minutes in this study versus 40 minutes in the earlier ones) are difficult to anticipate. Is the effect of a shortened discussion a lowered adoption threshold, thus yielding smaller valence values? Or is it to reduce conflict and focus discussion on the evaluation of a particular solution? The latter effect would probably generate valence values in the discussion comparable with those obtained under the longer time limit.

Both of these variations—the prediscussion, individual decisions and the shorter time limit—might be expected to reduce the correlations between members' valence and satisfaction with the group's solution. If the valence generated in the discussion is attenuated, the observed index may underestimate the member's true valence for that solution. An exploratory attempt to estimate each member's prediscussion valence for his preferred solution is included in this study.

METHOD

Subjects

Eighty-seven male introductory psychology students constituted fifteen four-man groups and nine three-man groups. The three-man groups resulted from the failure of one member to appear for each of those nine experimental sessions.

Problems

Two problems of each type—reasoning and value—were used. The Horse Trading Problem (Maier and Solem 1952) and the Bracelet Problem (Milton 1958) each have a correct solution. Neither the Traffic Problem nor the Cheating Problem (Schutz 1958), on the other hand, has a definite correct answer, the solutions being a function of the values or attitudes of the individual group members. Each problem had at least three solutions that were favored by a substantial proportion of the students.

Experimental Procedure

The order of presentation of the four problems was varied from group to group, to control for order effects. Each member solved the first problem individually and indicated his degree of confidence concerning the correctness of (or his strength of feeling about) his solution. The group then discussed the problem for a maximum of eight minutes, to try to agree on a single solution. The experimenter presented the value problems for group solutions with the admonition, "I recognize that there are no right answers to this problem, but see whether you can agree on a single answer," so members were aware that they were permitted to fail to agree after eight minutes. At the end of eight minutes, each member indicated his individual satisfaction with the group's solution and with his influence over it. This procedure was repeated for each of the four problems in succession, with no feedback to the group about its performance. Upon completion of the fourth problem, each member again gave his preferred answer to each of the four problems, "regardless of the group's decision." Feedback about the experiment and their results was provided at the end.

Measures

Valence Index

The solution-relevant statements of the group members were recorded in coded form by two independent observers while the subjects solved each problem as a group. The statements were coded on the basis of a modification of the procedure described in Appendix B.1.

The valence index for each solution discussed is the algebraic sum of the number of positive acts minus the number of negative acts made by each member. The group valence for each solution is the algebraic sum of the individual indexes of the members for that solution. The average intercoder reliability was .87, approximately the same level of proficiency as in the earlier studies (see Chapter 2).

Prediscussion Valence

Ratings were obtained from each person following his initial individual solution for each problem. A more complete procedure would have included measures of the subjects' feelings about each of the alternative solutions, but it was not administratively feasible to do so. For the reasoning problems, ratings were made on an

11-point probability scale (0 probability to 1 probability) in response to the question, "How confident are you that your answer is correct?" For the value problems, a five-point scale from "not at all strong" to "very strong" was used with the question "How strong are your feelings about the position you have taken with respect to your answer?"

Satisfaction with the Group Solution and with Influence in the Group

Each member rated his satisfaction individually after each problem had been solved by the group. A six-point scale was used, from "very dissatisfied" to "very satisfied," for responses to two questions: "How satisfied are you with the solution reached by your group?" and "How satisfied are you with the amount of say or influence you had over your group's solution?" Values ranging from 1 to 6 were assigned to the responses to indicate increasing degrees of satisfaction.

RESULTS

Solution Valence, Adoption, and Satisfaction

The first question to be answered is whether groups solved the reasoning and value problems in similar or different ways. We were struck immediately by the fact that all groups (100 percent) agreed on an answer to the reasoning problems, but four groups (16.7 percent) failed to agree on answers to one or both of the value problems (six failures altogether).

However, when only those groups that adopted solutions to the problems are analyzed, the results for the two types of problems are quite similar. The solution with the highest valence index was adopted in 47 (98 percent) of the 48 reasoning problems and in 40 (95 percent) of the 42 value problems. Similarly, the relationship between the valence index achieved by a solution and the percentage of times it was adopted was also almost identical for the two types of problems, as shown in Table 5.1. In both cases the percentage of adoptions increased with increasing valence values beyond a minimum value of about 5. None of the differences between problems in the percentage adopted is statistically significant. In both of these comparisons it should be noted that in each of the four groups that failed to produce a solution, there was at least one solution with more than five valence points and some with more than ten, values sufficient for adoption in other groups. Thus, except for these four groups, the valence-adoption process seemed to operate in similar

TABLE 5.1

Valence and Solution Adoption

	Reasoning Problems			Value Problems			
	Percent of Solutions			Percent of Solutions			
Valence Index	Adopted	Not Adopted	Number of Solutions	Adopted	Not Adopted	No Decision*	Number of Solutions
25 to 29	—	—	0	100.0	0.0	0.0	2
20 to 24	100.0	0.0	3	100.0	0.0	0.0	1
15 to 19	83.3	16.7	6	100.0	0.0	0.0	6
10 to 14	88.9	10.1	18	65.0	25.0	15.0	20
5 to 9	76.7	23.3	30	69.2	11.5	19.2	26
0 to 4	1.4	98.6	69	3.8	80.8	15.4	52
-5 to -1	0.0	100.0	4	0.0	87.5	12.5	40
-10 to -6	—	—	0	0.0	100.0	0.0	1
Total			130				148

*These data are for four groups that reached no decision on six problems. They were classified as "not adopted" for the chi-square test.

Source: Compiled by the authors.

fashion on the two types of problems. Furthermore, these results generally replicate those of the studies with the Assembly Problem and the Personnel Selection Problem. The similarities lie in the proportions of groups that adopted the highest valence solution and in the general shape of the valence-adoption relationship (compare Table 5.1 with Table 4.1). We should also note that there were no differences in the valence-adoption relationship on the reasoning problems for groups that adopted the correct answer and those that did not.

There was also a similarity in the relationship of individual valence for the adopted solution and members' satisfaction with the solution and their influence over it. The positive correlations in Table 5.2 between valence and satisfaction with both the adopted solution and the members' influence over the solution are significant for all four problems. They varied insignificantly from problem to problem, despite the different character of each problem. Moreover, the values are very close to those of .41 and .40, respectively, obtained in the earlier study.

TABLE 5.2

Individual Valence for and Satisfaction with the Adopted Group Solution

		Correlations Between Valence and	
Problem	N	Satisfaction with Solution	Satisfaction with Influence
Horse Trading	86	0.38**	0.38**
Bracelet	85	0.34**	0.29**
Traffic	80	0.26**	0.29**
Cheating	71	0.38**	0.35**

Note: N's vary because some groups failed to arrive at a solution and some members did not answer the questions.

**Significantly different from zero at the .01 level.

Source: Compiled by the authors.

An Exploration of Prediscussion Valence

The results presented thus far have supported the generality of the relationships between the valence index and members' adoption of and satisfaction with solutions found in Chapters 2, 3, and 4.

However, the absolute valence values of the present study are less than those obtained in the other studies. The majority (81.1 percent) of adopted solutions to the reasoning and value problems accumulated less valence than the previously identified adoption threshold of 15 valence points—the minimum value for adopted solutions in those studies. Furthermore, none of the solutions to the present problems attained valences of more than 29 points, in comparison with 74 percent of the solutions in previous studies. Whether the values obtained here are a function of the shorter period of problem solving permitted (8 minutes compared with 40 minutes) or of the prediscussion valence generated during the individual problem solving is an open question.

We attempted a partial examination of the latter possibility by using the members' ratings of their confidence in or strength of feeling about their individual solutions as estimates of the valence they brought into the meeting. The values 1-10 assigned to these ratings were purely arbitrary and intended only to provide a preliminary test of the hypothesis that such prediscussion valence contributed to both the adoption and the acceptance of solutions. The test is limited by three factors:

1. Ratings were obtained only for the solution offered by the member as his individual solution, whereas he might also have generated positive or negative valence for other possibilities as well.
2. This failure to obtain complete ratings also means that the solutions for which prediscussion valence was estimated could be different from one member to the next in a particular group.
3. The values assigned to each scale point, as well as the upper limit of 10 placed on the rating scale, being entirely arbitrary, may have unpredictable effects on the relationships obtained and may underestimate the true importance of prediscussion valence compared with valence generated by the discussion itself.

Despite these important limitations, a combined valence index was created for each solution put forth either as an individual solution or in the group discussion. The combined index is the sum of the valence measured during the group discussion and the rating of confidence or strength of feeling assigned by each member to his initial individual solution. The same analyses performed previously on the discussion-based valence index were repeated with the combined valence index. The following results were obtained:

TABLE 5.3

Combined Valence Index and Solution Adoption

Combined Valence Index	Reasoning Problems: Percent of Solutions: Adopted	Reasoning Problems: Percent of Solutions: Not Adopted	Reasoning Problems: Number of Solutions	Value Problems: Percent of Solutions: Adopted	Value Problems: Percent of Solutions: Not Adopted	Value Problems: Percent of Solutions: No Decision*	Value Problems: Number of Solutions
≥ 40	100.0	0.0	2	100.0	0.0	0.0	7
30 to 39	95.0	5.0	20	90.9	9.1	0.0	11
15 to 29	59.5	40.5	37	62.9	14.3	22.9	35
5 to 14	7.8	92.2	64	9.4	78.1	12.5	32
0 to 4	0.0	100.0	17	0.0	88.5	11.5	26
-5 to -1	0.0	100.0	2	0.0	86.1	13.9	36
≤ -6	—	—	0	0.0	100.0	0.0	1
Total			142				148

*These data are for four groups that reached no decision on six problems. They were classified as "not adopted" fcr the chi-square test.

Source: Compiled by the authors.

1. The combined valence index for adopted solutions ranged from 6 to 49. These values are higher than the discussion-based values, but are still substantially lower than those obtained in previous studies (range: 14 to 110).

2. Almost all (92 percent for reasoning problems, 83 percent for value problems) of the solutions that were adopted had the highest combined valence index in their group. These results are comparable with those shown in Table 5.1 for the discussion-based index alone, although the percentage for the reasoning problems was slightly smaller.

3. Examination of the quantitative relationship between the combined valence index and solution adoption in Table 5.3 shows that as the combined valence value increased, the proportion of adopted solutions increased. This relationship is similar to the one shown in Table 5.1, except that the combined valence values are more comparable with those obtained in previous studies.

4. The product-moment correlations shown in Table 5.4 support the hypothesized positive relationships between individuals' valence indexes and (a) their satisfaction with the solution and (b) their influence over it. The larger correlations found with the combined index, as compared with the discussion-based valence index (see Table 5.2), suggest that the prediscussion ratings of individual solutions measure some part of the valence that members brought into the meeting. The combined valence index, by summing the discussion-based valence and the prediscussion valence, appears to have yielded a better measure of each member's feelings about his solution than did the observed valence alone.

TABLE 5.4

Correlations between Individual Revised Valence for the Adopted Group Solution and Satisfaction with the Solution and with Influence in the Group

Problem	N	Revised Valence and Satisfaction with Solution	Revised Valence and Satisfaction with Influence
Horse Trading	86	0.45**	0.65**
Bracelet	85	0.47**	0.51**
Traffic	70	0.48**	0.37**
Cheating	71	0.62**	0.48**

Note: N's vary because some groups failed to arrive at a solution and some members did not answer the questions.

**Significant at .01 level.

Source: Compiled by the authors.

DISCUSSION

The principal purpose of this study was to determine whether the successful earlier tests of the valence model of the group problem-solving process would extend to problems of quite different character. The present results confirm the value of the valence model and its operations for both arithmetic reasoning and value problems. Although one might easily have expected that groups would approach these two types of problems in quite different ways, there seems to be a substantial similarity in the mechanism used. In attempting to arrive at some form of consensus, group members offer solution possibilities, and justifications for and against the solutions, and express agreement and disagreement with the alternatives proposed. In the laboratory context and the given time constraints, the group seems to respond to the frequency with which such comments are offered in deciding which solution to adopt. More specifically, whether the problem involves reasoning or a choice among value positions, the more valence a solution accumulates, the more likely is it to be adopted. Moreover, although the arguments favoring a particular solution to the Horse Trading Problem might refer to arithmetic processes and the arguments in the Traffic Problem refer to the social functions of the law, the valence values required for adopting a solution were almost identical for both types of problem.

The adopted solution, however, appears really to represent primarily those members who actively promoted it. The positive correlations between individual valence for the adopted solution and a member's satisfaction with the solution support this contention. Those who argued in favor and gained the decision had the satisfaction of being "winners," while those who favored an alternative "lost." In ad hoc groups like these, the problem provides an arena for playing out the struggle for leadership that marks the early stages of group development (Tuckman 1965). However, the valence-adoption relationships also must reflect the members' beliefs about the merits of the various solutions, since they hold as well for groups with correct and incorrect solutions to the reasoning problems.

The fact that the absolute valence values marking the relationships in this study were less than those of other studies, and that some groups failed to produce a solution to the value problems, may have related explanations. On the one hand, groups may reduce the value of their adoption threshold to meet a shortened time limit. Recognizing the impossibility of a protracted examination of the problem, they adopt the decision argued most strongly by some members. Members opposed to the growing consensus may withdraw more quickly, recognizing the diminished period in which to convince the others and lacking the commitment to their own solution or to the group's success to maintain a sustained opposition. Thus, the valence value needed to adopt a solution would appear to be smaller.

When, however, members are strongly committed to their solutions, as they were in the groups that failed to agree on the value problems, opposing members may not withdraw so easily. Their valence for their value position may outweigh their valence for arriving at a group decision. Hoffman (in Chapter 1) has suggested that conflict will not be resolved if the boundary conditions on the group cannot contain it. In this case the usual forces toward uniformity in laboratory groups (Thomas and Fink 1961) had been weakened by the experimenter's instruction to the group that they might not be able to agree on the value problems. By reporting no decision, they avoided a conflict within the group that could not be resolved successfully within the imposed time limit, yet they still met the group's external response to the experimenter. Research is needed to identify the conditions that contain but do not suppress conflict to promote the creative potential of groups (Hoffman, Harburg, and Maier 1962).

One factor that is likely to set the stage for such conflict is the commitment (valence) of members for or against particular decisions before the meeting begins. Our exploratory attempt to measure such valence through the ratings of individual solutions to these problems seems very promising. The index formed by adding the arbitrarily scaled ratings to the discussion-based valence predicted adoptions and produced relationships approximating those of the earlier studies. The most compelling evidence for the importance of prediscussion valence comes from the increased magnitude of the correlations between the combined valence index for each member and his rated satisfaction with the group decision. In most ongoing groups, members enter discussions of important matters with strong valences for some alternatives. Sometimes these may exceed their valence for the continued existence of the group, as when politicians change parties on matters of principle or when the personal ambitions of a member are opposed by the other members. Unless we understand and can assess such valence, our measures of valence from the discussion alone will be underestimates of the true values. Thus, the commitment of members to an adopted solution may be incorrectly estimated from such a measure, as may be the degree of conflict latent in the group. A more complete assessment of prediscussion valence for all solutions in the present study would provide greater insight into the relative importance of that factor versus the shortened time allowed for problem solving.

6

A NOTE ON SOLUTION VALENCE, THE AMOUNT OF DISCUSSION, AND STAGES IN PROBLEM SOLVING GROUPS

L. Richard Hoffman

The first empirical study (see Chapter 2) distinguished how much a solution is discussed from the valence it accumulates as determinants of its probability of being adopted. Nevertheless, there seems to be some confusion between the two concepts and their operational measures that needs to be removed. The distinction between the amount of discussion and the relative favorability or unfavorability (valence) of the comments made is critical both conceptually and operationally.

Conceptually, the valence concept was adapted from Kurt Lewin (1935) to describe the force on the group to adopt (or reject) a cognition (see Chapter 1). It rests on the assumption that the group as a social system moves toward certain beliefs and away from others as it solves problems. With special regard to solutions to a group problem, the group moves toward adopting a particular solution by attempting to develop consensus about the merits of that solution (Thomas and Fink 1961). Arguments are presented in its favor, opposing arguments are discredited, and support for it among the members is elicited until sufficient valence for its adoption has accumulated. How much valence is necessary for a solution to be adopted was not specified in the original model, although some minimum valence value—now known as the adoption threshold—was hypothesized to prevent the group from failing to adopt any solution.

Solution valence has been operationalized in several studies by recording the frequency of comments made in favor of and against each solution discussed by a group. The valence index equals the algebraic difference between these frequencies. Symbolically,

$$V_{i.} = \sum_{j}^{r}(P_{ij} - N_{ij}),$$

where i = the number of a solution, j = the number of a person, r = the size of the group, $V_{i.}$ = the group valence for solution i, P_{ij} = the number of positive comments made about solution i by person j, N_{ij} = the number of negative comments made about solution i by person j. The amount of discussion, on the other hand, is the total number of comments, regardless of whether they are positive or negative. The amount of discussion about a solution ($T_{i.}$), in terms of the above symbols, is

$$\sum_{j}^{r}(P_{ij} + N_{ij}),$$

and the total amount of discussion ($T_{..}$) is

$$\sum\sum_{ij}^{Kr}(P_{ij} + N_{i}),$$

where K is the number of solutions discussed by the group.

Thus, mathematically, there is no necessary relationship between the group valence for a solution and the amount of discussion either about it or about all solutions. However, we have already seen that the group valence index has shown strong relationships to the adoption of solutions by problem-solving groups. Therefore, we would expect some correlation between valence for the adopted solution and the amount of discussion about it. On the two problems with which the group members were unfamiliar before the meeting, (1) more than 80 percent of the groups adopted the solution with the highest valence; (2) no group adopted a solution with less than 15 valence points (the adoption threshold); and (3) the probability of a solution being adopted increased consistently with increases in cumulative valence, as shown for the generative and choice problems in Table 4.1. The same relationship shown for the generative problem in that table was found in groups with appointed leaders in which the leaders and members had identical or different goals (see Chapter 3).

Despite these consistencies in the relationship between the valence and adoption of solutions, nothing in the group problem-solving model to this point has dealt with the issue of how long it would take for a solution to be adopted or what relationship there might be between the amount of discussion and the rate of accumulation of valence for the adopted solution. The solution ultimately adopted is usually discussed at length. But all of the relationships between valence and adoption imply that the number of positive acts exceeds the number of negative acts for the adopted solution, which in turn produces an artifactually inflated correlation between the valence index and the total amount of discussion about the adopted solution. Furthermore, Bales and Strodtbeck (1951) have suggested that much of a group's closing activity is spent confirming the wisdom of the group's choice, thus adding valence to that solution. However, experience indicates that meetings often continue when there is conflict about alternative solutions or when there is very little support for any solution. The relationship between the total amount of solution-related activity in a meeting and the valence accumulated for the adopted solution seemed worth examining to clarify their possible overlap and distinctiveness.

PROCEDURE

The data for this analysis were obtained from groups that solved the two different problems that generated the data shown in Table 6.1. These problems are described in detail in Appendixes A.1 and A.2. The generative (Assembly) problem required the group to invent a solution to a case of industrial underproduction. Groups typically discussed 10 to 12 possibilities. The choice (Personnel Selection) problem asked the group to select the best from among five hypothetical candidates for a mythical job. In both cases groups were given up to 40 minutes to solve the problem.

Subjects

Fifteen groups each of three and four persons and 14 groups of five persons recruited from introductory psychology classes solved the generative problem. Thirty-nine groups of MBA students solved the choice problem in six three-person, 24 four-person, and nine five-person groups.

Length of Discussion

All groups were given up to 40 minutes to solve each problem, a time limit designed to permit all but the slowest groups to reach a decision. Many groups finished before time was called, but we did not record the actual time they took. Instead, for this analysis we have used the total number of comments made about solutions as our proxy measure of the length of the meeting. This measure was correlated .85 with the timed amount of participation of each group member in 20 groups on the generative problem. Since most groups spent most of their meeting in discussion of alternative solutions, we felt that the total number of acts coded would be an adequate estimate of the length of these discussions. Furthermore, to the extent that this measure is task-focused and does not measure comments made about nontask matters, its relationship to the valence for the adopted solution will tend to overestimate that relationship.

Symbolically,

$$V_{A\cdot} = \sum_{A1}^{r} (P_{Ai} - N_{Ai}),$$

where $V_{A\cdot}$ = valence for the adopted solution, P_{Ai} = the number of positive comments made about that solution by person i, N_{Ai} = the number of negative comments made about that solution by person i, and r = the number of people in the group.

On the other hand

$$T_{\cdot\cdot} = \sum_{ji}^{Kr} (P_{ji} + N_{ji}),$$

where $T_{\cdot\cdot}$ = total acts or number of comments made about all solutions, K = number of solutions (j = 1,···k) r = size of group (i = 1,···,r), and P and N are the number of positive and negative comments made about all solutions.

Operationally, then, the two measures should be related only to the extent that discussion of the adopted solution is relatively favorable and takes up a large proportion of the group's discussion.

RESULTS

The correlation between the total acts coded for the adopted solution and the valence it accumulated are shown in Table 6.1 for groups of each size and for all groups on each problem. The latter is significant for both problems, accounting for 52 percent and 41 percent of the common variance on the Assembly and Selection problems, respectively. The magnitudes of the correlations are similar for three- and four-person groups, but somewhat smaller for five persons, possibly due to slightly smaller variances on the variables. At the overall level, then, we see a substantial relationship between the amount of discussion about a solution and its total valence, but also about an equal amount of unique variance for each.

The separation between discussion and valence is augmented when we recognize that many of these groups spent the last part of the discussion making only positive comments about the adopted solution. In such groups the correlation between the valence for the adopted solution and the amount of discussion about it would be artificially inflated, since every positive comment added to both valence and the number of acts. Even in groups where two solutions were discussed at the end, as in Figures 4.2 and 4.3, the comments made about the adopted solution were almost uniformly positive. This phenomenon appeared to exemplify the Bales and Strodtbeck (1951) control phase in which the group affirmed its choice.

TABLE 6.1

Correlations between Amount of Discussion about Adopted Solutions and Their Valence

Problem		Group Size 3	4	5	Total
Assembly	r	.66**	.89**	.34	.72**
	N	15	15	14	44
Selection	r	.66	.64**	.46	.64**
	N	6	24	9	39

**$p < .01$.
Source: Compiled by author.

To test the hypothesis that the correlation between valence and amount of discussion was smaller than was apparent in Table 6.1, we attempted to identify such a control phase on each problem. The criterion for the beginning of the control phase on the Selection Problem was the last point at which each comment made about the adopted solution added positive valence, with no failure to add valence for more than ten acts. In most groups this point was clearly identifiable, but in a few cases an arbitrary decision had to be made. Some groups added valence to their favored solution almost continuously from its first mention, and in those cases a point was chosen near the end of the meeting where only that solution was being discussed. In other deviant cases, groups concluded their discussions with comments about candidates other than the one adopted, and that part of the discussion was considered the control phase. In all cases the point chosen for the beginning of the control phase was designed to work against the hypothesis that removal of that part of the discussion would reduce the correlation between the amount of discussion and the valence for the adopted solution. On the Assembly Problem, because the data had been retained in aggregated form, a similarly precise criterion could not be applied. The last segment of the group discussion was identified as the control phase, unless the criterion used on the Selection Problem was violated. In that case the second-to-last segment was defined as the control phase.

The validity of this means of identifying the control phase is attested to by the correlations between the number of comments made about the adopted solution and the valence it accumulated during the control phase only (see Table 6.2).

TABLE 6.2

Correlations between Amount of Discussion about Adopted Solutions and Their Valence: Control Phase Only

Problem		Group Size 3	4	5	Total
Assembly	r	.58*	.84**	.72**	.74**
	N	15	15	14	44
Selection	r	.96**	.92**	.87**	.91**
	N	6	24	9	39

*$p < .05$; **$p < .01$.
Source: Compiled by the author.

The correlations are all substantial, but especially large for groups of all sizes on the Selection Problem. Since the identification of the beginning of the control phase was more accurately made on that problem than on the Assembly Problem (where the last segment often was much larger than the control phase itself), those data should probably be considered as more significant.

Another important point in the group's discussion is the one where the adopted solution first passed the adoption threshold—that is, where its valence index exceeded 15. Again, this point could be identified reasonably precisely on the Selection Problem, within the limits of the intercoder reliability. But on the Assembly Problem, because the data were organized into segments, the identification of the threshold point was more difficult. For exploratory purposes that point was the end of the segment in which the adopted solution accumulated valence greater than 15. Because the "segments" were aggregates of between 60 and 90 acts, the end of a segment was often well past the true point for which we were searching. The error attached to this identification of the adoption threshold is revealed in the fact that the mean valence for the adopted solution to the Assembly Problem "at threshold" was 19.6 with a standard deviation of 9.80. On the Selection Problem the mean was 14.3 (compared with 15) with a standard deviation of only 1.97.

Despite this "error" in estimating the point at which the adopted solution passed threshold on the Assembly Problem, it is informative to examine the correlations between the number of acts for the adopted solution and the latter's valence at that point. These were .55 for three-person groups, .19 for four-person groups, .19 for five-person groups, and .72 for all groups combined. Thus, again, for all groups combined, about half the variance in the valence for the adopted solution was accounted for by the amount of discussion about it. Since the mean number of acts for the adopted solution "at threshold" was 39.9 and the mean valence was 19.6, the mean number of positive acts was 29.8. The ratio of the latter to the total acts reflects an artifactual aspect of the correlation between the measures of valence and amount of discussion, which reduces the significance of the obtained correlation even further.

The lack of necessary relationship between the number of acts for the adopted solution and its attainment of the adoption threshold of 15 is seen more clearly in the data for the Selection Problem. The threshold was identified so precisely on that problem that there was little variance (standard deviation = 1.97) in the mean valence across groups. The standard deviation of the number of acts coded for the adopted solution to that point (mean = 25.1) was 16.86. Clearly the ratio of these two variances is highly significant ($F_{39,39} = 73.29$), so the notion that the valence accumulated and the amount of discussion of the adopted solution are identical is refuted. A similar conclusion is reached when the prediction of the total group valence is made from the number of acts needed for the adopted solution to pass the adoption threshold. The correlations between the "acts to threshold" and the final valence for the adopted solution were -.29 (6 three-person groups), -.29 (24 four-person groups), -.59 (9 five-person groups), and -.32 for all 24 groups on the Selection Problem. All the correlations are negative, supporting the intuitive assumption that the longer a group takes to support the ultimately adopted solution beyond the adoption threshold, the more in conflict it is about the solution's merits. Nevertheless, the modest size of the correlation ($r^2 = .1024$), indicates that many groups deviated from that general trend.

The separation of the discussion into three parts—before threshold is passed by the adopted solution, from threshold to control phase, and the control phase alone—is further reinforced by the correlations among the acts for the adopted solution in each part and between those acts and the valence accumulated for the adopted solution. (This analysis could be done only on the Selection Problem, since the segmented nature of the data for the Assembly Problem often made the "threshold" and "control" data identical.) The relevant correlations are displayed in Table 6.3. The first correlation in each pairing is between the number of acts about the adopted solution in one period and those in another. Although these are slightly negative, indicating less discussion in a period following an above-average period of discussion, the correlations are all rather small. The same is true of the bottom correlations in each pairing, in which the number of acts for the adopted solution is correlated with the valence accumulated subsequently. The largest absolute value of all these correlations is only .32, which shows only about 10 percent of the variance in common. Thus, the rate at which valence accumulates for the adopted solution was relatively independent of the amount of discussion that solution received in each period. The amount of discussion on the adopted solution was also unrelated from period to period. Therefore, we should not be surprised that the amount of valence accumulated by the adopted solution before the control phase was correlated only .19 with the amount it accumulated during that phase.

TABLE 6.3

Relationships among Acts and Valence for the Adopted Solution at Various Stages of the Process

Correlations between acts for the adopted solution to threshold and	
Acts after threshold:	-.27
Valence after threshold:	-.32*
Acts from threshold to control phase:	-.10
Valence from threshold to control phase:	-.21
Correlations between acts for the adopted solution from threshold to control phase and	
In control phase:	-.05
Valence in control phase:	-.02

Note: Selection Problem only, 39 groups.

*$p < .05$.

Source: Compiled by the author.

With these strong suggestions that the rate of movement of the group toward adopting a particular solution is independent of the amount of discussion about that solution in particular, we can still ask how such movement is related to the total discussion. For the Assembly Problem, the length of the discussion—as measured by the total acts coded for all solutions—was correlated only slightly with the valence for the adopted solution, while on the Selection Problem the correlations were significant and somewhat stronger (Table 6.4).

TABLE 6.4

Total Acts for All Solutions and Valence for the Adopted Solution

Problem		Group Size 3	4	5	Total
Assembly	r	.15	.14	-.22	.22
	N	15	15	14	44
Selection	r	.78	.54**	.34	.58**
	N	6	24	9	39

**$p < .01$.
Source: Compiled by the author.

When the relationship on the Selection Problem between valence for the adopted solution and the amount of discussion is examined in more detail, however, their independence again becomes apparent. For example, the mean number of acts for all solutions at the point the adopted solution passed the adoption threshold was 132.7, about halfway (46.4 percent) through the total meeting. However, the standard deviation of such acts was 73.15, which is almost as large as the standard deviation of total acts for the entire meeting (97.16). In other words, the rate at which adopted solutions passed the adoption threshold was not determined by the amount of general solution-related discussion. Some groups pushed the adoption solution past threshold within the first 60 acts, while others waited for 200 acts.

Furthermore, the rate at which the adopted solution passed threshold showed only modest correlation with both the amount of subsequent discussion (-.44) and the subsequent valence accumulation

(-.26) by the adopted solution. Breaking the discussion down further, the correlation between number of acts before threshold with the number from threshold to control phase was -.38, and the latter with the length of the control phase was .05.

The valence accumulations for the adopted solutions were also relatively independent of the amount of general discussion from period to period. The correlation between the number of acts to threshold and the valence accumulated between the threshold and the control phase was -.24, and between the number of acts to the control phase and the valence during that phase was .07. Similarly, the valence accumulated before the control phase was correlated only .19 with the valence accumulated during the control phase. Thus, we see a pattern of independence in the rate at which the group accumulates valence for its to-be-adopted solution and the general level of discussion in these different parts of the meeting.

DISCUSSION

In the absence of an independent measure of the length of discussion, the findings presented here strongly suggest that the valence index charts a facet of the group's activity that is not reflected in mere discussion. In conjunction with the evidence presented previously concerning the relationship between the valence index and the probability of a solution's adoption, we now see that the valence index records the rate of the group's progress toward a decision, independent of the amount of discussion in the group. A long discussion does not mean high valence, nor does little discussion preclude high valence for the adopted solution. Rather, these results raise questions about the effects of different patterns of relationships between the length of discussion and the rate of accumulation of valence. For example, do groups that accumulate valence rapidly for their ultimately adopted solution tend to define the problem less well than groups that have extensive discussions before any solution passes the adoption threshold? The latter would appear to conform to the principle of deferred judgment so central to brainstorming (Osborn 1957). Or are groups that hold extended discussions so locked in conflict that the members are unable to agree on the bases for adopting a solution to the problem? Unfortunately, the Personnel Selection Problem did not lend itself to answering questions of this sort, and the segmented form of the data for the Assembly Problem lacked the precision necessary for such analysis.

The results of using the valence index to divide the discussion into phases showed very promising parallels to the phase sequence suggested originally by Bales and Strodtbeck (1951). The evidence for the control phase was very striking in almost every group. It was rare that less than 70 percent of the comments about the adopted solution were positive at the end, and very common were groups where only positive comments were being made. Even when a second solution had passed the adoption threshold and was a true contender—as in groups like Figure 4.3, the final comments were almost uniformly favorable.

The period before which the adopted solution has passed the adoption threshold seems to be a good candidate as an orientation phase. Since until that time the group has not made its ultimately adopted solution a real candidate for adoption, we may assume that they are still searching for an acceptable possibility. However, that definition of the orientation phase is probably too restrictive. Some groups continued to accumulate valence for the adopted solution well beyond the threshold, before turning to other solutions. Others accumulated valence of greater than 15 points for several solutions before limiting themselves to choosing among them. Thus, it may be necessary to apply a rule that the orientation phase ends when all solutions have passed the adoption threshold or when the first one past the threshold has an inflection point in its cumulative valence curve indicating a period of slower accumulation.

Despite these variations, the use of the adoption threshold as a means of identifying the orientation phase seems preferable to the arbitrary division of the total discussion into thirds, as Bales and Strodtbeck (1951) did. Conceptually, as indicated above, it is consistent with the group's searching for an acceptable solution. Empirically, we know that solutions must pass that threshold to be adopted.

Furthermore, the period between the orientation and control phases also seems to have characteristics of an evaluation phase. Once one solution has passed the adoption threshold, the group seems to use it as a standard against which to compare other prospective solutions. Thus, while there may still be a search for new solutions or for new bases on which to evaluate existing ones, these searches usually result in increasing valence for only one or two possibilities, leading to the decision confirmed in the control phase.

7

VALENCE FOR CRITERIA: A PRELIMINARY EXPLORATION

L. Richard Hoffman
Gary R. Bond
Gideon Falk

The studies reported thus far have focused exclusively on the valence attached to possible solutions to problems. However, the valence model presented in Chapter 1 is completely general with regard to the nature of the cognitions referred to. Our research began with the study of solution valence because groups tend to spend most of their time discussing solutions, and we could be sure of identifying the final outcome—that is, which solution the group adopted. The question of whether groups "adopt" other cognitions—such as a particular definition of a problem—is more uncertain.

The stability of the solution valence-adoption relationships raised the possibility of testing the model further. We asked ourselves why certain solutions accumulated valence very rapidly—some almost from their first mention in the group—while others were discussed at length but never accumulated any positive valence. Cognitive consistency theories (such as Rosenberg 1960) would suggest that solutions accumulate valence according to their perceived consistency with the underlying beliefs and attitudes of the group members. Thus the "reasons" given for supporting or rejecting solution alternatives would reflect these underlying beliefs about the nature of the problem and would provide a basis for the group to act rationally, that is, to adopt the solution that best fits their shared definition of the problem. The definition of the problem, however, also raises questions for the group, as it does for individuals (Hoffman, Burke, and Maier 1963). In order to justify the adoption or rejection of solutions, the group members must agree that the reasons offered for such actions are valid. Groups often solve problems without clearly defining the problem to be solved. Rather, in acting to adopt or reject particular solutions, they define the problem implicitly. We assume, therefore, that the definition of the problem, being another type of cognition, would be subject to a valence-adoption process similar to the one already shown for solutions. Prior to, or coincident with, the accumulation of valence for and against solutions, we hypothesize that sufficient valence for a definition of the problem accumulates for the group to use it in evaluating solutions. This study will explore that possibility.

We recognize, however, that there are difficulties inherent in this investigation that were not barriers to the study of the solution valence-adoption process. The first of these is that there is no objective method for determining whether a particular definition of a problem has been adopted by the group. Whereas, at the end of their meetings, laboratory groups typically provide some attempted solution to the experimenter, few groups announce systematically that they have adopted a particular definition of the problem. For example, groups solve the Personnel Selection Problem by telling us their preferred candidate, but they never report the criteria they used in his selection. Whether a criterion has been adopted will have to be inferred from the action taken subsequent to it. For example, some candidates on the Personnel Selection Problem have changed jobs more often than others. If the criterion adopted by the group is job stability, then we might expect the less mobile candidates to be retained or adopted. If action consistent with the criterion is not taken, this would be a partial refutation of the hypothesis.

The second problem in studying criterion valence is that groups need not develop a complete set of criteria against which all candidates are to be measured. Only as many criteria need to be adopted as are required to complete the problem—that is, to permit a solution to be adopted (Simon 1956). The latter arises from the fact that groups tend to be "solution-minded" (Maier 1963). Since nobody requires them to identify a problem completely and publicly, they need only define it sufficiently to create and adopt a solution that will solve it. On the Personnel Selection Problem the selection criteria need only be specified in the detail needed to choose among the available candidates. Once that can be done, further listing of criteria would be superfluous.

Despite these recognized constraints on the possibility of discovering any relationships between the valences generated for criteria and their effect on group decision making, we decided to explore the available data to begin to understand this phenomenon. In that respect this study is avowedly exploratory, somewhat like the first empirical test of the model (see Chapter 2).

METHOD

Task

The Personnel Selection Problem (Appendix A.2) was used in this study. The group was asked to choose the best candidate from among five résumés presented for a hypothetical job. The job is described in general terms. The information in the résumés had to be interpreted by the members in assessing the candidates' qualifications, since it was not presented in a form commensurate with the job description. Furthermore, the résumés were designed for the purpose of the principal study (Chapters 4, 10) to prevent any one candidate from being particularly outstanding by balancing the qualities thought relevant to the job from candidate to candidate. The dimensions on which the resumes were designed to vary among candidates are summarized in Table 7.1. Thus, one candidate might have an MBA degree but little job experience, while another would have good job experience but only a bachelor's degree from a mediocre college. For purposes of this study, the overlapping qualifications of the candidates thus created made the difficulty of relating criterion valence to the group's selection of a particular candidate even greater.

Subjects

Twenty-eight three-, four-, and five-person MBA groups solved the problem as part of a classroom exercise. Their problem-solving sessions were tape-recorded and transcribed. The results for groups of different sizes seemed quite similar, and were combined in these analyses.

Criterion Valence

The reasons given by group members for wanting to reject or adopt each candidate were organized into the 28 categories shown in Table 7.2. Having no a priori reason for weighting the criteria or comments made about them differentially, we scored one positive point for each time a criterion was used by the group and a negative point each time a criterion was rejected. The reader must recognize the distinction between criterion valence and solution valence. The comment "Godep has a good record of staying with the same company for many years" would be scored positively for Godep as a candidate (solution valence) and positively for job stability as a

TABLE 7.1

Summary of the Systematically Varied Résumés

	Stanley Godep	David Kroll	Roger O'Brien	Walter Tinneman	Howard Winston
Age	44	30	34	33	40
Sex	M	M	M	M	M
Race	white	white	white	white	white
Years of job-related experience	20	6	6 (4 sales)	2 (7 nonrelated)	15
Stability of experience	good	bad	good	good	bad
Highest degree earned	BA	MBA	BA	MBA	BA
Quality of undergraduate school	mod.	mod.	mod.	high	high
Quality of graduate school		mod.		high	
Major as undergraduate	bus.	pol.sci.	bus.	Acctng.	bus.
Years on present job	8	1	2	2	6 mos.
Marital status	marr.	single	marr.	single	single
Children	5		3		
Military background	active duty	1Y	active duty	Army Reserve	4F

Source: Compiled by the authors.

TABLE 7.2

Criterion Valence by Criterion
(28 groups)

Criterion	Mean	S.D.
Job diversity	15.4	10.14
Job stability	24.7	15.35
Depth of experience	14.5	9.15
Mobility	7.2	7.48
Sales background	7.4	8.39
Quantitative background	-0.1	9.48
Research experience	8.1	9.50
Management experience	14.2	8.82
Planning experience	10.0	8.32
Implementing experience	4.7	3.63
Market entry	7.2	7.00
Marketing experience	6.4	5.24
Has been promoted	9.8	11.52
MBA	2.6	4.25
Younger age	5.2	6.36
Single—could travel	2.9	6.30
Willing to move	3.2	5.56

Analysis of Variance

Source	df	SS	MS	F
Between criteria	16	16,408	1,025	14.94**
Between groups	27	3,488	129	1.88*
Criteria x groups	432	29,642	68.6	
Total	475	49,538		

*$p < .05$; ** $p < .01$.

Source: Compiled by the authors.

criterion (criterion valence). However, the comment "Godep has not had enough experience with other products" would be scored negatively for Godep as a candidate (solution valence), but positively for the criterion of job diversity (criterion valence). The coding manual describing the rules used to code criterion valence is included in Appendix B.2.*

The reliability of the criterion valence scoring system was estimated by correlating the total acts scored by two coders in each of the 24 most-used categories for the first 120 acts in each group. The correlations ranged from .57 to .97, with a median of .83. The five groups with intercoder reliabilities below .70 were recoded before this analysis was undertaken, and intercoder agreement was improved. We note that there is a bias in criterion valence scoring toward positive valence, since members tended to invoke criteria that they favored for evaluation, whether the candidate was favored or not. Thus, unlike the coding of solution valence, where candidates were discussed pro and con, errors of omission in criterion valence coding were not compensated for by errors of commission in measuring criterion valence. Nevertheless, to improve the stability of the criterion valence scores, we have averaged them for the two coders in each group at identifiable points of interest for most analyses.

RESULTS

The first questions we asked were whether the criteria accumulated valence in ways that differentiated among them and that showed differential patterns across groups. Table 7.2 shows the means and standard deviations of the valence scores for the 17 most-discussed criteria. A one-way analysis of variance ($F_{16,431} = 11.64$, $\underline{p} < .01$) shows that the criteria accumulated valence at differential rates. Whether a candidate had remained in his various jobs for a reasonable amount of time and was not a "job hopper"—job stability—received the highest valence (mean = 24.7). But the need for diverse experiences (mean = 15.4) and particular experiences (management and planning) were also favored by groups. (We should note here that the level of valence achieved by a criterion may not be completely indicative of its importance on this problem. Some criteria may be so obvious that their mere

---

*Orville Madden joined Drs. Falk and Bond in developing the criterion categories and the coding manual.

mention is sufficient to reject a candidate. At the extreme, for example, it is unnecessary to mention that the candidate must be a male, since all the candidates were. Nevertheless, it is likely that the magnitude of criterion valence generated reflects its importance in any group's definition of the job requirements.)

Despite these overall differences among the criterion means, the sizable standard deviations of almost all of them suggest that groups varied substantially in their use of each one. We might expect this result from the varied patterns of rejections and adoptions of solutions obtained from group to group (illustrated in part by Figures 4.1-4.4). Before examining the possible relationships between the accumulation of criterion valence and such adoption-rejection patterns, let us look at the relationship between criterion valence and solution valence.

Criterion valence accumulated in three different ways:

1. Criteria were discussed without specific reference to particular candidates ("We need someone who can open up new markets").
2. Candidates were matched against criteria, either favorably or unfavorably ("Godep has been part of the promotion of a very good product" or "Tinneman is too quantitative for this job").
3. Candidates were compared with each other as to their degree of match with a criterion ("Winston is more promotable than Kroll").

Method 1 clearly generates valence for criteria independent of the solution valence generated for particular candidates. However, methods 2 and 3 have potential overlap, since the use of particular criteria to justify the adoption of a candidate and agreements with those reasons add valence both to the solution and to the criterion. On the other hand, negative evaluations of candidates and agreements with them add positive valence to the criterion, but negative valence to the solution. In addition, there are many acts that contribute valence to the solutions—both positive and negative—such as eliciting support or asking questions, that do not refer to criteria at all.

The question, then is what degree of overlap or independence is therebetween solution valence and criterion valence? Comparisons between the total number of criterion-valence acts and total number of solution-valence acts were made at four different points in the group meeting: the total meeting, the point at which the first candidate was actively rejected, the point at which the adopted solution passed the adoption threshold, and the end of the rejection phase (in those groups that had two phases).

These comparisons are displayed in Table 7.3. There we see that there were significantly fewer criterion acts than solution acts for the discussion taken as a whole (means of 242.0 vs. 303.7). However, both seem to reflect the level of active discussion in the group, as indicated by the correlation between them of .72 ($p < .01$).

TABLE 7.3

Numbers of Solution-Valence and Criterion-Valence Acts at Different Points in the Group Meeting

		Number of	
Comparison Point		Solution-Valence Acts	Criterion-Valence Acts
Total meeting[a]	Mean	303.7**	242.0**
	S.D.	86.61	68.67
First active rejection of a candidate[a]	Mean	78.5	74.5
	S.D.	74.98	59.83
Early active rejections first 50 acts[b]	Mean	24.3	38.8
	S.D.	11.75	26.55
Adopted solution passed threshold[a]	Mean	129.7	123.6
	S.D.	73.41	70.82
End of Rejection phase[c]	Mean	155.4**	126.0**
	S.D.	99.11	79.08

[a]N = 28 groups.

[b]N = 15 groups whose first rejection (solution valence < -8 for that candidate) occurred during the first 50 solution-valence acts.

[c]Four groups had no announced end, so N = 24 groups.

** p difference < .01.

Source: Compiled by the authors.

Noteworthy also, however, is the fact that the surplus of solution-valence acts was not apparent in the early parts of the discussion. At the time the first candidate had been actively rejected—that is, dropped below a valence of -8 (see Chapter 4)—there was hardly any difference in the numbers of solution- and criterion-valence acts (means of 78.5 and 74.5), and they were highly correlated with each other ($r = .74$, $p < .01$). Even somewhat later, when the adopted solution first passed the adoption threshold, the numbers of solution- and criterion-valence acts were very similar (means of 129.7 and 123.6) and were even more highly correlated ($r = .89$, $p < .01$). However, by the end of the rejection phase, in the 24 groups that had two identifiable phases, the number of solution-valence acts (mean = 155.4) significantly ($p < .01$) exceeded the number of criterion-valence acts (mean = 126.0). The correlation between them at that point was again high (.84 $p < .01$).

Unfortunately, solution valence was coded only for positive and negative comments, so the actual overlap between the two measures produced by the number of times a criterion was used to justify a solution could not be determined. There is some indication that that must have occurred fairly frequently, however. If the high correlations between the numbers of solution- and criterion-valence acts merely represented their respective correlations with the total level of activity in the group, there would be similar correlations among the numbers of valence acts generated at different points in time. Table 7.4 shows that such is not the case. Thus, until we can obtain more definitive data, we assume that the groups acted "rationally" in attempting to justify the adoption or rejection of solutions on the basis of criteria. The possibility that some groups may have generated valence for some criteria before they began to generate solution valence is indicated by the surplus of criterion-valence acts over solution-valence acts in groups that rejected their first candidate early, in the first 50 acts (Table 7.3). However, even that difference falls short of the .05 level of statistical significance. So, the more frequent pattern seems to be the simultaneous generation of valence for criteria as they are used to reject or support (provide negative and positive valence for) the various solutions.

While the overall relationship between the numbers of solution-valence and criterion-valence acts gives us some insight into the problem-solving process, the ultimate test of the validity of the criterion-valence index is its relationship to the solution-adoption process. The complexity of this relationship is illustrated in the following attempt at such an analysis. We examined the data for some form of adoption threshold that would exist for criterion valence as it does for solution valence. We asked whether there was an association between a candidate's adoption and whether criterion valence for any criteria exceeded 11 or dropped below -3. These values were chosen arbitrarily, on the assumption that criteria are adopted or rejected with less absolute valence than are solutions, since the former do not have to be justified to some nonmember of the group. Table 7.5 shows the percentage of groups that adopted each candidate whose valence for the specified criterion either exceeded 11—and could be considered adopted—or dropped below -3 and was rejected. It is clear that in all four groups that adopted Winston, valence for the criteria of job diversity and job stability exceeded 11, and that valence for quantitative background was less than -3. However, in most of the Tinneman-adopting groups (six of seven) job diversity and depth of job experience also exceeded 11. On the low side, too, Winston overlapped with other candidates, but this time with Godep on the criteria of research experience and having been promoted. Thus, merely looking at the total accumulation of valence for a criterion across the entire meeting identifies criteria that probably accumulated valence for candidates other than the one finally adopted. The picture thereby becomes blurred. Yet it is clear that some differential association exists between the adoption of particular candidates and the amount of valence accumulated for certain criteria.

TABLE 7.4

Correlations between Numbers of Solution-Valence and Criterion-Valence Acts at Various Points in the Meeting

	RS	RC	AS	AC	TOS	TOC
RS	—					
RC	.74*	—				
AS	-.29	-.09	—			
AC	-.27	.16	.89**	—		
TOS	.47*	.47*	.18	.16	—	
TOC	.17	.61**	.28	.50**	.72**	—

R = First active rejection of candidate.
S = Number of solution-valence acts.
C = Number of criterion-valence acts.
A = Adopted solution passed threshold.
TO = Total meeting.
N = 28 groups.
* $p < .05$; ** $p < .01$.

Source: Compiled by the authors.

TABLE 7.5

Percentage of Groups "Adopting" (+11) or "Rejecting" (-3) Criteria, by Candidate Adopted

	Candidate Adopted					
	O'Brien	Kroll	Godep	Winston	Tinneman	All Groups
Diversity	50.0	25.0	33.3	100.0	85.7	60.7
Stability	80.0	75.0	66.7	100.0	71.4	78.6
Depth	90.0	75.0	66.7	75.0	85.7	82.1
Sales	40.0	0.0	0.0	25.0	0.0	17.9
Research	30.0	75.0	0.0	0.0	42.9	32.1
Management	60.0	25.0	100.0	50.0	71.4	60.7
Planning	30.0	0.0	0.0	25.0	14.3	17.9
Implementing	30.0	25.0	33.3	0.0	14.3	21.4
Market entry	30.0	75.0	33.3	50.0	28.6	39.3
Promoted	40.0	75.0	33.3	0.0	14.3	32.1
Quantitative (-3)	40.0	50.0	66.7	100.0	0.0	42.9
Number of groups	10	4	3	4	7	28

Source: Compiled by the authors.

A similar, but slightly less aggregated, analysis was also possible with these data. At the last act for each candidate, we tested in each group for an association between the solution-valence status (positive or negative) of the candidate and whether the criterion valence for each criterion was above or below the mean for that criterion. Our hypothesis was that some such candidate-criterion associations would be found and that they would be different for different candidates.

Again, although the results were far from uniform, differential candidate-criterion associations were uncovered. Samples of those results are shown in Table 7.6. The numbers of groups in which the candidate, for example, Winston, had positive or negative valence and whether the valence for job diversity at that point was above the overall mean for diversity were entered in the appropriate cells. The relationships shown are consistent with the characteristics of the candidates built originally into their résumés (see Table 7.1). However, we found no relationships for O'Brien. This was due primarily to the fact that he received negative valence so seldom and was so often retained so long into the meeting that by the time they discarded O'Brien, all criteria that had been used to reject other candidates were associated with him in this analysis.

DISCUSSION

This exploratory attempt to generalize the valence model from solutions to criteria seems very promising. Given the many difficulties outlined earlier—including the basic design of the résumés themselves—that worked against finding any associations between criterion valence and solution-related action, the study tends to suggest several propositions. First, criterion valence, like solution valence, accumulates as an implicit process. Second, the accumulation of solution valence rests on the concomitant generation of criterion valence, and more rarely on the prior generation of such valence. In other words, these groups seemed to define the problem as a means of justifying the solution, rather than defining the problem first and then matching the solutions to it. Perhaps that was a function, in this case, of the paucity of information about the job.

Third, it appears that criteria accumulate valence only to the level needed to take action on a particular candidate. A set of criteria is not necessarily built up during the discussion and then applied systematically to all candidates.

These propositions obviously require further testing and more convincing statistical evidence for their validity. Fortunately, as

TABLE 7.6

Selected Associations, by Groups, between Candidates and Criteria at the Last Act for that Candidate

Candidate		
	Valence for Job Diversity	
Valence for Winston	< Mean	≥ Mean
Positive	2*	8
Zero or negative	13	5
	Valence for Management Experience	
Valence for Kroll	< Mean	≥ Mean
Positive	3	9
Negative	12	4
	Valence for Research Experience	
Valence for Tinneman	< Mean	≥ Mean
Positive	3	7
Negative	11	7
	Valence for Job Stability	
Valence for Godep	< Mean	≥ Mean
Positive	6	7
Negative	11	4

*Cell entries are numbers of groups. No statistical tests were performed on these tables, since they were not selected randomly.

Source: Compiled by the authors.

we prepared this chapter (unfortunately, not soon enough to be able to report the results) a new program became available by which more detailed analyses at different points in the process will be possible. However, data from a problem in which the definition of the problem is more clearly associated with particular solutions will be needed to test these propositions.

PART III

VALENCE AND ACCEPTANCE OF THE DECISION

8

PARTICIPATION, INFLUENCE, AND SATISFACTION AMONG MEMBERS OF PROBLEM-SOLVING GROUPS

L. Richard Hoffman
Ronald J. Burke
Norman R. F. Maier

Research findings show that members accept the decisions resulting from group problem solving, but there is disagreement regarding what aspects of the process are critical in determining acceptance. Edith Bennett (1955) concluded from her study that the act of making the decision itself is the principal factor. Others have suggested that the amount of participation (Barnlund and Haiman 1960) or the amount of felt or psychological participation (French, Israel, and Ås 1960) are the crucial variables. Still other research (Hoffman and Maier 1959; 1961a; 1961) has pointed to the member's feelings of satisfaction with his/her influence over the solution as an important factor in his/her satisfaction with the solution. All of these explanations imply that the level of member's satisfaction is independent of the quality of the solution.

In the present study we examined the relationship of each member's satisfaction with the group's solution to three aspects of his participation in the discussion: (1) the total amount of his participation, (2) the amount of influence he attempted over the solution, and (3) the amount he actually influenced the solution. These three aspects were measured with the use of a newly developed observational system for recording the character of statements made about specific solutions to a problem. It was hypothesized that the amount of actual influence over the final solution is more

---

The research reported was supported by Grant no. MH-02704, U.S. Public Health Service. An abbreviated version of the paper was given at the meetings of the Midwestern Psychological Association, Chicago, 1963.

highly related to satisfaction than is level of total participation in the meeting or attempted influence. It is assumed that the more a member argues in favor of a solution, the more positively valent it is for him and the more satisfied he is with its adoption by the group (see Chapter 1).

METHOD

Subjects

Seventy-five male subjects, recruited from an introductory psychology class, solved the Assembly Problem in fifteen four-person and five three-person groups.* Each group was allowed up to 40 minutes to solve the problem, and most groups took the entire time.

Problem

The Assembly Problem has been adapted from a role-playing version developed by Maier (1952) to a problem without roles. The problem concerns a seven-man group of workers who assemble carburetors in a series of sequential operations. An instance of inadequate production is described, and the problem consists of discovering the best means of achieving maximum productivity. The problem is quite difficult, and a wide variety of solutions are offered and discussed.

Measures of Participation and Influence

At least two observers coded the statements of each group member in all but one of the 20 groups, using a newly developed

---

*The three-person groups occurred because one person assigned to each of these groups did not report for the experimental session.

The assistance of Donald Worley, who did all the time measurements, and of Paul Kimmel and Bruce Springborn, who helped in developing the process observational system, in coding the groups, and in analyzing the data, is greatly appreciated.

coding system designed to measure the verbal support given to each solution proposed in the group. The development of the system and evidence for its high interobserver reliability and for its usefulness in predicting the adoption of solutions by the group have been reported in Chapter 2.

In brief, the observers coded each member's statements about a particular solution with a number, corresponding to the person speaking, and a letter, corresponding to one of seven categories of statements, on a row representing that solution. Only statements that could be associated with a specific solution were coded, so much of the group process was ignored. The coding categories were constructed such that four reflected support for a particular solution (positive acts), two indicated criticism (negative acts), and one was neutral. A valence index, representing the algebraic sum of the number of positive acts minus the number of negative acts, was shown to be highly related to the adoption of solutions by the groups. The higher the valence value a solution achieved in a group, summed across the values for the individual members, the greater was the probability that the solution would be adopted. Previously it had been found that the solution with the highest positive valence in the group was adopted in 17 of the 20 groups (see Chapter 2).

On the basis of these relationships, it is assumed that each individual's valence for the adopted solution is an index of his actual influence over the solution. A member's valence index is computed from the number of times he supported the adopted solution minus the number of times he criticized it. (Thus, each member's valence can be either positive or negative.) Similarly, the sum of the individual valence indexes becomes the total group valence index for the adopted solution.

Each member's attempted influence was measured by summing his valence indexes for all the solutions he discussed, including the solution finally adopted. Attempted influence is thus a measure of the extent to which a person argued for solutions rather than criticizing them (cf. Bass 1961).

The members' level of total participation in the discussion was measured in two ways. The duration of each person's verbal participation in the discussion was recorded on a clock corresponding to that person. Thus a measure of each member's total participation was derived from the sum of all the times he talked, regardless of whether his comments were related to the problem or not. The total number of solution-related acts recorded by the observers was also used as a measure of total participation. The latter has been used in the analysis to represent total participation, since it correlated so highly with the timed measures. The correlation, for the 75 subjects, between total time and total acts was .85, and between percent time and percent acts in the group was .92. The mean *tau* between the rank orders of time and acts within each group was .76, with 11 of the 20 *taus* being greater than .90. The total number of solution-related acts is clearly an excellent sample of a member's participation in the discussion. All relationships shown in this report between total acts and other measures were almost identical to those found when the timed measures of participation were used.

Each of these measures—(1) total individual participation, (2) individual attempted influence, (3) individual actual influence (valence), and (4) group support (valence) for the adopted solution—was correlated separately with each member's rated satisfactions with the solution and with his influence over the solution.

Measures of Satisfaction

After each group arrived at a solution to the problem, the members responded individually to two questions: "How satisfied are you with the solution reached by your group?" and "How satisfied are you with the amount of say or influence you had over the solution?" Responses to both questions were made to a six-point scale: very dissatisfied, somewhat dissatisfied, neither satisfied nor dissatisfied, fairly satisfied, quite satisfied, very satisfied. Values from 1 to 6 were assigned to the responses, reflecting increasing degrees of satisfaction. These questions have been shown, in previous studies, to reflect the character of the problem-solving process; higher levels of satisfaction usually represent more open discussion (for instance, Hoffman and Maier 1959; 1961a).

RESULTS

The intercorrelations among the three aspects of individual participation in the discussion, as shown in Table 8.1, are moderately high and significantly different from zero. On the average, the more a member participated in the discussion, the more influence he attempted and the more influence he had over the decision. Also, the more influence he attempted, the more influence he actually had.

The correlations of each of these variables with the measures of satisfaction with influence over the solution and with the solution itself are shown in Table 8.2. Of the three participation measures, only the index of actual influence over the solution was significantly correlated with the members' satisfaction with their influence over

TABLE 8.1

Pearson Intercorrelations among Member's Total Participation, Attempted Influence, and Actual Influence

	Attempted Influence	Actual Influence
Total participation	.62**	.52**
Attempted influence		.71**

Note: N = 75 for all correlations.
**Correlation significantly different from zero at p - .01.
Source: Compiled by the authors.

TABLE 8.2

Pearson Correlations of Member's Participation, Attempted Influence, and Actual Influence with Satisfaction with Influence and with the Solution

	Satisfaction with Influence	Satisfaction with Solution
Total participation	.19	-.01
Attempted influence	.22	.12
Actual influence	.40**	.41**
Actual influence, with total participation and attempted influence controlled	.35**	.48**

Note: N = 75 for all correlations.
**Correlation significantly different from zero at p = .01.
Source: Compiled by the authors.

the solution and with the solution itself. As shown by the significant partial correlations of actual influence with the two satisfaction measures, this relationship was unaffected by the significant correlations of actual influence with total participation and attempted influence. Even though the persons who participated most actively in the discussion attempted to influence the decision most, and actually exercised the most influence over the decision, only the amount of influence they actually exercised was correlated with their satisfaction.

The data were then examined to determine whether the total valence for the adopted solution in the group affected the individual member's satisfaction with the solution. Since the probability that a solution would be adopted varied directly with the level of total support it received, the question was asked, "Does the level of group support for the adopted solution contribute to the members' satisfaction with the solution?" The correlation between the group valence index and individual members' satisfaction with the solution was .26, significant at the .05 level of confidence. When, however, the individual member's actual influence was partialed out, the correlation between group support for the adopted solution and member satisfaction with the solution dropped to .10, which is not significantly different from zero. Conversely, the correlation between individual actual influence and satisfaction with the solution (.40) was reduced only to .34 ($p < .01$) when the total group support was partialed out (see Table 8.3). Thus each member's satisfaction with the adopted solution was determined by his own level of support for it, regardless of the other members' feelings about it.

TABLE 8.3

Group Support for the Adopted Solution and Members' Satisfaction with the Solution

Pearson correlations between individual satisfaction with the solution and group support	.26*
Group support with individual influence partialed out	.10
Individual influence with group support partialed out	.34**

Note: N = 75 for all correlations.
*Correlation significantly different from zero at $p = .05$.
**Correlation significantly different from zero at $p = .01$.
Source: Compiled by the authors.

The relationship between the quality of the groups' solutions and the members' satisfaction was also examined. Only 6 of the 20 groups produced solutions that were considered to have potentially productive effects. The mean satisfaction of the members of these groups with their solutions was 4.3, while that of the members of the 14 groups with poor solutions was 4.4, an insignificant difference.

DISCUSSION

This study was designed to evaluate the relative contributions of various aspects of members' participation in the group problem-solving process to their satisfaction with their influence over the solution and with the solution itself. The results appear clear-cut in establishing the actual influence exercised by each member over the solution as an important determinant of his satisfaction with his influence and with the solution. The member's level of participation in the discussion and his attempts to influence the decision, while moderately correlated with his actual influence, were relatively unrelated to his satisfaction. Thus the important ingredient of participation is influence.

Advocates of group decision have stressed the importance of participation in the discussion for gaining members' acceptance (such as Barnlund and Haiman 1960; Thibaut and Kelley 1961). Others have pointed to the opportunity to participate as critical (French, Israel, and Ås 1960; Marquis, Guetzkow, and Heyns 1951). The present results suggest that neither the amount of participation nor the opportunity to participate is as important as is the ability to have one's own opinion reflected in the decision. Confusion about the meaning of the term "participation" has led several writers for management (such as Jones 1957) to propose the use of meetings to give workers a feeling of participation in accepting decisions that have already been made by the supervisor. Such pseudo-participative procedures should fail to gain the workers' acceptance, according to these results, since the workers would not be permitted truly to influence the decision.

A certain type of participation by all the members in making a group decision should be encouraged, however, to gain acceptance. Since a member's satisfaction with the decision reflects the number of positive comments he/she makes about it, the feelings of each member about the solution should be solicited. The favorable comments would, presumably, promote satisfaction with and commitment to the adopted solution. Expressions of criticism would prevent the adoption of a solution that lacks the acceptance of all the members and would encourage the group to search for a different solution. Such a search for a solution that would reconcile the different viewpoints of the members might produce an even more effective solution than the ones already considered (see Chapter 1; see also Hoffman, Harburg, and Maier 1962). Thus, soliciting the opinions of all group members should increase the acceptance of group decisions, and might even improve their quality.

The fact that satisfaction was not related to the quality of solutions raises a serious problem for the participative approach in untrained groups. Satisfaction is often essential to ensuring that the decision is carried out, but quality considerations cannot be ignored. In order to ensure decisions of high quality, it is necessary to find discussion procedures that will reject poor-quality decisions. Progress along this line has been reported elsewhere (Maier 1963; Maier and Hoffman 1960a, 1960b). Unskilled participation can upgrade acceptance, but the use of group processes to protect quality and to generate innovative solutions requires refinements in group problem-solving processes.

9

VALENCE, SATISFACTION, AND COMMITMENT TO THE GROUP'S SOLUTION

Gary Coleite
L. Richard Hoffman

Consistent with the concept of valence as a force representing the members' attraction to a solution, in Chapter 8 we found that the valence index was positively correlated with members' rated satisfaction with the solution adopted by their groups. This result indicates only, however, that people will report more satisfaction with an adopted group solution when they have expressed high valence for it. We have also suggested that reported satisfaction and valence represent the strength of a member's acceptance of and commitment to the solution reached by his group. There is no behavioral evidence, however, that shows that people with high measured valence for, or satisfaction with, a group's adopted solution will continue to be committed to it beyond the immediate problem-solving situation.

The importance of gaining members' commitment lies in their willingness to implement the decision. Often in organizational settings decisions made at meetings must be carried out without the surveillance of the others in the group. Unless members are committed to the decision, they are unlikely to invest much energy in such actions. Often, too, members must represent the group's decision to others, either inside or outside the organization. The enthusiasm with which they perform this representational function will again be a function of their commitment to the group's decision.

The present experiment provides a behavioral test of the hypothesis that measured valence and rated satisfaction for the group's decision reflect the members' commitment to that decision. It is a partial simulation of the representational situation. After people have solved a problem in one group, they will be asked to solve it again in a different group. Each member's valence for and rated satisfaction with the solution adopted in the first group is hypothesized to determine the strength of his arguments for that solution in the second group. By composing the second groups according to the amount of valence generated by each member in his first group, we were able to compare the effects of the amount of valence generated with the rank order of valence and, at the same time, partially to control for the general level of activity. The question is whether commitment is a function merely of being the most influential (see Chapter 11) or of the amount of valence generated.

METHOD

Subjects

Thirty-six male undergraduates selected from introductory psychology classes served as subjects. Nine subjects were run in each session, assigned randomly to one of three three-man groups to solve the Assembly Problem (Appendix A.1). The three groups solved the problem at the same time in separate rooms.

Task

The Assembly Problem presents a case of industrial underproduction. The group is asked to produce the single solution they think is best for increasing production. The typical group mentions 10 to 12 possibilities, but more than 50 different solutions have been identified in our research. Groups had 40 minutes to solve the problem, which is usually sufficient for all groups to finish.

Procedure

Two coders observed each discussion, recording each subject's valence toward the solutions discussed by the group. After the first solution a 10-minute break was given and subjects were instructed not to discuss the problem. Each subject's valence for the adopted solution was tabulated during this period so he could be placed in his second group. After the break new groups were formed, given the same instructions as before, and allowed 40 minutes to solve the problem again.

The three new groups contained one member from each of the old groups. The "high valence" group contained the three subjects who had the highest valence for their first group's adopted solution. The "medium valence" group consisted of the three subjects who had the second-highest valence for their first group's adopted solution, while the "low valence" group contained the subjects who had the lowest valence for their first group's adopted solution. We note that this method of assigning members to the new groups occasionally resulted in placing people in "medium valence" groups who had valences for their first group's adopted solution higher than those from other groups who were placed in "high valence" groups. Thus high, medium, and low refer to rank orders, not to the absolute amount of valence generated.

Even though groups were instructed to recommend a single action step, many groups adopted more than one solution. One of these was usually a principal solution and the others were subordinate solutions. In cases where this happened, valences for both principal and subordinate solutions were combined algebraically to measure a person's commitment. The rationale for this procedure lies in the assumption that the subordinate solution was usually adopted in order to pacify a deviant member. The results obtained in using the principal solution alone were quite similar, but will not be presented.

In all, four replications of this design were run. Thus, the experiment totaled 36 subjects who served in 12 first-round groups, and in one of the four second-round "high valence," "medium valence," or "low valence" groups. In each replication coders were rotated so that no pair of coders coded more than two high-, medium-, or low-valence second-round groups. Most of the statistical analyses use an analysis-of-variance design in which the "treatments" are the members' ranks and the replications are treated as fixed-effects levels.

Commitment

The measure of commitment was an individual subject's valence in his second-round group toward the solution adopted in his first-round group.

Measures of Satisfaction

After the first-round groups had arrived at a solution, the members individually answered the question "How satisfied are you with the solution reached by your group?" Responses to the question were made on a six-point scale from "very satisfied" to "very dissatisfied."

RESULTS

The assignment of members to second-round high-, medium-, and low-valence groups was based on the rank order of the valence each generated for the adopted solution in his first group. As a partial validation of this assignment, the valence indexes associated with these assignments are shown in Table 9.1. The mean valences parallel the rank orders, and are all significantly different from each other. However, the mean difference between the members assigned to the high-valence groups and those assigned to medium-valence groups is small compared with the difference between the medium-valence and low-valence means. Thus, the members of high-, medium-, and low-valence groups did differ significantly in their valences for their first group's adopted solution and, presumably, in their commitment to that decision. (The lack of difference among replications is as fortunate as is the fact that no two of the first-round groups adopted the same solution.)

TABLE 9.1

Valence for the First Group's Adopted Solutions

	High-Valence Subjects	Medium-Valence Subjects	Low-Valence Subjects
Mean	29.00*	20.83*	4.92*
S.D.	9.74	7.75	7.32

Analysis of Variance

Source	SS	df	MS	F
Between replications				
Replications (A)	117.63	3	39.2	.23
Error	1,361.12	8	170.1	
Within original groups				
Valence rank (B)	31,600.17	2	1,800.09	52.05**
A x B	414.28	6	69.05	1.99
Error	553.55	16	34.56	

*All significantly different from each other at the .05 level of confidence by a post hoc comparison.

**$p < .01$.

Source: Compiled by the authors.

Several behavioral tests of the members' commitment to their first group's solution were conducted. Each test assumed that such commitment would be demonstrated by willingness to promote the first group's solution in the second group. Thus, the principal dependent variable is the amount of valence generated by a person for his first solution in the second group.

Table 9.2 shows the mean total valence in the second group for the first group's solutions, by conditions. Although the ordering of the means is consistent with the hypothesis—high > medium > low—the analysis of variance shows that these differences are not statistically significant.

TABLE 9.2

Valence in the Second Groups for Solutions Adopted by First Groups

	High-Valence Subjects	Medium-Valence Subjects	Low-Valence Subjects
Mean	27.08	14.08	12.50
S.D.	32.49	12.15	16.05

Analysis of Variance

Source	SS	df	MS	F
Between replications				
Replications (A)	1,874.89	3	624.96	.69
Error	7,195.34	8	899.42	
Within original groups				
Valence rank (B)	1,536.73	2	768.36	2.06
A x B	2,493.27	6	415.54	
Error	5,971.33	16	373.21	

Source: Compiled by the authors.

The preceding analysis is a less sensitive test of members' commitment than it appears initially. Recognizing that the second-round groups also produced solutions to the problem, the members ultimately had to compromise in some way and abandon their initial positions before the end of the meeting. Therefore, we attempted to capture their expression of commitment before the point at which they began to compromise. In each second-round group we selected a point at about the first 60 acts (because of the unreliability of the act-by-act coding, we chose a point of obvious correspondence in the two coders' protocols very close to the first 60 acts) to analyze each member's valence for his first group's solution. The means and associated analysis of variance are shown in Table 9.3. Although the overall F-test for first-group valence rank was significant, the principal effect was the low valence generated by the low-valence members. The differences in the means between the high-valence and medium-valence members were not statistically significant. The relative magnitudes of these means parallel those shown in Table 9.1 for valence in the first groups.

TABLE 9.3

First-Segment Valence in the Second Group for Solutions Adopted by First Groups

	High-Valence Subjects	Medium-Valence Subjects	Low-Valence Subjects
Mean	8.58	8.25	4.00
S.D.	3.65	8.12	2.85

Analysis of Variance

Source	SS	df	MS	F
Between replications				
Replications (A)	181.00	3	60.33	1.54
Error	314.22	8	39.29	
Within original groups				
Valence rank (B)	156.72	2	78.46	4.56*
A x B	268.84	6	44.81	2.50
Error	287.11	16	17.94	

*Significant beyond .05 level of confidence.
Source: Compiled by the authors.

In an attempt to ensure that the results of this analysis of the first segment were not some form of artifact, the analysis was repeated with several different variables as covariates. On the possibility that the valence differences were merely a function of the differences in participation rates, each member's total number of acts in the first segment was used as a covariate. Its effect was to enhance the differences among the conditions ($F_{2,15} = 8.69$, $p < .01$). Thus, the valence-commitment relationship was not a function of mere activity in the second group.

Even more insight was provided by an analysis of covariance in which the covariate was the amount of valence for the adopted solution in the first group. The differences among conditions in mean second-round valence in the first segment almost completely disappeared ($F_{2,15} = 0.77$). Thus, the amount of valence generated in the first group, not the person's relative contribution to his group's valence, was the principal determinant of his expressed commitment to that solution in the early part of the new group's discussion.

Finally, the members' rated satisfaction with their first group's decision was also used as a covariate in an analysis of covariance of the new group's first-segment valence. The results of that analysis were mixed. The F-test for ranks dropped to 3.14, substantial but below the value needed at the .05 level of confidence. The interaction between the ranks and the replications had a similar F-value (3.10, $p < .10$). Nevertheless, there was no interpretable consistency in this effect.

As one might anticipate from the latter two analyses, the correlations between valence for and satisfaction with solutions in the first group (which correlated .64 with each other) were correlated .58 and .62 with valence for that solution in the second group. Partial correlations suggest that the valence-commitment relationship is mediated through the valence-satisfaction relationship. The satisfaction-commitment relationship held at .38 even when initial valence was partialed out.

DISCUSSION

The principal purpose of this experiment was to test the proposition that a person's expressed valence for his group's adopted solution would determine his commitment to that decision. The behavioral evidence presented here is striking in its confirmation of that proposition. The more valence the person contributed personally to the group's adopted solution, the more likely he was to argue for that solution in his new group. Although the total mean valences for the first solution in the second group showed only directional differences consistent with the hypothesis, they suggest that the members' commitment caused them to resist abandoning their initial positions until quite late in the discussion. Most impressive, of course, was the initial level of commitment displayed by the members with high valence in the first round.

Also notable in that respect is the fact that the level of valence contributed by each member in the first-round groups was such an important determinant of commitment. Being the most influential in the first-round group was not sufficient to ensure a high level of commitment. Unless a person spoke frequently in favor of his group's solution, he was not terribly committed to it. The related finding was that people who were only second most influential in their first group often showed high commitment to their initial solutions in the second group, if their first-round valence had been very high.

The major conclusions to be drawn from this study, despite the small number of groups involved, is that the valence expressed by a member for the solution adopted by a group and the associated ratings of satisfaction with it are good estimates of that person's commitment to the decision. Thus, groups should encourage all their members to express their views about a solution before it is finally adopted by a group, for example, as a self-conscious part of the control phase. Although such a procedure may be considered a waste of the group's time, it may prove to be time well invested in gaining everyone's understanding of and commitment to the final decision.

Such a procedure runs one "risk." It may uncover the development of a false consensus due to the accumulation of valence for a solution by a dominant few. By systematically calling for the views of each member in turn, the doubts of the dissenters may be revealed and a new round of problem solving required. We labeled this a "risk" because the procedure may help the group to improve both the quality and the acceptance of the solution it reaches, even though the meeting may take longer.

10

THE EFFECTS OF VALENCE OF SOLUTIONS AND GROUP COHESIVENESS ON MEMBERS' COMMITMENT TO GROUP DECISIONS

Myron W. Block
L. Richard Hoffman

Ever since Lewin's (1947) World War II research demonstrated the effectiveness of group decision making for getting housewives to alter their food-consumption habits, the use of groups for obtaining people's commitment to decisions has been advocated as part of the participative management of organizations (Maier 1952; 1963; Likert 1967; Vroom and Yetton 1973). Reviewing the many studies of organizational change, Greiner (1967) concluded that successful changes were accompanied by management's concern for employees' acceptance of the change and the use of group decision in effecting it.

Although the effectiveness of gaining members' commitment to change through the use of group decision is unquestioned, the mechanism by which such commitment is achieved has been a matter of controversy. Bennett (1955) concluded that "the process of making a decision and the degree to which group consensus is obtained . . ." were the important factors. But Vroom (1960) and French, Israel, and As (1966) identify "the felt opportunity to participate" in the decision as most significant.

Several experiments in this volume have shown that group members were more satisfied with their group's decision the more they, individually, had influenced its adoption by contributing valence to it. The magnitudes of the correlations obtained between individual valence for the adopted solution and rated satisfaction with the solution have varied from .20 to about .64. (See Chapters 2, 3, 8, 9.) Chapter 9 showed that individual valence and rated satisfaction with the decision both predicted a group member's valence for that solution in a subsequent group, thereby confirming the satisfaction rating as an estimate of the member's commitment to the decision.

These studies were all performed, however, in ad hoc experimental groups, which had neither prior history nor any expectations of future interactions. Thus, the members had little connection to each other or commitment to the group as a whole. A member's commitment to a decision produced by a group could have been determined solely by whether the group adopted his/her preferred solution or even whether he/she was able to influence the group's decision. The question of whether the member's standing in the group would be enhanced by "going along" with the group's solution or be jeopardized by opposing it was probably not as important as it might be in an ongoing group (Thomas and Fink 1961).

The importance of a person's relationship to a group in influencing his/her opinions and attitudes has been studied extensively (Hare 1978). Deutsch and Gerard (1955) showed that a person's reference group may serve both informational and normative functions in influencing a member's judgments. The group provides both "social reality" (Festinger 1954) to guide the member's interpretation of information and norms to identify the group's preferences. The pressures on members to conform to such norms have been well documented even under laboratory conditions (Schachter 1951; Thomas and Fink 1961). However, when the group is cohesive or when the members are particularly dependent on the group, the forces to conformity become even more severe (Seashore 1954; Jackson and Saltzstein 1958). Seashore showed that members of cohesive groups in a factory produced at the group norm, regardless of what they individually considered to be a reasonable day's production.

The present study is designed to examine whether members of cohesive groups are committed to their group's decision, regardless of the solution valence contributed by each of them individually, or whether the members' attraction to the group mediates the valence-satisfaction relationship in any way.

METHOD

Problem

The Personnel Selection Problem, in which the best of five hypothetical candidates for a mythical position is to be chosen by the group, was used in this study (Appendix A. 2).

Subjects

Two samples of students from advanced programs in management education provided the groups for this experiment. In the first sample 115 MBA students from four sections of an introductory course in management were composed into 28 groups. The second sample consisted of the 72 members of an executive program, from which 15 groups were formed. While the MBA students were generally recent college graduates and the students in the executive program were mostly middle managers, the valence-adoption process described their problem-solving processes about equally well (see Chapter 4).

Cohesiveness and Attraction to the Group

Two different methods were used to vary the cohesiveness of the groups in this study. In the MBA sample students in two course sections were told one week before the experiment, which was conducted during the middle of the term, to form ten groups of four people to perform a group project. The project was to constitute 30 percent of their course grade, so it was assumed that students would pick others whom they thought were competent and with whom they could work. Ten such "high cohesive" groups were formed. In the other two class sections 19 groups of three, four, and five persons were formed randomly for the experiment. Since these groups had not existed before, had no anticipated future, and had members randomly assigned to them, we assumed that they would be less cohesive.

The effectiveness of this method of varying cohesiveness was assessed by four questions administered just prior to the experiment. They were modified to fit the present conditions from questions used by Jackson (1959) and Schachter et al. (1951). On seven-point, bipolar scales members rated (1) their satisfaction with their group; (2) their anticipated liking of the other members; (3) the knowledgeability of the group members; and (4) their desire to be part of a different group (scored negatively). An index of attraction to the group was created from the mean of the four ratings. The mean attraction of members of groups who chose each other ("high cohesive" groups) was 22.6 (S.D. = 1.63), while the mean attraction of those who were assigned randomly ("low cohesive" groups) was 20.3 (S.D. = 2.46; $F_{1,28} = 8.59$; $\underline{p} < .01$). Despite the statistical significance of this difference in means, however, there was a high degree of overlap between the two distributions. The range of the "low cohesive" groups was from 17.5 to 23.6, while that for the "high cohesive" groups was from 18.3 to 26.3. Thus, although permitting students to choose their own work groups produced a somewhat higher level of attraction to the group, the effect was not strong. Therefore, in the analyses to be presented, the measured level of attraction to the group will be used, rather than the experimental treatment, as the independent variable.

In the executive program class 15 study groups had been formed at the beginning of the academic year on the basis of their place of residence in the Chicago area, to assist the students in preparing for class. These groups were entirely voluntary and usually met at least once a week, according to the needs of the members. By the time of the experiment, the groups had been in existence for about eight months, and their measured level of cohesiveness served as the independent variable.

The mean cohesiveness in the ongoing groups was 23.4, which is slightly higher than the MBA sample (mean = 21.1). But both the range (from 15.0 to 28.0) and the standard deviation ($S.D._{Exec}$ = 2.54, $S.D._{MBA}$ = 2.19) were somewhat larger, suggesting possibly more intense reactions in both directions in these ongoing groups. Because these distributions were somewhat different, they were divided into thirds in each sample for comparability in the analyses (Table 10.1).

TABLE 10.1

Categories of Attraction to the Group

	Attraction to Group		
Sample	Low	Medium	High
Executive	0-21	22-25	26-28
	N = 21	N = 21	N = 27
MBA	0-20	21-22	23-28
	N = 40	N = 32	N = 35

Note: N's vary slightly from table to table because of nonresponse to each item.

Source: Compiled by the authors.

Influence over the Decision

As in Chapter 11, the measure of actual influence was the member's individual contribution to group valence for the adopted solution. The valence index was the algebraic sum of the positive minus the negative statements made by the member about the candidate adopted by the group.

These measures were obtained from two coders, who coded the discussion in progress (executive program groups), or from transcripts made from recordings of the groups (MBA groups). These differences in the method of coding produced somewhat different distributions of valence at the individual level in the two samples, which caused us to divide the valence indexes for the adopted solutions into quartiles to be able to perform comparable analyses on the two samples. The values identifying the quartiles are shown in Table 10.2.

TABLE 10.2

Distribution of Valence Scores for the Adopted Solution, by Quartile

	Valence Score Quartile			
Sample	Low	2	3	High
Executive	-14.5 to 2	2.5 to 8	8.5 to 13.5	14.0 and higher
	N = 17	N = 16	N = 17	N = 20
MBA	-6.5 to 4	4.5 to 11.5	12 to 20	20.5 and higher
	N = 25	N = 29	N = 27	N = 28

Note: N's vary slightly from table to table because of nonresponse to each item.

Source: Compiled by the authors.

Commitment to the Decision

Two measures of commitment were used. One was a rating of satisfaction with the decision on a seven-point bipolar scale, comparable with those used in previous studies. Each of the five candidates was also rated on a nine-point bipolar scale of acceptability for the job. The rating of the adopted candidate was added to the rating of satisfaction with the decision as a measure of members' commitment.

RESULTS

The first question to be asked in this study is whether the individual valence generated for the solution adopted by the group is related to the member's commitment to the decision. The overall relationships between individual solution valence and commitment are shown for the two samples in Table 10.3. The *tau* for both samples is significant at the .05 level of confidence, replicating previous studies. (The Pearson correlations between valence for the adopted solution and member's satisfaction with the decision alone were .44 for the 72 subjects in the executive sample and .21 for 113 members of MBA groups. Both are significantly different from zero, but the latter is smaller than the values obtained in previous studies. This reduced size may be due in part to the small number of MBA students who expressed low commitment to their group's decision.)

TABLE 10.3

Relationship between Member Valence for the Group Decision and Degree of Commitment

Degree of Member Commitment to Group Decision	Member Valence for Group Decision Quartile				Total	Kendall's Tau
	Low	2	3	High		
	Executive Sample					
High	4	12	12	17	45	
Medium	5	2	3	2	12	
Low	8	2	2	1	13	
Total	17	16	17	20	70	.39*
	MBA Sample					
High	14	13	22	24	73	
Medium	9	9	5	4	27	
Low	2	7	0	0	9	
Total	25	29	27	28	109	.28*

*$p < .05$.

Source: Compiled by the authors.

The relationship between members' attraction to their group and their commitment to the decision, shown in Table 10.4, is also statistically significant in both samples. The more attracted members were to their groups, the higher was their commitment to the decision.

TABLE 10.4

Relationship between Member Attraction to the Group and Commitment to the Group Decision

Degree of Member Commitment to Group Decision	Member Attraction to the Group: Low	Medium	High	Total	Kendall's Tau
	Executive Sample				
High	10	13	21	44	
Medium	4	2	6	12	
Low	7	6	0	13	
Total	21	21	27	69	.28*
	MBA Sample				
High	20	25	26	71	
Medium	14	6	7	27	
Low	6	1	2	9	
Total	40	32	35	107	.21*

*$p < .05$.
Source: Compiled by the authors.

The joint effects of group cohesiveness and individual valence for the adopted solution on members' commitment are shown in Table 10.5. In that table, for each sample separately, the relationship between individuals' valence for the adopted solution and their commitment to the decision is shown in "high cohesive" and "low cohesive" groups. (Separation into "high cohesive" and "low cohesive" groups was accomplished by dividing the group cohesiveness scores at the median for each sample.) The *taus* in all four parts of the table are statistically significant, indicating that the valence-commitment relationship was maintained even when the level of cohesiveness was controlled. In both samples, however, the *tau* was larger in the "low cohesive" groups. Unfortunately, there is no statistical test for the significance of differences between *taus*, so we were unable to determine the stability of the differences obtained. Nevertheless, it is clear that the members of cohesive groups almost invariably indicated commitment to the decision, regardless of their level of expressed support for it during the discussion. The members' individual influence over the decision was more important in the "low cohesive" groups.

TABLE 10.5

Moderating Effect of Group Cohesion on the Valence-Commitment Relationship

Degree of Member Commitment to Group Decision	Members of "High Cohesive" Groups: Member Valence for Group Decision Quartile						Members of "Low Cohesive" Groups: Member Valence for Group Decision Quartile					
	Low	2	3	4	Total	Kendall's Tau	Low	2	3	4	Total	Kendall's Tau
Executive Sample												
High	3	9	8	7	27		1	3	3	10	17	
Medium	1	1	0	1	3		4	1	3	1	9	
Low	1	2	0	0	3		7	1	2	0	10	
Total	5	12	8	8	33	.25*	12	5	8	11	36	.57*
MBA Sample												
High	8	9	13	13	43		6	4	10	10	30	
Medium	6	6	2	2	16		4	3	5	0	12	
Low	0	2	0	0	2		2	5	0	0	7	
Total	14	17	15	15	61	.27*	12	12	15	10	49	.36*

*$p < .05$.
Source: Compiled by the authors.

The commitment reported by the members of "high cohesive" groups did not stem, however, from a lack of variation among the members' valence for the adopted decision. Chi-square tests comparing the quartile distributions of valence between "high cohesive" and "low cohesive" groups—the bottom rows in each of the tables—did not approach statistical significance ($\chi^2_{Exec} = 3.26$, $\chi^2_{MBA} = 0.24$, 3 d.f.). Thus, high group cohesiveness did not inhibit the expression of conflicting points of view, but did produce commitment even though the conflict had not been resolved.

DISCUSSION

Consistent with the results of previous studies (see Chapters 8, 9), a positive relationship was found between a member's expressed valence for the adopted solution and degree of post-discussion commitment to it. The more influence members have in causing the group to adopt a decision, the more strongly they identify with it. Thus, one value of the use of group decision making is in permitting members to persuade the group of the virtues of their preferences. In so doing, they seem also to persuade themselves in a process of self-reinforcement and to become even more committed to the decision. However, it is clear that the potential danger of such unilateral dominance of the influence process reduces the level of commitment potentially available from the other group members. By "winning the battle" of convincing the group to adopt a particular decision, a member may "lose the war" by failing to gain the commitment of others necessary for its implementation. Group decision making does not guarantee high commitment if the dominance of some members prevents others from truly influencing the final outcome (see Chapter 9).

The effects of group cohesiveness and members' attraction to the group on their commitment to the decision moderate this conclusion somewhat. Members of "high cohesive" groups, especially those in the executive program, which were ongoing groups, showed a high level of commitment to the decision even when they had negative valence for it. We might conjecture that the valence these members had for the group's solidarity was more important to them than was their valence for the group's decision. Since the experimental task was clearly peripheral to the central concerns of the members, the need to present a uniform stand to the world (or at least to the experimenter) may have been greater than the need to be personally correct on this problem. This type of interpersonal conflict was not created in less cohesive groups. Dependence on the group was less, so individual attitudes toward the solution and toward the process of adopting it assumed greater importance in obtaining members' commitment.

The conclusion that one way to ensure members' commitment to decisions is to create a cohesive group, while basically true, has certain dangers inherent in it. The principal short-term threat is to the quality of the solution to any particular problem. Invoking loyalty to the group may prevent the expression of divergent views and the suppression of substantive conflict so important to creative problem solving (see Chapter 1; see also Hoffman, Harburg, and Maier 1962). If a member feels too dependent on the group and is fearful of losing the group's rewards, he/she may censor thoughts and information that cast doubt on the prevailing view. Unless the cohesiveness of the group demands conformity to only the limited set of norms necessary for the group's survival, it may gain commitment only through compliance and at the sacrifice of effective problem solving. Commitment based on true conviction about the merits of the solution is a desirable goal for the effectiveness even of cohesive groups.

PART IV

PARTICIPATION, POWER, AND INFLUENCE

11

PARTICIPATION AND INFLUENCE IN PROBLEM-SOLVING GROUPS

L. Richard Hoffman
Molly Mooney Clark

Research on equal-status small groups has generally assumed that the participation rankings of group members are identical with the distribution of influence in the group. The basis for the assumption of identity comes from Bales's work (Bales et al. 1951; Bales 1953). He found a strong relationship between the participation rates (measured in terms of acts initiated) of group members and their judgments about who exercised influence within the group.

Riecken's (1958) study of the effects of talkativeness is also cited in support of the identity of participation and influence. He demonstrated that the elegant solution to the Assembly Problem was adopted by the group more often when the most talkative member promoted it. The most talkative member, again, was identified most frequently as the most influential member of the group.

With this identity in mind, many studies of the regularities in the distribution of participation in groups have been based on the assumption that the identification of the shape of such a curve would also identify the nature of the distribution of influence. Beginning with Stephan and Mishler's (1952) demonstration of the fit of the exponential distribution to individual participation rates, controversy has raged over the possibly better fit of alternative mathematical models (Kadane and Lewis 1969; Reynolds 1971; Fisek and Ofshe 1970; Berger, Connor, and Fisek 1974).

Both common sense and a substantial amount of empirical evidence, however, suggest that participation and influence, even in ad hoc, experimental, problem-solving groups, are quite different concepts. Most of the studies cited earlier in support of the identity actually demonstrate very modest correlations. The correlations between participation and nominations for leadership tend to be moderate (about .40), and even Riecken's most talkative leaders often failed to convince their groups to adopt the elegant solution.

March (1956) concluded that participation was used as a surrogate for influence primarily because it was easily available and was visible by judges to make inferences, rather than really reflecting the true influence process.

The earlier studies in this volume on valence in group problem solving have added to the data suggesting a separation of participation and influence. Chapter 6 showed that the amount of discussion concerning a particular solution is not predictive of that solution's adoption by the group. Rather, the valence, the net frequency of positive comments for a particular solution, is strongly associated with its adoption. Furthermore, Chapter 8 demonstrated that each member's valence index for the adopted solution, not his amount of participation, was correlated with his satisfaction with the solution. Thus, while it is likely that participation and influence are related, since a person must participate in order to influence, differences can be demonstrated between the two.

The present study is designed to examine the relationship between participation and influence, in order to determine how much and in what ways they are different. On both problems used in this study, the valence index for a solution has shown strong correlation with the probability of its being adopted by the group. The form and magnitude of this relationship for the two problems was shown in Table 4.1. For both problems the proportion of solutions adopted increased with increasing values of the valence index beyond the adoption threshold of 15. Solutions that achieved a valence index greater than 40 were adopted more than 80 percent of the time; solutions with valences between 30 and 39, between 50 and 60 percent; and at lesser rates for valences between 15 and 30. The magnitude of the valence index for a solution is an indication, therefore, of the probability of its adoption by the group.

Our measure of individual influence will assume that the group valence index measures the forces promoting the adoption of that solution. Each individual's contribution to the group valence will be assumed to measure his/her degree of influence over the group decision. In this way we can ask a number of questions about participation and influence, concerning their distributions among the group members, the relationship of participation to influence, and the emergence of participation and influence structures. These questions will be specified in the presentation of our results.

Tasks

Two problem-solving tasks were studied. The Assembly Problem (Appendix A.1) requires the generation of alternative solutions to a production problem and the selection of the best one by the group. The Personnel Selection Problem (Appendix A.2) asks the group to select one of five hypothetical job applicants to recommend for a hypothetical position.

Subjects

The Assembly Problem was solved by 175 introductory psychology students divided into 15 three-person groups, 15 four-person groups, and 14 five-person groups.

The Personnel Selection Problem was solved by 159 MBA students in 6 three-person groups, 24 four-person groups, and 9 five-person groups.

Participation and Influence Measures

All groups were coded by two observers using a modification of Hoffman's valence system for both participation and influence (see Chapter 2). Each solution-related comment (act) was identified with (1) the person making the comment, (2) the particular solution referred to; and (3) the sign, positive or negative, with regard to the speaker's feelings about the solution. Participation is the total number of acts, regardless of sign, for each group member. This measure correlates about .85 with the amount of timed participation (see Chapter 8). Influence is the valence—the number of positive comments minus the number of negative comments—contributed by each member for the solution adopted by the group. This index is the individual portion of the group valence index. For any particular group member, then, total participation is the absolute sum of his/her positive and negative acts for all solutions. Influence is the algebraic difference between his/her positive and negative acts only for the adopted solution in the group. The intercoder reliability of these indexes exceeds .80 in almost all groups.

Although these measures are conceptually and operationally distinct, some overlap between them arises due to the nature of the control phase (see Chapter 6). As noted in Chapter 6, in the last portion of most groups' discussions, almost all comments made about the to-be-adopted solution are positive. Each such comment, thus, adds both to the participation and to the influence measures, artifactually inflating their overall correlation.

RESULTS

In presenting the results we must first demonstrate that our measure of participation is comparable with those used in other studies. (We have mentioned that our measure of solution-related acts correlates .85 with timed participation.) The left three columns of Table 11.1 compare the distributions of participation rates

TABLE 11.1

Proportions of Participation and Influence

Group Size	Member Rank	Participation			Influence	
		Kadane and Lewis	Assembly	Selection	Assembly	Selection
3	1	.438	.434	.493	.559	.596
	2	.330	.349	.298	.327	.350
	3	.232	.216	.209	.114	.054
4	1	.367	.370	.386	.560	.463
	2	.273	.282	.280	.303	.300
	3	.216	.210	.203	.133	.167
	4	.144	.137	.132	.005	.069
5	1	.354	.341	.335	.526	.457
	2	.261	.260	.258	.307	.267
	3	.191	.197	.181	.151	.177
	4	.126	.135	.137	.073	.103
	5	.068	.066	.090	-.057	-.004

Source: Compiled by the authors.

for the two problems of the present study with leaderless groups reported by Kadane and Lewis (1969). Participation rate equals the ratio of the number of individual acts to the total number of acts in the group. The three columns show a marked similarity for each group size, despite variations in the samples, activities, and measures of participation. Note, however, that the proportion of participation initiated by the most active member declined with increasing group size, especially in the groups that solved the Assembly and Selection problems. The highest participator accounted for 43 and 49 percent in three-person groups, for 37 and 39 percent in four-person groups, and for only 34 percent in the five-person groups.

The proportions of influence were calculated in exactly the same way as the participation rates, but they are not exactly comparable with them. Since individual valences for the adopted solution were sometimes negative, the group valence index is of the algebraic sum of positive and negative numbers. The "proportion" of influence is the ratio of individual valence to group valence. While these ratios are not strictly proportions to be compared directly with the participation rates, they are comparable with each other on the problems and in groups of different sizes.

The two right-hand columns of Table 11.1 show the distributions of influence for each of the two problems for the three group sizes. They show two important things: (1) there is a high degree of similarity in the proportions for the two problems; (2) the proportion of influence exercised by the most influential member did not decline with increasing group size. Unlike the decline in participation rates, approximately half of the influence for the adopted solution was exercised by the most influential member in groups of all three sizes on both problems.

The modest, but significant, correlations obtained between individual measures of participation and influence parallel these differences in the distributions. They varied from .28 to .64 (see Table 11.2), despite the built-in correlation resulting from the artifact discussed in the "Method" section. The rank orders of the participation and influence measures within each group also show only a modest relationship with each other, as shown in Table 11.3. This analysis controls for the levels of general activity and valence in a group. There we see that the rank orders were often inconsistent, even regarding only the highest participator. In 11 of the 15 three-person groups (73 percent) on the Assembly Problem, the highest participator was the most influential. In the four-person groups it was 60 percent, while in only 50 percent of the five-person groups was the most active person the most influential one. The relationships on the Personnel Selection Problem showed a similar, but even more precipitous, drop from three-person to five-person groups. The percentages of times the same person was the most active and most influential were 67 percent, 58 percent, and 33 percent for three-person, four-person, and five-person groups, respectively. Although there is no statistical test for these types of interdependent relationships, the relative independence of participation and influence seems obvious.

TABLE 11.2

Correlations between Participation and Influence

		Group Size		
Problem		Three-Person	Four-Person	Five-Person
Assembly	r	.28	.54**	.58**
	N	45	60	70
Personnel selection	r	.64**	.32**	.34*
	N	18	96	45

*$p < .05$; **$p < .01$.
Source: Compiled by the authors.

Our ability to divide the Personnel Selection Problem into phases paralleling Bales and Strodtbeck's (1951) orientation, evaluation, and control phases (see Chapter 6) allowed us to examine the development of the influence and participation structures in finer detail. It was shown in Chapter 6 for the entire group that the control phase was marked by high correlations among the total number of acts and the number of acts and valence for the adopted solution. The correlations in the first row of Table 11.4 between participation and influence for the control phase show that the most active person in that phase contributed most valence to the adopted solution. However, the magnitude of the relationship drops sharply from three-person to five-person groups.

When the participation-influence relationship is examined during the discussion up to the control phase, however, the correlations are all much smaller. Since the variances of the two variables were actually larger in this phase than in the control phase, the difference in the sizes of the correlations is impressive.

TABLE 11.3

Congruence between Rank Orders of Participation and Influence

		Participation Rank													
		Group Size 3				Group Size 4					Group Size 5				
		1	2	3		1	2	3	4		1	2	3	4	5
						Assembly Problem									
Influence	1	11	2	2	1	9	5	1	0	1	7	4	3	0	0
rank	2	2.5	8	4.5	2	3	4	5	3	2	6	2	4	1.5	.5
	3	1.5	5	8.5	3	2	2.5	5	5.5	3	0	3	2	6.5	2.5
					4	1	3.5	4	6.5	4	1	.5	3	5	4.5
										5	0	4.5	2	1	6.5
Percent		1:1	73.3				60							50	
						Selection Problem									
Influence	1	4	1	1	1	14	2	4	4	1	3	3	1	1	1
rank	2	1	5	0	2	4	12	6	2	2	4	1	2	0	2
	3	1	0	5	3	4	7	7	6	3	2	0	3	1	3
					4	2	3	7	12	4	0	3	1	3	2
										5	0	2	2	4	1
Percent		1:1	67				58							33	

Source: Compiled by the authors.

TABLE 11.4

Correlations between Participation and Influence at Different Points in the Discussion (Personnel Selection Problem)

	Group Size		
Correlation	Three-Person (N = 18)	Four-Person (N = 96)	Five-Person (N = 45)
Between P and I in control phase	.82*	.51*	.33*
Between P and I to control phase	.17	.34*	.34*
Between P before and during control phase	.35	.15	-.53*
Between I before and during control phase	-.34	.16	-.22

P = participation.
I = influence.
*$p < .01$.
Source: Compiled by the authors.

Finally, we correlated the participation before the control phase with participation during the control phase. The influence measures in those two phases were also correlated with each other. Those are shown in the third and fourth rows, respectively, of Table 11.4. The correlations for the participation measures were much smaller than anticipated from the results of the study by M. Fisek and R. Ofshe (1970). They had shown that a stable participation structure developed early and was maintained throughout in most groups. The correlations in Table 11.4 show that the level of activity of the person most active for most of the meeting was unrelated to his/her activity during the control phase.

The same seems to be true of the influence measure (line 4 in Table 11.4). The person who was most influential in bringing the group to its decision was often least active in contributing to its final confirmation.

DISCUSSION

When influence is measured in terms of a person's actual contribution to the group's adoption of a solution, its relationship to participation becomes much more complex. The usual assumption that the two are identical is obviously false. It arises from the modest and significant correlations usually found between participation rates and post-meeting ratings of influence and leadership by the group members.

The source of this misleading perception may be a recency effect arising from the correlations between participation and influence in the control phase. Perhaps the person who leads the group in confirming its decision receives the credit for having helped them make it. The subtle influence of the less-active person who contributes the most valence to the adopted solution before the control phase goes unrecognized. That person may also be active in eliciting others' support for the solution during the earlier period as well (Stein et al. 1979).

The independence of the participation and influence aspects of members' functioning in the group is probably even more pronounced than is evident in these data, since the participation measure was limited to solution-related acts. Although, in problem-solving groups in the laboratory, most of the discussion is task-centered, this bias in our estimate of participation probably enhances its correlation with influence beyond the artifacts already noted.

The regularity of the participation rate may reflect some social structure that the group develops to maintain members in the group. People follow norms of politeness and taking turns to permit everyone to feel part of the group. However, the actual group movement to a decision is reflected in the valence index and may be short or long, depending on factors as yet unidentified.

The results also further emphasize the value of studying the process by which groups actually move from the beginning of a problem to its final adoption. The questions raised by these data would not be revealed by any input-outcome experimental design. Even merely measuring participation and relating it in an aggregate way to a post-meeting measure of members' post hoc perception of influence may be inadequate and misleading.

12

A VALENCE ANALYSIS OF THE IMPACT OF DECISION RULES IN UNEQUAL POWER GROUPS

Gideon Falk
L. Richard Hoffman

Many studies have shown that the dominance of a powerful group member over the group process frequently interferes with the free expression of ideas by group members with low power. Power differences have been shown to be an obstacle to effective group problem solving (Torrance 1955; Maier and Hoffman 1960b; Hoffman, Harburg, and Maier 1962). the more powerful person's preferences tend to carry more weight in the group's deliberations, in part, because he/she asserts himself/herself more often, contributes more valence (see Chapter 2), and causes the group to adopt his/her preference (Pepinsky, Hemphill, and Shevitz 1958). However, especially in formal groups, the members accept domination by the leader as legitimate and often withdraw their opposition to the leader's suggested solutions (Maier and Hoffman 1960b). The burden of the group's effectiveness, then, rests heavily on the leader's ability, rather than on the total resources of the group. When the leader is wrong, the group is wrong too (Torrance 1955).

Various methods have been introduced to reduce the untoward impact of the leader's power on the group's effectiveness. Maier (1953) trained leaders to be more permissive and to invite the members to express their views. Hoffman, Harburg, and Maier (1962) increased the commitment of the members to a solution opposed to the leader's preference. In both cases the opposition of the members' point of view to the leader's created a conflict from which creative solutions to the problem often emerged. Conceptually, in the terms of this volume, the first two "conditions for creative problem solving" (Chapter 1) were created by allowing the valence for the members' preferred solution to balance the power-based valence of the leader's favored solution. The conflict thus generated often motivated the group to search for or invent a third alternative that would be acceptable to the entire group. By increasing the members' incentive to express their valence for their preferences and by reducing the leader's reliance on his/her power to overcome their opposition, the group's problem-solving effectiveness was often increased.

More formal methods have also been proposed for increasing the expressed valence for minority and other low-power preferences. The Delphi method (Dalkey 1969) provides anonymity for the source of opinions. Bouchard (1972) recommended that each member present an opinion in turn, thus reducing the tendency of more dominant members to generate undue valence. The most widely recognized and accepted methods, however, are the use of formal decision rules such as unanimity and majority rule.

The value of a unanimous rule in ensuring the expression of minority opinion is so well accepted that the Supreme Court only reluctantly agreed to relax that rule for juries in civil cases. Research is almost unanimous in supporting the utility of a unanimous-decision rule for improving the problem-solving effectiveness of groups (Bower 1963; Hall and Watson 1970; Holloman and Hendrick 1972). Although the process by which the unanimous-decision rule effects such improvement has not been studied directly, its proponents have assumed that all members are encouraged to express their opinions and that deviation cannot be overruled by the more powerful members or by the majority of the group. In this way the valence for all significant options may be presumed to rise above the adoption threshold, ensuring them a serious hearing by the group. Also, under unanimous rule, therefore, the valences of opposing points of view are more likely to become balanced and encourage creative conflict.

The research supporting the value of a unanimous-decision rule rests, however, almost entirely on experiments with equal-status groups whose members have no formal power over each other. The unequal distribution of influence exercised by the more dominant members in such groups, in the absence of formal decision rules, has been demonstrated in many studies (see Chapter 11; see also Riecken 1958).

Where there are formal power differences in a group, however, unanimity may not be the universal panacea it seems to be in equal-status groups. If we consider a formal decision rule as one of the group's norms, it may come into conflict with other group norms—such as formal leadership—in affecting the members' participation in the group discussion. In formal organizational groups the leader's power to reward or punish subordinates may still influence the willingness of the members to invoke the rule of unanimity and oppose his/her position publicly. Recognizing that the leader can defend his/her position by invoking the rule of unanimity, the rule may have little influence on the distribution of power established by the formal hierarchy. Each member, including the leader, may be considered to have had an equal increment of power, by virtue of the decision rule, with no change in the resulting distribution of forces (Lewin 1947).

If, on the other hand, the opposition to the formal leader is shared by the members, the formal power of the leader may be opposed successfully (Hoffman, Harburg, and Maier 1962). A decision rule that promoted the members' perception of mutual interest could provide the security for them to express their valence for their opposition. Under certain circumstances a majority-decision rule could perform that function. By assuring each member that the other low-power people would join together formally to oppose the leader, sufficient valence for the low-power preferences could be generated to balance the valence generated by the leader. Instead of the ambiguity and insecurity of individually invoking the decision rule of unanimity, majority rule fosters the perception of social support from the other low-power members. Furthermore, since under majority rule the low-power members can carry the decision without the consent of the powerful person, they may perceive an opportunity to have a real input into the decision if they coalesce. The threat of a possible coalition against the powerful person is likely to induce him/her to generate less valence for his/her preferred solution and against the opposing alternative. Falk (1978) has demonstrated that the self-perceived power and influence of the formal leader was lower in groups with majority rules than in groups with unanimous rule or no decision rule. Also, the self-perceived power of the low-power members was higher.

The Change of Worl Procedures (CWP) Problem—a role-playing case involving a foreman and three subordinate workers—simulates some conditions of group problem solving in which formal power differences exist within the group. In an attempt to persuade the workers to change their present work methods so as to increase group productivity, the foreman presents a new work procedure. Two of the workers usually resist the change strongly, while a third is somewhat more ambivalent. While the third is willing to adopt the new method, his loyalty to the other workers may cause him to join them in opposing the foreman. The central role of the foreman's power to induce the workers to adopt the new work method has been illustrated in a number of studies (Maier and Hoffman 1960b; 1961). The value of the workers' collective opposition to the foreman in inducing both resistance to change and constructive conflict has also been shown (Hoffman, Harburg, and Maier 1962).

This case offers the opportunity to test the proposition, then, that a majority rule may be more effective than a unanimous rule in promoting effective problem solving in groups where power differences are associated with incompatible solutions to a problem. By encouraging the expression of valence for the workers' preferred solution through the security of a shared position and by reducing the foreman's dominance through the threat of a coalition vote, the majority rule is more likely than a unanimous one or no formal rule to promote effective problem solving.

The hypotheses to be tested in this experiment, then, are linked. As compared with the results for groups with no formal decision rule or a unanimous rule, under a majority rule in the early stages of the meeting:

1. The foreman will generate less positive valence for the new work method, and/or the workers will generate more negative valence for it.

2. The workers will generate more positive valence for the old work method, and the foreman will generate less negative valence for it.

3. The group valence for the new method will be less positive, and it will be more positive for the old method.

METHOD

Task

The CWP contains four roles—a foreman and three workers. The foreman calls a meeting to persuade the workers to adopt a new work method, to work only on their best position (based on time-study data) to increase their group's productivity. The three workers have worked as a team for a long time and have developed a method of rotating on three different positions every hour. Two workers' roles call for resistance to the change, and favor retention of the old work method. A third worker has a built-in role conflict. Being the slowest among the three workers, he feels comfortable working on the position designated for him and favors the recommended change. On the other hand, he feels loyalty to his peers, which encourages him to oppose the proposed change. The integrative and compromise solutions shown in Table 12.1 are alternate work methods designed to capitalize on the differences in ability while avoiding boredom.

Procedure

Data for this study were collected from 18 groups of four persons each whose role-playing of the CWP Problem (Maier 1952, Appendix A.3) was tape-recorded to permit valence analysis of the discussions. These groups were part of a larger study of the effects of decision rules on group problem solving (Falk 1978). In that study 62 groups solved the CWP, but their discussions were not recorded, so the valence data needed for this analysis are not available. The 18 groups that provided these data were assigned randomly to the different experimental conditions and tape-recorded in a separate room while the other groups were also role-playing the problem. Groups were given 40 minutes to solve the problem. There were eight groups with majority rule, four groups with unanimous rule, and six groups with no formal decision rule. While any conclusions reached with such a small sample are, of course, quite tentative, the overall results for these groups parallel those for the larger sample, so an examination of these valence-based hypotheses should be informative. Table 12.1 shows the distribution of types of solutions adopted by the 62 groups in the total study and by the 18 groups included in this analysis, according to the three experimental conditions. It is clear from the table that overall, the majority rule produced more integrative solutions, while the unanimous rule was little different from no decision rule. The valence analysis presented here is an attempt to examine the mechanisms underlying these results.

The experimental conditions were created by adding a pertinent paragraph to each person's standard role (Appendix A.3):

Unanimity rule—"It has been the company's policy and this team's practice to arrive at all group decisions by reaching consensus and unanimity of all four group members. Using a unanimous rule for the total group, including the foreman, seems to contribute to effective work."

Majority rule—"It has been the company's policy and this team's practice to arrive at all group decisions by using a majority rule of all four group members. The majority rule for the total group, including the foreman, seems to be a practical decision rule for your groups. It has proven to be a good way to resolve conflict, avoid wasting time in endless discussion."

No decision rule—The groups with no decision rule received the standard roles.

TABLE 12.1

Distribution of Solutions by Assigned Decision Rules

Type of Solution	Majority Rule		Unanimous Rule		No Decision Rule	
	Total	Valence	Total	Valence	Total	Valence
Old	39%	3	23%	1	12%	2
New	9	1	50	2	59	3
Compromise	9	0	18	1	12	1
Integrative	43	4	9	0	18	0
	100		100		100	
	(N = 23)	(N = 8)	(N = 22)	(N = 4)	(N = 17)	(N = 6)

Note: "Total" columns show the percentage of solutions of each type in the entire sample. "Valence" columns show the number of solutions of each type produced by groups in the valence analysis.

Source: Compiled by the authors.

Subjects

The subjects were mostly part-time students of business administration in a small midwestern state university. Most were undergraduates between the ages of 25 and 35, working full-time, from suburban and urban backgrounds.

Solution Valence

A coding system was developed by Falk to measure the valence accumulated for each of the possible solutions to the CWP. For purposes of this analysis, only positive and negative comments about each solution were recorded. The identification of different solutions on the CWP is particularly difficult because elements of the old and new solutions form the basis of the compromise and integrative solutions. For example, the principal compromise solution has one worker working only on his best position according to the time study (an element of the new work method), while the other two workers rotate between the remaining two positions (an element of the old method). Before this new solution is proposed, the slow worker's willingness to work on the one position is coded to favor the new method and the others' preferences for rotating as positive for the old method. After the compromise method has been proposed, a judgment has to be made as to whether such comments should be coded as above or in favor of the compromise method. These judgments were made with reasonable consistency. The intercoder reliability of the valence coding within each group was .80 or greater, about comparable with levels achieved on other problems.

RESULTS

Foreman's Solution Valence

Since we anticipated that the decision rules would have greatest impact on valence in the early parts of the discussion—before their actual use could be tested—the valence generated in the first 50 solution acts was examined. Table 12.2 shows the two valence measures of interest for each experimental condition: (1) foreman's mean valence for the new method and (2) foreman's mean valence for the old method. While the foremen in the majority-rule groups had substantially less valence for the new solution than did foremen in the unanimous groups, their valence was slightly greater than that for the standard foremen. An opposite, but similar, pattern held for the foremen's valence for the old method. The foremen of unanimous-rule groups had the most negative valence, majority-rule foremen the next, and the standard foremen the least. Thus the majority-rule foremen attempted to persuade their workers to adopt the new method as strongly as did the foremen with no formal decision rule.

Workers' Solution Valence

Table 12.3 shows the valence for the old and new solutions generated by the workers in the three experimental conditions during the first 50 acts. Here the patterns are clearly consistent with the hypothesis. Workers in majority-rule groups produced more negative valence for the new work method and more positive valence for the old method than did the workers in the other conditions. Both in their opposition to the foreman's preference and in their willingness to support the present work method, the workers

TABLE 12.2

Foreman's Valence, by Decision Rule
(in first 50 acts)

Foreman's Mean Valence		Majority Rule (N = 8)	Unanimous Rule (N = 4)	No Decision Rule (N = 6)	p*
For new solution	M	10.6	17.8	9.8	N.S.
	S.D.	4.87	3.34	4.22	
For old solution	M	-1.4	-2.2	-0.8	N.S.
	S.D.	2.64	2.17	2.48	

*t-test comparisons of means: majority-rule vs. combined others—N.S. = $p > .05$.

Source: Compiled by the authors.

TABLE 12.3

Workers' Valence, by Decision Rule
(in first 50 acts)

Workers' Total Valence[a]		Majority Rule (N = 8	Unanimous Rule (N = 4)	No Decision Rule (N = 6)	p[b]
For new solution	M	-9.1	-4.3	+1.0	.06
	S.D.	7.41	14.27	6.98	
For old solution	M	7.0	1.8	2.7	.05
	S.D.	5.45	3.9	5.53	

[a]Since there were three workers in each group, the "total" equals the algebraic sum of each worker's valence for the solution.

[b]t-test of means: majority-rule vs. combined other groups—$p < .05$.

Source: Compiled by the authors.

reflected the increased power given them by the majority-decision rule. In contrast, the workers in the unanimous-decision groups opposed the foreman to the same extent as did those in the standard situation.

Group Valence

The interactive effects of the foreman's reduced self-perceived power and the workers' increased self-perceived power resulting from the majority rule resulted in much less positive valence for the new method and greater positive valence for the old method during the first 50 acts (Table 12.4). Many of the groups with unanimous rules and no decision rules had accumulated substantial positive valence for the new method. In half of them the new method had already passed the adoption threshold. By contrast, in only one of the majority-rule groups did the new method pass the adoption threshold by the end of 50 acts. The workers and foremen essentially balanced each other's valences for the new and old solutions in the early stages of the majority-rule discussions. The workers in groups with majority rule early demonstrated their willingness to use their power collectively in opposing the foreman's attempts to induce change, and forced his willingness to consider solutions other than his preferred new one.

TABLE 12.4

Group Valence, by Decision Rule
(in first 50 acts)

Group Valence		Majority Rule (N = 8)	Unanimous Rule (N = 4)	No Decision Rule (N = 6)	*p**
For new solution	M	1.5	13.5	10.8	.05
	S.D.	7.63	14.53	7.89	
For old solution	M	5.6	-0.4	1.9	.05
	S.D.	5.15	6.02	7.24	

**t*-test of means: majority rule vs. combined other groups.
Source: Compiled by the authors.

The groups with no formal decision rule displayed a third pattern of valence contributions, with group results similar to the groups with unanimous rule. While the foremen argued for the new method with only about the same strength as those in the majority-rule groups, the workers, instead of resisting the change, actually contributed a small amount of positive valence. At the same time, the workers often supported the old method, but the foremen offered almost no resistance. As noted before, however, the group valence for the new method had passed the adoption threshold at 50 acts in three of these six groups, while the old method had not passed in any.

In summary, then, the effects of a majority-decision rule were felt early in the discussion, and were not limited to the resolution of conflict at the end. The effect of the rule in reducing the power of the foreman and increasing the power of the workers was reflected in the first 50 acts in an impasse on the new method and positive valence for the old one. These early effects, as compared with the groups with unanimous and no decision rules, forecast the ultimate retention of the old method or the development of integrative solutions.

The Total Process

The effects of these early differences among the three experimental conditions were reflected in certain aspects of the total discussion. Valence for the new solution passed the adoption threshold in only three of the eight majority-rule groups, but did so in three of the four unanimous-rule and in five of the six standard groups. In none of the majority-rule groups did the new method have the highest valence at the end, despite the fact that one group adopted it. In contrast, half the groups in each of the other conditions gave more valence to the new method than to any other one. Thus, the early resistance by the majority-rule workers to the foreman's attempts to adopt the new method continued throughout most of the meeting.

The Slow Worker

Finally, we should note that the hypothesized conflict in the slow worker between his personal preference for the new method and his loyalty to his co-workers was revealed early by the valence analysis. If this worker sided with the foreman, then his valence for the new method should be greater than his valence for the old method. Conversely, if he sided with his co-workers, his valence for the old method should exceed his valence for the new one. The majority rule was hypothesized to induce a coalition among the workers, whereas the other conditions left the slow worker more at the foreman's mercy.

The results confirm the hypothesis. In the first 50 acts the slow worker sided with the foreman in only two of the eight majority-rule groups, but in three of the four unanimous groups and in four of the six groups with no decision rule. Such an early commitment to one side or the other tends to forecast whether the group will subordinate itself to the foreman or provide itself an opportunity for a creative outcome.

DISCUSSION

There are several promising insights arising from this study despite the modest number of groups observed. Their potential import for the valence model of group problem solving prompted us to include these data here in this avowedly preliminary form.

The foremost effect is the early impact that the decision rules had on the power relations in the group. By the first 50 acts the valences for the two ostensible alternative work methods (old and new) already reflected strongly the differential impact of the majority and unanimous rules. Most discussions of formal decision rules tend to emphasize their value in resolving conflict after it has arisen (Davis 1973). The valence analysis reveals their power to determine the decision early and even to increase conflict under the unequal power conditions of this study.

The effects of particular decision rules are not unidirectional, as has been implied by many of the discussions of the benefits of unanimous rules. Rules have their effects as they mediate the accumulation of valence for different outcomes. Unanimous rules are beneficial in equal-status groups, since they are congruent with members' assumptions that equal status implies equal rights to influence the decision. In groups with differentiated, legitimated power positions, a rule of unanimity conflicts with the power differential and cannot overcome it. Thus, the foremen in groups with unanimous rules immediately took the offensive by promoting their preferred solution and the workers seem generally to have knuckled under to this display of power.

In the groups with majority rule, on the other hand, the foremen's recognition of the potential formation of a coalition among the workers made them more cautious than the foremen in unanimous-rule groups, both in espousing the new method and in opposing the old one. The workers in those groups, sensing the power they derived from the majority-decision rule, opposed the new method and insisted on retaining the old one. Both the foremen and, especially, the workers were guided by the majority-decision rule toward contributing valence for their preferred solutions in a way different from their counterparts with identical role information in groups with different decusion rules. Thus, with these types of early effects of decision rules on the members' solution-valence behavior, there is little need to invoke the decision rule to resolve conflict later, and few groups actually did.

The last point we wish to make concerns the implicit way in which the decision rules affected people's behavior. Although members occasionally said, "You know, we have a majority rule," as a not-so-subtle reminder to the foreman of its existence, it was rarely mentioned in the early parts of the meetings, that is, in the first 50 acts we were examining. We assume that all members were aware of the decision rule under which their group operated or that, possibly, because everyone assumed that everyone knew the rule, there was no need to discuss it. Yet, without discussion, the profound valence effects produced by the rules attest to their functioning at an implicit level. It is likely that other norms, especially in ongoing groups, also regulate the group's activities at an implicit level. In this case, for example, the leadership norm (Stein et al. 1979) also affected the members, but in ways that were rarely made explicit. To understand the likely effects of any formal change in a group's procedures, then, requires an understanding of their interaction with the central norms of the group (Humpal and Hoffman 1979). The naive assumption that any new method of group operation will have universally beneficial effects ignores the fact that groups develop norms suited to their own unique requirements.

PART V

AN EXTENDED VALENCE MODEL OF GROUP PROBLEM SOLVING AND ITS IMPLICATIONS FOR APPLIED SETTINGS

13

THE BEGINNINGS OF A HIERARCHICAL MODEL OF GROUP PROBLEM SOLVING

L. Richard Hoffman

I began this book with a theoretical model of group problem solving. The basic ingredients of that model were (1) the concept of valence as a force on the group to adopt a particular cognition; (2) the representation of substantive conflict by the opposition of such forces attached to different cognitions; and (3) the need for a boundary around the social system, to contain the conflict. The studies reported in the subsequent chapters have sustained the importance of those ingredients, have given us greater insight into their meaning and the way they affect group and individual outcomes of problem-solving meetings, and have suggested a more elaborate model of the group problem-solving process. This more elaborate model will be described in this chapter. I offer it very tentatively, as a guide to areas of exploration and empirical test. I present the model in an attempt to show the connections among the various studies reported earlier.

THE HIERARCHICAL MODEL

Traditional approaches to problem solving in groups have treated it as essentially an extension of individual problem solving with a group-maintenance function added on. Thus, N. R. F. Maier (1963) recommends that groups follow a procedure that starts with defining the problem, then goes on to generating solution possibilities and evaluating the alternatives generated, and finally choosing the best one or a combination of alternatives. Group leaders are instructed to follow this procedure to produce more effective solutions to problems and to gain the members' commitment to the decision.

Bales and Strodtbeck (1951) defined a "full-fledged" problem as one in which groups proceed from a relative emphasis on orientation, to evaluation, to control activities. In their original study a small proportion of the groups seem to have satisfied those conditions.

While these formulations may have prescriptive value for effective problem solving and may be descriptive of the gross outline of group movement, they are insufficient to account for the variety of phenomena observed in such groups. The present model is basically consistent with both the Maier and the Bales formulations. But it attempts to provide a framework that is integrative and descriptive of a greater variety of phenomena, and should lead to greater precision in their measurement.

Although it is difficult to depict the dynamic character of the hierarchical model in a static presentation, Figure 13.1 will outline the general framework. The border around the figure represents the group's boundary. The nature of the membership requirements may be loosely defined by the dashed lines. The ad hoc groups of the experimental laboratory are formed in response to the experimenter's power and remain in existence only until the members are released or until the required time has passed. Nevertheless, the members do perceive themselves as a group, with collective responsibility for meeting the experimenter's requests—"serving as good subjects" (Orne 1962) - as shown by the almost universal production of a solution by such groups. Even on the value problems in Chapter 5 the groups attempted to reach consensus and only a few failed to do so.

FIGURE 13.1

A Skeleton of the Hierarchical Model

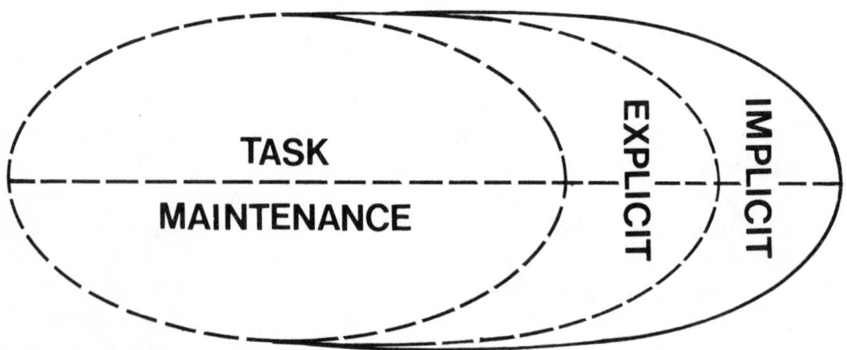

Source: Compiled by the author.

The boundary around more formal groups may be quite impermeable (Hemphill and Westie 1950), allowing inside only people with very specific characteristics—age, sex, socioeconomic status, achievements, and so on. Even in such groups, however, members are only partially included in the group (Katz and Kahn 1978). They also belong to other groups, which may place conflicting demands on them, and all retain a certain area of privacy that they choose not (or are unable) to share with the other members (Luft 1969). The "size" of the group may be considered, then, as determined by how many potential members are motivated to invest their energy and resources in helping the group accomplish its task and continue to survive.

We begin, then, by defining a group as an open system in which many processes go on simultaneously. For the moment, following Bales (1953), we will divide these processes into task (concerned with maintaining the boundary of the group in relation to its environment) and maintenance (concerned with holding the members within the boundary and with the general ability of the members to interact effectively with each other). Both of these functions are activated when a group comes into existence and operate simultaneously in interaction, as will be specified later on. We assume also that groups strive toward some quasi-stationary equilibrium (Lewin 1947) with the environment through these processes, and typically attain it for some time.

We then define a "problem" as a disturbance of that equilibrium. The disturbance creates the motivation among the members to restore a state of equilibrium, either the original state or some other acceptable level. This level may be viewed as either a contraction or an expansion of the boundary. The group contracts when it defends itself against environmental incursion by, for example, denying relevant information or by losing a member through withdrawal from the discussion or resignation from the group (Bion 1959). The boundary may expand by the group's developing a novel solution to a problem, which gives it greater control of its environment, or by facilitating the cooperative, synergistic efforts of the group members. In both cases the examples given indicate that the group's "problem" may occur at either the task or the maintenance level.

Crosscutting the task and maintenance process is the dimension of explicitness (see Figure 13.1). The model assumes that only one of these processes is being attended to explicitly at any particular time, while the other is implicit. In most laboratory experiments the manifest task is to solve the problem presented, but a social structure develops, as exhibited in the differential rates of members' participation (Tuckman 1965).

In contrast, team-building activities in organizations are designed to improve the quality of interactions among the members, although task issues are often handled implicitly. Often members' acceptance of their group's decision—made at the task level—reflects the implicit socioemotional process by which the decision was reached (see Chapters 8, 9, 10). By identifying a manifest level and an implicit level of functioning, I am indicating that the task and maintenance processes are both occurring at all times, even though the group attends explicitly to only one of them at any particular time.

One way in which the model is hierarchical, then, is in positing the dominance of the explicit level of group functioning over the implicit level. When group phenomena occur at the explicit level, they are presumed to be the legitimate function of the group and to have an overlapping meaning to all group members. They are thereby discussable and under the self-conscious control of the group. When matters that affect the group remain at the implicit level, they are more open to differential interpretation by each group member. Often such matters are thereby relegated to prohibited status as members decide individually—"in their heads"—that it would be risky to raise them in the group.

The distinction between the explicit and implicit levels is analogous to the distinction Argyris and Schön (1974) make between espoused theory and theory in use. However, the hierarchical model does not specify as they do, the content of the norms at each level, since that content varies from group to group. Even the groups which Argyris and Schön define as operating on Model 2 norms also have implicit norms.

The broad definition of a problem as a disturbance of the group's equilibrium makes us aware of both task and maintenance types of problem and of the fact that a group may have more than one problem to cope with at any particular time. The same group—a group of sales managers—might, simultaneously, have the manifest problem (problem 1) of forecasting sales accurately for the following year, but also (problem 2) have to cope with the absence of its formal leader and (problem 3) to ensure that the jobs of all members are secure. These may be quite conflicting problems, in that an acceptable solution to problem 1—such as an estimate that sales will decrease by 15 percent—may imply a probably unacceptable solution to problem 3—a reduction in the sales force. Such a conflict in the character of the group's problems can clearly affect the adequacy of the "answer" to the group's manifest problem. While this conflict between problems is apparent in the example, such conflicts also exist in the experimental groups on which most of the research on problem solving has been done. In such ad hoc groups, the processes of resolving such conflicts have not stabilized and come under normative control, so they are more likely to be observable than in ongoing groups.

Before going further into the issue of how such conflicts are resolved, let us return to the definition of a problem as a disturbance of the group's equilibrium. An examination of the procedure in typical problem-solving experiments reduces this issue to its primitive manifestations. In most studies a group of strangers is brought together to participate in "an experiment on group problem solving," often to satisfy each person's course requirement to gain experience as a subject in a psychological experiment. In most cases the subjects are positively motivated to cooperate with the experimenter (Orne 1962; Rosenberg 1969). Furthermore, with college students at least, the intrinsic value of solving problems ensures substantial positive motivation toward solving the manifest problem. Nevertheless, the group's "problem" is imposed by the experimenter, in his/her terms. The group does not initiate the problem, so we may consider it as having entered the group from the environment. The form it takes as it crosses the boundary is usually specified by each member privately and, occasionally, by the group as a whole publicly. The more complicated the problem, the more likely there are to be difficulties in defining it and differences between the experimenter's perception of the problem and the problem actually defined by the group.

Let us take, for example, the Personnel Selection Problem, in which the group is given the résumés of five hypothetical people from which to select the best one for the imaginary job of assistant market planning manager (see Chapters 4, 7). Although the job description supplied (see Appendix A.2) specifies that the desired candidate should have "ingenuity, foresight, and marketing capabilities" among other qualities, groups take 30 minutes or more to arrive at a decision. It is clear that the experimenter's description of the problem—"Select the one applicant who appears to be most suitable"—must be transformed in some way to provide an answer. A "simple-minded" computer might define the problem as "Pick one of the five candidates, toss a five-headed coin, and print out whichever name appears as its solution." No group ever determines the answer to this problem simply by lot.

Yet it is not clear that such a solution would be ineffective in restoring equilibrium, since it would provide the experimenter with a group solution to the problem and might permit the members' release from the experimental situation. An equivalent minimum response might be given to a custodian who entered the experimental room to check the temperature. He might be told "It's warm enough" or "Come back later; we're busy." Such a group response to an external threat to its equilibrium would restore it to its previous state. Ad hoc groups in a problem-solving experiment rarely treat the experimenter's problem so cursorily, although an ongoing group took only 15 minutes to solve the Personnel Selection Problem "so they could go to lunch earlier."

Groups more typically go through a lengthy process of generating and evaluating alternative solutions to a problem until one is adopted. The group accepts the legitimacy of the experimenter's imposition of the task, which then activates implicitly a set of rules by which such problems are to be solved. These rules involve defining the problem, offering solutions, and giving reasons for their relevance to the problem. The majority of such comments are proposed justifications of the solution—that is, why it will work, what advantages it offers, how it will be received by outsiders, and so on. In more than 85 percent of all groups studied, the adopted solution had the highest valence index, that is, more net positive comments were made about it than about any alternative solutions. The latter part of the problem-solving process consists almost invariably and exclusively of comments that express support for the final solution and agreement with people who make such comments (Bales and Strodtbeck 1951; see also Chapter 6). Thus the end of a problem-solving process may be considered to be a restoration of the group's equilibrium by a verification of the match between the nature of the initial disturbance and the proposed method of reducing it. The latter may be termed the solution to the manifest problem. It usually contains some form of the solution the experimenter is seeking, but also may be designed to solve certain maintenance problems in the group. Certainly the tension involved in having to choose among different possible solutions and the collective anxiety about possibly being wrong are reduced by this final affirmation of the solution (Festinger 1957).

This definition of a solution raises the question of how a group defined the disturbance. Some insight is again obtained from the Personnel Selection Problem. Chapter 7 showed that the "problem" was defined in piecemeal fashion in most groups. The criteria supplied by the experimenter—foresight, ingenuity—were too vague to be translated into items on the résumés, so the groups had to develop a set of job requirements by interpreting the information in the résumés. Each group generated valence for a different set of criteria, as they justified the rejection or adoption of each candidate. Most groups developed only sufficient criteria to enable them to choose among the candidates. Often, once a criterion had been used to reject a candidate, it was never used again. Other criteria, on the other hand, accumulated large valence values, presumably through discussion of the relative match between the candidates retained and the particular criterion. It is clear that the "solution-mindedness" (Maier 1963) of the group permitted the members to reject and adopt candidates without explicitly declaring a general set of criteria against which all candidates would be compared. Thus, as Duncker (1945) showed to be true in individual problem solving, groups define the problem in terms commensurate with the solution until they discover a match between the two.

Between the presentation of the problem and the adoption of a solution the manifest problem-solving process occurs. The modal process for the Assembly Problem, as mapped by solution-related valence, shows an early accumulation of valence for the to-be-adopted solution, followed by a consideration of other alternatives, and concluding with an almost single-minded confirmation of the adopted solution. In contrast, there was no modal process for the Selection Problem, although all groups began by identifying unacceptable candidates. Some also implicitly adopted one candidate during that same period, while others waited until all candidates had been reviewed. Almost all groups ended with a rapid accumulation of valence for the adopted candidate.

These contrasting processes may be considered within a single framework, as depicted in Figure 13.2, which is a more detailed representation of the model, essentially a further specification of Figure 13.1. Several "stages" in the problem-solving process are depicted there for purposes of discussion. They are not to be taken literally as being the number of stages in a "complete" problem (Bales and Strodtbeck 1951), but merely as a means of indicating different levels of generality at which a group may discuss a problem—from the vague level of defining the problem to the very specific level of taking some action, such as offering a solution to a problem. Each problem, however, may have a different number of stages, depending on its severity and complexity and the ability and willingness of the group to recognize these dimensions of the problem. For example, one group may adopt a piece-rate incentive system as a solution to the Assembly Problem, while another will debate the merits of a straight-line piece-rate versus an exponential system before adopting one as their solution. The second group would have more "stages" than the first one.

A group may enter the problem-solving process at any stage. As noted earlier, the Personnel Selection Problem was entered at the evaluating stage, since all candidates were given to the group by the experimenter. On the Assembly Problem, on the other hand, the group needed to invent its own solutions before it was able to evaluate them—thus entering at the generating stage. The arrows in Figure 13.2 indicate a general strain toward remaining as close to the final stages of evaluating and implementing solutions as

FIGURE 13.2

Task-Level Stages in the Problem-Solving Process

Defining	Specifying	Generating	Evaluating	Implementing
General nature of problem	Barriers to be overcome	Alternative solutions	Solutions	Solution adopted
Goals to be achieved	Criteria to be met	Characteristics of candidates	Candidates	Solution adopted

<u>Source</u>: Compiled by the author.

possible. Thus the dominance of those stages over the earlier stages of goal and problem identification is a second way in which the model is hierarchical. In both cited problems, the group's end state was reached by adopting the solution that was evaluated most favorably in the implementing stage. Since most such groups operate on a norm of rationality, we may assume that the justifications for the adopted solution were offered against the group's criteria for an acceptable solution.

The model also assumes, however, that there is a tendency toward minimizing the needed reaction to a disturbance. On the Personnel Selection Problem this resulted in a minimal specification of criteria, consistent with previous evidence that groups tend to be "solution-minded" rather than "problem-minded" (Maier 1963; Maier and Solem 1962). We found in Chapter 7 that on that problem as many as 28 different criteria were used to describe the merits and demerits of candidates for the hypothetical job. Yet any particular group was likely to employ principally five or six of these to reject and adopt the candidates. Rarely were all candidates evaluated against the entire set of criteria employed by the group by the end of its discussion. Rather, a few criteria were applied to reject one or two candidates, some others to reject a third, and another set to adopt the final candidate.

Groups at each stage should be considered as attempting to move to the next stage, that is, successively to the right, toward adopting and implementing a solution. In so doing they are presumed to have sufficient valence for some possibility in the preceding stage to provide a basis for evaluating—adding positive and negative valence to—alternatives at the present stage. For example, groups could not attempt to solve the Assembly Problem if they did not assume that increased productivity was a desirable goal. As this example indicates, however, that assumption is so "obvious"—that is, there is so much valence for that goal activated by the experimental setting and the statement of the problem—that the group never needs to discuss it explicitly. Evidence for its existence is clear, however, when members reject solutions "because production won't change." If other members object to rejecting that solution, it is usually because they think the method will improve productivity, not because the goal is wrong. Thus, criteria must be adopted at a previous stage to permit the group to move through the next stage. Between each stage there is a valence-adoption process that takes place at the implicit level, before the group can move through the following stage. In stages before the final one, a group can move from one stage to the next once a criterion's valence passes the adoption threshold. The criterion need not attain a high level of valence, since all that is needed is sufficient force for the group to add to that which is moving the group generally toward attaining a solution. The valence for criteria used on the Personnel Selection Problem to reject unacceptable candidates often had very small values.

The valence model presented in Chapter 1 may be applied to any stage of the problem-solving process. If one definition of the problem—such as the workers on the Assembly Problem lack motivation—accumulates substantial valence, it will be adopted. Thereafter, only solutions that increase workers' motivation will accumulate positive valence, while those that attempt to improve productivity by changing the workers' abilities will be rejected.

However, there may be conflict between two solutions, which reflects the group's failure to have adopted an adequate definition of the "problem." Such conflict at the evaluating stage may be resolved by "moving back" to the specifying or defining stage and reexamining the definition of the problem. The "back-and-forth" between defining the problem and generating solutions, described by Duncker (1945) for individuals, can be seen here to operate at the group level.

For example, Figure 13.3 schematically illustrates a potential conflict in adopting a solution (lettered candidates) to a personnel selection problem. Candidates B and D are favored because they both have adequate amounts of criteria I, II, and IV. The group can resolve the conflict in several different ways: (1) in favor of B by discovering that he also has III; (2) in favor of D because he also has V; (3) in favor of B by noting that D also has V, an undesirable characteristic; (4) in favor of D because B has III, another criterion for rejection; (5) by differentially weighting the importance of the criteria; or (6) by convincing themselves that B or D has more of I, II, or IV than does the other.

Methods (1) through (5) denote an expansion of or change in the problem definition resulting from an examination of the characteristics of available solutions. The group would then be working at the specifying stage, thus illustrating a reversal in the direction of the usual problem-solving movement. Methods (1) and (2) identify additional desirable elements, while methods (3) and (4) consider undesirable ones. Method 6 allows the group to resolve the conflict at the evaluation stage, add valence to the favored candidate, and move to the implementing stage. Other methods for resolving conflict are possible, but they require shifts to other levels of the process and will be discussed later.

One final point of importance regarding the movement of groups from stage to stage should be noted. While conceptually we can characterize the group's movement from one stage to another, we should recognize that all members of the group may not have moved together. Just as the group's adoption of a particular solution may

FIGURE 13.3

A Cognitive Hierarchy of Problem Solving

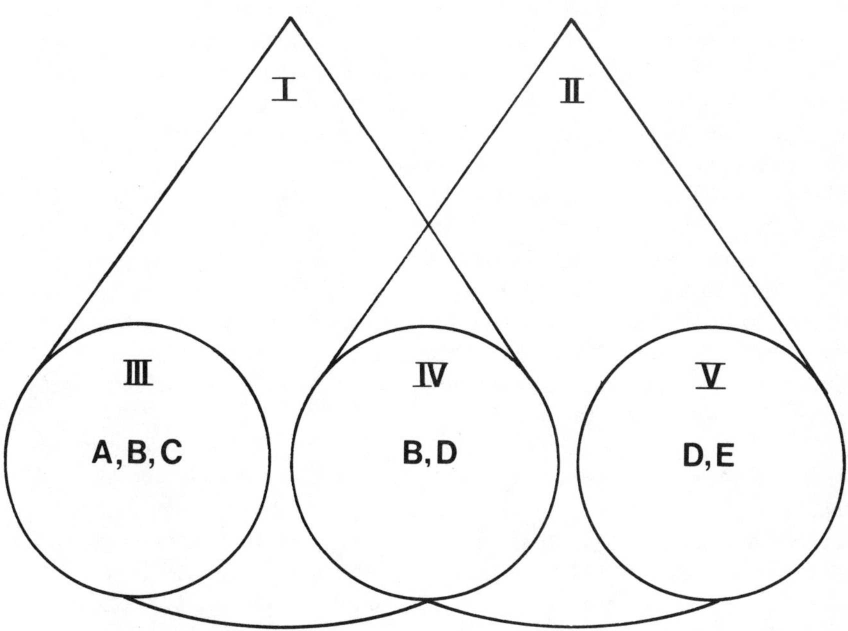

Letters are solution possibilities.
Roman numerals are criteria or definitions of problem elements.
Criterion I satisfied by solutions A, B, C, D; E excluded.
Criterion II satisfied by solutions B, D, E; A, C excluded.
Source: Compiled by the author.

be accomplished with varying degrees of members' acceptance, the group may change stages through the valence generated by only a few of the members. Those members who were not prepared to move may reduce their participation in the later discussion or actively sabotage it if they feel particularly resentful about being ignoted. Their acceptance of the final decision may be threatened by their lack of acceptance of earlier definitions of the problem.

Explicitness

The discussion to this point has assumed that movement from stage to stage occurs implicitly through the valence-adoption process at each stage. However, groups can abort that process by making some facet of their activity the focus of the discussion. For example, the announcement by a group member that "We have only these two candidates left"—the end of the rejection phase on the Personnel Selection Problem (Chapter 4)—typically limited the subsequent discussion to evaluations of those two candidates. In some groups such an announcement merely confirmed explicitly what was apparent from the valence accumulations, but in others the group moved forward via this announcement before the valence for any solution had passed the adoption threshold. The group limited the number of solutions it discussed, thus reducing the number of possibilities of passing the adoption threshold.

Explicitness raises a procedure from the level of habitual control of the group's operations to the level of self-conscious, shared choice. The first is based on experience, as it provides each member with valence for or against its existence as an operating rule in the group. Each member must interpret the rule individually and determine how closely to adhere to it (Jackson 1960). When the rule is made explicit, the members know that all are bound by it. The rule becomes a temporary norm in the group, at least for dealing with the problem at hand.

Procedures (Task)

The preceding discussion calls our attention to the operation of another level of group functioning that we have not identified in Figures 13.1 and 13.2 of the hierarchical model. Attached to each task is a set of procedures that vary in their level of specificity. At the most general level are the stages that define the hierarchy from goals to implementation. These stages may be referred to explicitly, as when a member says, "First, we have to define the problem" or "We have to decide on which type of piece-rate system to use," or the group may move from stage to stage through an implicit valence process related to its movement down the "decision-tree" at the task level. The valence for a particular stage may accumulate from the concentration of the group's activities at that stage, without a public announcement. Each time a member offers a new solution alternative, the valence for the group's being in the generating stage—and not the specifying stage—increases. Members become increasingly wary of attempting to redefine the problem as such valence increases, whether the valence was generated with or without an explicit statement.

All the various task-related procedures developed to facilitate group problem solving operate at the procedural level. Brainstorming (Osborn 1957), for example, is a technique for holding a group at the generating stage before it develops enough valence for any solution for it to move to the evaluating stage. Maier's (1963) screening principles were designed to focus the group on the factual basis for matching the solution alternatives to criteria as they accumulate valence in the evaluating stage. One principal advantage of these techniques is that they make explicit what the group is doing, so all the members can focus on the same activity. In this way the group has greater control over its own activities and is less subject to the forces moving it too quickly toward an inadequate solution.

Anticipating our discussion of the maintenance level of the model, we should also recognize that many techniques are also designed to prevent the confounding effects of "maintenance problems" and "task problems." For example, the anonymous form in which members contribute judgments in the Delphi technique (Dalkey 1969) is designed to reduce the impact of differential status and to focus attention on the cognitive dimensions of the contributions. Chapter 12 showed that the use of majority voting rules can interact with the power structure of the group to prevent the leader from accumulating too much valence for his/her preferred, but inadequate, solution.

Certain problems may have very idiosyncratic procedures associated with them, which we learn through socialization. Most groups solved the Personnel Selection Problem explicitly by first attempting to reject unsatisfactory candidates, then choosing among the remainder (see Chapter 4). The conformity to the announced end of the rejection phase presumably reflects the members' prediscussion valence for the legitimacy of the division of the process in this way.

Our empirical support for Maier's (1963) contention that groups are solution-minded, causing them to react minimally to a disturbance of equilibrium, may be primarily a product of American culture. There seems to be much prediscussion valence for the assumption that implementation should dominate introspection, causing groups to focus on decision making rather than problem identification. As Janis and Mann (1977) so eloquently attest, in a group with shared beliefs about the definition of the problem or about valued goals, the discussion need not, and typically does not, include a discussion of those beliefs. Rather, the beliefs serve as criteria against which the proposed solutions are evaluated. For example, in Chapter 5, if all four group members had the same individual answers to the reasoning problems, it was rare that the group discussed the problem further, examining the process by which they arrived at their answers. It was as if everyone assumed that because they had agreed on the answer, they agreed on the method of achieving it. In most groups the first question was usually "What answer did you get?" rather than starting the problem anew. Unfortunately, this lack of reexamination was equally true for groups with unanimously correct and incorrect answers. Thus, groups whose members hold different wrong answers are more likely than are unanimously incorrect groups to generate correct answers to a problem, because they generate conflict. They are forced to examine the assumptions underlying their answers (Hoffman and Maier 1961b).

Such conflict is likely to raise issues from the implicit level to the explicit level, since the assumed consensus among the members has obviously been violated. This process is analogous to our discovery in individual problem solving that only when new information is clearly in violation of the solutions people are attempting, will it be effective in changing their definition of the problem. Otherwise, they tend to distort the information to make it compatible with the ongoing definition (Hoffman, Burke, and Maier 1963; Burke, Maier, and Hoffman 1966). Unless the valence of the new information can compete with the valence of the old definition, the inadequacy of the latter will not be recognized and the need to redefine the problem will not be acknowledged.

In summary, a model of the task level of group problem solving has been offered that adopts more traditional models as its basic framework. It incorporates mechanisms by which the group may move back and forth between stages until a final match is effected between the group's definition of a problem and a proposed solution. The top part of Figure 13.4 describes the model to this point, illustrating some of the methods and their relationship to the various stages. The basic contributions it makes are to suggest (1) that the different stages represent a successive narrowing of the gap between the definition of the problem and the definition of the solution adopted; (2) that progression from stage to stage involves a series of tests or evaluations of the adequacy with which the solution to that stage's

FIGURE 13.4

Task-Level Stages in the Problem-Solving Process

Level	Defining	Specifying	Generating	Evaluating	Implementing
Task	General nature of problem	Barriers to be overcome	Alternative solutions	Solutions	Solution
	Goals to be achieved	Criteria to be met	Characteristics of candidates	Candidates	Adopted
Procedure (task)		Analogies	Brainstorming	Screening principles	Decision rule

Source: Compiled by the author.

problem fits criteria established earlier; (3) that the process may be entered at any stage with a tendency to strive toward the "adoption" end, but often necessitating some further definition of the problem at least to fit the dimensions of available solutions. Finally, the model permits us to understand how the task and procedural levels interact. Methods may be designed to perform particular functions that are indicated by the model. The model also helps us to recognize why methods effective for one function may fail to satisfy other criteria of group effectiveness.

MAINTENANCE LEVEL

Although the division of Figure 13.1 into task and maintenance activities is traditional, I have implied already that these two aspects of group problem solving are so commingled that they must be treated together in order to understand the outcomes of the task level. Because the maintenance process and, certainly, the interaction between task and maintenance processes are not so well charted as is the task level of the diagram, I shall discuss some aspects of maintenance and this commingling based on data already collected. The inadequacies of laboratory groups for studying group problem-solving phenomena are revealed in this examination. The fact that they have no history and no future means that they have little need to maintain themselves for longer than the one-hour experimental session (Lorge et al. 1958).

As Tuckman (1965) has pointed out, groups begin with members only loosely attached to the group, thus requiring the development of a social structure to perform task activities. Members enter the group with individual needs to be met and idiosyncratic beliefs about the norms appropriate to that particular group. In the experimental groups in the laboratory, the maintenance requirements are ordinarily minimal. The group is required only to survive for an hour, the people have little to gain personally from the group, the general norms of the culture are sufficient guides to proper behavior, and the laws of the state provide safety from physical attack. Nevertheless, indicative of the importance of the maintenance process for task activity, even in these groups certain phenomena are apparent that may be generalized easily to ongoing groups. I shall discuss these categorically before attempting to relate them systematically to the hierarchical model.

Belief and Value Systems

The general value system of a group will determine whether it accepts a problem given to it and how the members will define that problem. For example, on the Assembly Problem the group has to share the belief that productivity can be improved and that such improvement would be a desirable objective in order to enter the first stage of the problem. Furthermore, people who think workers are generally lazy would be more likely to define the problem as a motivational one than would people who have more favorable attitudes toward workers. The Change of Work Procedures Problem, the role-playing case involving a conflict over work methods between a foreman and his three workers, is clearly one in which the group as a whole does not share the foreman's desire to increase productivity (Hoffman, Harburg, and Maier 1962; see also Chapter 12). Workers also value job interest and their group's solidarity, which may conflict with the foreman's singular goal. To the extent that all members' different definitions of the problem are not incorporated in the total definition, the group will solve only a part of the problem (Maier 1963). Unless there is agreement among members about the desired goals, they may be unwilling to invest in trying to solve the problem at all. Groups of college women often only make pro forma attempts to solve arithmetic reasoning problems, thus failing to solve them, unless circumstances can be created in which such activity is legitimized as "feminine" (Hoffman and Maier 1961b; 1966).

Norms

Both Tuckman (1965) and Thibaut and Kelley (1961) indicate that norms serve as substitutes for direct interpersonal influence to regulate members' behaviors. Throughout this discussion norms have been implicit in their effects on all phases of the task level of decision making. Most problem-solving groups operate under a norm of rationality, that is, that "reasons" must be given to justify members' suggestions. It is not important that what pass for reasons in a group would be unacceptable as facts to an external observer. Rather, facts are what is acceptable within the shared belief system. Thus, because Richard Nixon and his aides believed that there was a conspiracy to overthrow his presidency, they established a private investigative unit—"the Plumbers"—to uncover that conspiracy. Another group might have interpreted the lack of evidence from the established investigative sources as denying the existence of such a conspiracy. Nevertheless, both groups may operate under the same norm of rationality that our laboratory experimental groups do, since we socialize our students into believing that rationality is a useful avenue to truth.

The solution valence-adoption relationships, found consistently in the studies reported here, testify to the failure of groups to discriminate well among arguments based on objective facts and those based on opinion, judgment, and personal preference. The same relationships occur for groups with correct and incorrect answers to the reasoning problems (see Chapter 5) and with better and worse solutions to the Assembly Problem. Unpublished attempts to differentiate the valence generated by arguments based on facts in the case from valence generated otherwise in influencing the adoption of solutions have proved futile.

Groups also have implicit norms about the participation of members. In leaderless groups, members are not permitted to monopolize discussion completely and will frequently censure themselves by saying, "I'm afraid I am taking up too much of the group's time." Nor are members permitted to be completely silent, since that would provide concrete evidence that the implicit decision rule of unanimity has not been achieved. However, there is no norm for complete equality of participation, since almost every such group develops an ordering of participation rates. These differential rates probably reflect the group's use of general social norms of taking turns and politeness (Duncan and Fiske 1977) to regulate the propensities of members to speak in group settings on the basis of their personalities (Willard and Strodtbeck 1972; Mann 1959), their stake in the group outcome (Hoffman 1965), and their desire to dominate the other group members (Blake and Mouton 1961; Stein et al. 1979).

In groups with formal roles, especially formal leadership roles, norms about participation are usually much less egalitarian. Even when leaders have only legitimate power (French and Raven 1959), they are expected and permitted to guide and direct the discussion, summarize progress, and have a greater influence in the final solution (see Chapter 3). A number of studies have revealed that such appointed leaders show great similarities in these activities, despite substantial differences in their personalities, thereby implying a strong role stereotype for formal leaders (Berkowitz 1956; Pepinsky, Hemphill, and Shevitz 1958; Hollander 1978). Since these behaviors are strongly influential in moving the group from one stage to the next, appointed leaders are likely to have undue weight in determining the solution adopted by a group, regardless of their other qualifications. Most of the advice given to leaders of problem-solving groups is directed at reducing this biasing factor (Maier 1963). Since the degree of influence exercised by the leader is a direct function of his/her power in the group, the more bases of power he/she has, the more difficult it is for the group to reduce his/her biasing effect (French and Raven 1959). In all studies done with the Change of Work Procedures Problem (Maier 1970), the power of the foreman was mitigated substantially only where the workers were made unanimously resistant to his proposed change by increasing their personal antagonism (Hoffman, Harburg, and Maier 1962) or through decision rules (Falk 1978).

Decision Rules

In discussing procedures affecting the task, I suggested that the decision rules used by a group may be considered as a type of group norm. Chapter 12 showed that they may affect the problem-solving process at many points. Often we limit our attention to a group's decision rules to those used in the final choice made among solution alternatives (Davis 1973). Even in groups where unanimity is sought concerning the final solution, however, the initial decision concerning the group's definition of the problem may be made in a highly unilateral way by its leader. Because such definitions of the problem focus the group's attention on a limited set of criteria, to the exclusion of others, the group's energies will be directed toward inventing solutions that fit that definition, to the exclusion of other, possibly more effective solutions. At the worst, the unilateral definition of the problem may create distrust in the other group members about the leader's concern for their opinions and feelings, thus reducing their motivation to participate in the decision.

One of the more interesting findings of the valence research is that the implicit adoption of a decision often occurs without the group's obvious awareness (see Chapter 4). Because a group strives for consensus, the information conveyed by the continued accumulation of valence for a particular decision seems to be interpreted as some representation of the "group mind." In a form of pluralistic ignorance (Schanck 1932), members begin to believe, in the absence of critical comments, that "everyone must be in favor." Most studies of the effects of a formal decision rule of unanimity, as distinct from the implicit unanimous rule usually found in laboratory groups, have shown that members would resist more strongly the inference that they must go along with the rest of the group. Chapter 12 showed that in groups with formal leaders, an explicit majority-decision rule unified subordinates to resist the leader's strongly espoused solution. In both the equal-status and differential-power situations the formal decision rules prevented groups from adopting inferior solutions by providing the opportunity for valence to accumulate for better ones.

Laboratory groups, it has often been noted, tend to strive for unanimity (Thomas and Fink 1961). Although I have never heard any group adopt that decision rule explicitly at the beginning of their discussion, the members' attempts to persuade each other, to offer arguments, to elicit support, and so on imply their search for unanimity. As the group nears the stated time limit, expressions of concern about the possibility of not arriving at a solution appear in the discussion. (I have seen lunch time and train time serve similar functions in management groups.) As it becomes apparent that the true consensus cannot be reached, a majority rule is often invoked to produce a decision. Often the dissenting member will accept the majority's decision by saying, "Well we have to make a decision, so I guess if the majority agrees, I'll go along." Implicit in that statement is not only an adoption of the majority-decision rule as a procedure. It also shows the person's identification with the group as a problem-solving unit that should not fail to produce a solution to the problem.

Thus, the definition of the group's problem has been changed by the adoption of time as a constraint. The problem is now "Can we provide any solution to the manifest problem within the time remaining?" The solution to that problem is often "Let's adopt the solution that the majority favors." By including time as a paramount criterion, producing a decision becomes a way of maintaining the group. To save the group from failure, any decision is better than no decision, even though, from an external point of view, the group may have failed miserably in its attempt to solve the manifest problem.

Acceptance

Finally, essential to the success with which solutions are implemented is their acceptance by those responsible for such implementation. Acceptance seems to be a function of the members' identification with the group (see Chapter 10) and, especially as the problem affects each group member, his/her degree of identification with the solution (see Chapters 8, 9). In American culture we react defensively when we are imposed upon by illegitimate authority (Brehm 1966). On the other hand, we react enthusiastically to the adoption of our own ideas. Thus, fundamental to the successful acceptance of solutions by the members are the norms regulating the acceptance of members' feelings and differential goals. Group norms that permit the free expression of feelings, that promote substantive conflict, and that treat differences of opinion as opportunities for creativity often produce creative solutions with high degrees of member acceptance (Maier and Hoffman 1965). Suppression of such conflict and the unwillingness to tolerate members' objections generally have the opposite effect. Unfortunately, substantive conflict quite often turns into interpersonal conflict, which threatens the existence of the group. To prevent disharmony and avoid the threat of group dissolution, conflict-suppressing norms develop.

It is too early in the development of the hierarchical model to be more specific about the operation of norms concerning the maintenance functions of problem-solving groups. Reviews of the literature on norms highlight the diversity of definitions and operations used by different scholars. Jackson (1960) offered a social reinforcement model, which seems useful in understanding the way norms function at implicit levels. His model permits norms to be imprecisely defined and differentially interpreted by group members. It also points to the possibility of a norm being defined by a range of behaviors, each of which may be differentially acceptable to the members. These ideas are all useful in conceptualizing the ways in which members vary in their modes of conforming to group norms. As suggested earlier, members may all subscribe implicitly to a norm of equal participation in the group, but deviations from strict equality will be tolerated in both directions, within limits. Thus, we see a compatibility between Jackson's distribution of payoffs (positive and negative valences) for certain behaviors and the Sherifs' (1969) concept of the latitude of acceptance of behaviors for describing norms at the implicit level.

By contrast, Goffman's (1974) insightful use of frame analysis to describe the way people define situations helps us identify some mechanisms for the way norms are stated explicitly. His treatment is consistent with the present one in stating that while norms may be signaled by well-learned cues, or even stated explicitly, their operating significance for the group rests on the consistency of the members' subsequent experience with (positive valence for) that version of the norm. For example, a formal leader may state, "I want to hear everyone's point of view on this matter," which he may be legitimately empowered to say according to the group's norm for his role. Nevertheless, unless he accepts all contributions without evaluating them, the norm of universal participation will not be adhered to. Rather, the valence will be increased for the norm that states that his leadership role includes the power to make decisions unilaterally—and that norm will be the operative one. Thus, the mere enunciation of a norm in a group may be insufficient for its adoption if it conflicts with a norm of higher valence. Unless valence for the new norm can be accumulated through experience, its continued enunciation may only prove embarrassing to the speaker and to the other group members. The contradiction between the espoused message of the explicit level and the operative message of the implicit level may divert the members' energies from the explicit task. To maintain the fiction of the explicit norm while operating on the implicit one in attempting to solve a problem requires great care and concentration, lest the myth be revealed.

This discussion of norms has attempted to chart a direction for a systematic treatment of the interaction of the task and maintenance levels of activity in problem-solving groups. The basic assumptions of this approach view the maintenance functions of the group as a set of implicit problems, varying with the degree of "maturity" (Tuckman 1965) of the group. In the early stages of the group's development, issues of inclusion, control, and status are paramount (Schutz 1958). Later, issues of affection and actualization may become more urgent. However, the ramifications of all of these issues may become manifest at any point in the group's life if the environment changes and creates new "tasks" or if changes in the members or the group structure make the group's norms dysfunctional.

Norms, then, are the "procedures" for solving the maintenance problems of the group. As such, they may operate implicitly or explicitly. For example, the Environmental Protection Agency may create a new task for an executive group by declaring a plant in violation of certain pollution standards, when the members had all believed that the law would never be enforced. Some members might favor compliance while others might want to resist the government's intrusion—both as matters of principle. This conflict in values would have to be resolved for the group to solve the "task problem" created by the E.P.A.'s edict.

The introduction of women into an executive group usually creates similar problems at the maintenance level. The norms of most such groups rest on the implicit assumption that all members will be males. When such a group attempts to establish policies in the company that affect women, the mere presence of a woman in the group interferes with the formerly smooth flow of conversation. The usual ribald comments about women in the work force, used to make a point at the task level and sustained by masculine norms, would create substantial maintenance problems. New norms must be developed concerning references to gender before the group is capable of solving problems involving women's issues. A leader may say, "As the person responsible for this action, I will assume the risks of taking that action, so I don't want to discuss that matter any further." By this statement the leader states explicitly that part of his/her role is to take responsibility for the group, and implicitly that he/she can decide what matters the group can or cannot discuss. This example also illustrates an interaction between the task and maintenance levels of group functioning. The leader has called on the normative aspect of the leadership role (a maintenance function) to alter the content of the problem being discussed (a task function).

In describing the movement of a group through the stages at the task level, I suggested that substantive conflict could prevent the group from moving on to the next stage, since the valences for competing alternatives prevented either from being adopted. One way of resolving such conflict is to "move back" a stage to provide a better basis on which to evaluate the alternatives at issue. For example, solutions in conflict could be resolved by defining the problem more completely or by redefining it so the group can invent new, more adequate solutions.

Often, however, a group resolves its conflicts and moves toward a decision by invoking or relying on its maintenance norms. The group's acknowledged "expert" may be called on to arbitrate the dispute. On the Personnel Selection Problem, group members with marketing experience often served in this role, although the relevance of that experience to the problem was never examined. Formal leaders also often arbitrate disputes from their base of power by increasing the valence of one alternative, thus inhibiting the expression of opposition by the other members (see Chapter 3).

The use of maintenance norms to resolve substantive conflict clearly prevents a group from examining the elements of that conflict more thoroughly, and inhibits creativity. The whole group may collude in "moving on" to the next stage in this way, so as to avoid having to invest the energy necessary to return to a prior stage, for instance, by reconsidering the definition of the problem. Often norms serve a defensive function by permitting the leader to hide from group consideration certain aspects of the problem that he/she does not want everyone to recognize.

By adding his/her valence to a particular alternative sufficient to allow the group to move on or by "ruling" in favor of that alternative, the leader allows the group to deal with only that part of the problem he/she feels is safe. Note that when the leader uses his/her legitimate power to resolve substantive conflict in the group, the group's "adoption" of his/her solution not only moves it closer to a decision, but also adds valence at the implicit level to the legitimacy of the leader's use of power in that way. If conflict arises again, the group may look for the leader to conform to the leadership norm and resolve that conflict also, rather than "waste time" trying to solve the substantive problem.

Since in American culture we invest little time or effort in training groups, the norms developed by each group typically are adopted implicitly, on the basis of exogenous norms reinforced by experiences in the group. Rarely are the norms developed by a group open to change by the group members, since, especially in administrative groups, the discussion of norms is normatively prohibited (Argyris and Schön 1974).

With this discussion we round out our representation of the hierarchical model in Figure 13.5. Although we place the maintenance functions below the task functions, in some ways that is quite arbitrary. The group must maintain itself to survive, although it may continue as an entity even after some members have been lost. On the other hand, the group's survival may be crucially dependent on its ability to cope with its environment.

FIGURE 13.5

The Hierarchical Model, Schematically

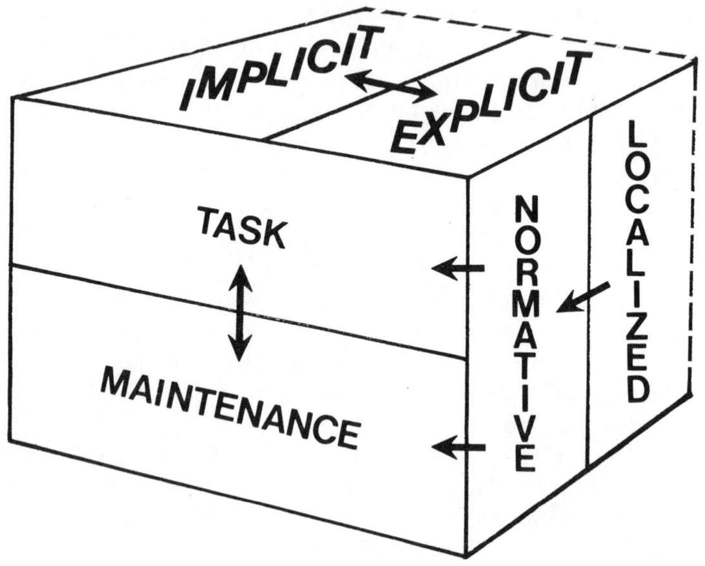

Source: Compiled by the author.

In similar vein, we remind the reader that either the task or the maintenance functions may become the explicit problem of the group. When the maintenance functions become explicit, the stages of Figures 13.2 and 13.3 become operative for that problem. "Task procedures" may be applied to its solution, although typically they are not.

A third implication of Figure 13.5 is that the character of a group as an emergent system is defined by its norms at both the task and maintenance levels. These define the legitimate (explicit) and operating (implicit) rules by which the group functions and continues as a total system. Even when the explicit and implicit norms are inconsistent or contradictory, we can describe the group as one which says one thing and does another. Then we will want to know what defensive mechanisms the group uses to deny this contradiction.

The localized dimension identifies the loosely linked nature of the elements of a problem-solving group. Although it is often convenient analytically to consider a group as a unified set of people who operate in a uniform manner, the relationships of each individual to the group are usually quite varied. Members join for different reasons, are willing to invest in the group's activities to varying degrees, and are rewarded or incur costs according to their individual experiences and personalities (Hoffman 1965). Chapters 8, 9, and 10 document the variation in members' acceptance of the group decision as a function of their individual expressed public support (valence) for it. The less cohesive the group is, the more the individuals' own needs and values determine their commitment to the decision.

Two people in the group may become particularly attracted to each other and share confidences, while another pair may become extremely antagonistic. Coalitions may form to dominate the group or to oppose the formal leader. The coalition of workers, encouraged by the majority decision rule in Chapter 12, effectively balanced the foreman's power, thus producing the conflict from which creative solutions often emerged.

These events, which affect only one or a few members of the group, constitute the localized dimension of the hierarchical model. They often have a substantial degree of regularity and the members develop valence for their existence. An outside observer will be told after a meeting, "Joe always supports Sam because they are close friends," although that basis for Joe's remark may have been disguised by some task-related reason offered by Joe during the meeting.

Finally, every group also has areas of randomness both in its internal functioning and in its relations with its environment. A member may become particularly fatigued or have a heart attack. The table in the meeting room may collapse or the lights may flicker. The "localized" aspects of group functioning provide the continuing rudiments of change. Each interaction of a group member with the environment or with another member either provides additional valence to maintain the current equilibrium or changes the balance of forces to create a "problem" for the group.

Unless the group adopts the problem, it may continue to react to the disburbance of its equilibrium in habitual ways. For example, a member may be picked on by the others, to his/her dissatisfaction. This behavior creates a force on the member to leave the group, thus raising a maintenance problem. If the behavior persists and the member fails to indicate displeasure or to retaliate against the others, the "problem" may be solved through the adoption of an implicit norm that picking on that person is an acceptable thing to do. Picking on this member becomes a group "habit," a poor solution to a maintenance problem never explicitly adopted and, therefore, never considered by the group as a whole.

In similar fashion a particular member of the group may begin to serve as the group's representative to a particular outsider, such as a client of a consulting group. The initial contact may happen fortuitously, but other meetings follow to the point where the client's valence for this member as the group's representative becomes so strong that the group is forced to adjust to it. If the group has no valence for that member to be its representative, the two forces can create a conflict, a problem for the group. Again the "solution" can occur implicitly, by the member's acting toward him/her as the representative to that client, without ever publicly acknowledging it. Or the group can hold a meeting to discuss the problem explicitly—the discrepancy between his/her legitimate role in the group and the function of representative to this client—and find some acceptable solution to it. The implicit "solution" may create confusion or dissatisfaction because it is a recurrent deviation from the legitimate practices. The explicit treatment of the problem may result in a different or the same solution, but be accepted as normative by the entire group.

SUMMARY

The dynamic character of the hierarchical model is only partially captured by the cube in Figure 13.5. The model is intended to describe the simultaneous functioning of the three aspects (dimensions) of the group. The arrows in the figure depict some of the interactive effects of one dimension on another and of one level on another within each dimension. These interactions are mediated by valences at an implicit level. For example, when the group's norm for protecting weak members from the leader's power acts to inhibit discussion of the problem a member created (effect of maintenance norm on task activity), it also strengthens (adds valence to) the protective norm itself (effect of task action on maintenance norms). The valence concept must be seen as Lewin (1947) conceived it, as a force on the group whose value may remain constant for only short periods. The force field created by the valences for each dimension and for their interactions provides a useful model for describing the total activity of the group. The model then becomes useful as a way of depicting the interactions of forces arising simultaneously from various sources. The hierarchical model in its present form provides many interesting avenues for research, but there is no denying the difficulty of testing many aspects of it. We were very fortunate in beginning this series of studies by concentrating on the valence for solutions which we could measure through the members' comments. Except for one study (Chapter 5), we could assume that the prediscussion valence of the members for different solutions was small relative to the valence generated during the discussion. It is rare that all the members of ongoing groups come to a meeting with no valence for a particular solution. In fact, leaders' identification with particular solutions to the problems they bring to groups are often major barriers to effective problem solving (Maier and Hoffman 1965; Chapter 12). Measuring the members' prediscussion valence for solutions is difficult even when the solutions are known in advance (see Chapter 5 for a preliminary attempt), but are obviously impossible when members "surprise" the group by proposing a solution to a problem of which the other members were unaware.

The difficulties become even greater when the maintenance aspects of the group are considered. Norms are rarely made explicit and years of socialization make many of them so automatic that they are never violated. They, therefore, can never be observed nor even described by the members unless we know enough to ask about them. Since they operate implicitly they vary in scope and strength from member to member and in different situations (Humpal and Hoffman 1979). We have begun to study leadership norms in newly forming, ad hoc groups with a method consistent with the hierarchical model (Stein et al. 1979). While the problem is difficult, the first results look very promising.

14

APPLICATIONS TO THE FUNCTIONING OF PROBLEM-SOLVING GROUPS

L. Richard Hoffman

Having begun this line of research not only from the pure-science base of merely "wanting to know," but also from a need for a model of groups that was useful to me in facilitating group functioning, I take this opportunity to speculate a bit on the practical implications of the results of these studies. The one striking conclusion I reach is that they imply much more than they can deliver at this point. The very fact that these studies are the first to track—through the solution-valence index—the movement of groups toward the adoption of solutions should create an expectation of beginnings, not conclusions. From a strictly scientific point of view, then, we are at the beginning. The hierarchical model is the best conclusion I can draw at this point, and its uncharted areas are manifold. What follows, then, are speculations, some of which have been tested informally in my consultations with groups in a variety of business settings. I make the assumption in all of them that the reader is interested in promoting a group's problem-solving effectiveness. There are, of course, implications in these studies for perverting the group's activities for personal ends, but I shall not provide a guide to them.

SOLUTION VALENCE

Probably the most useful way to benefit from our studies of solution valence is to become aware that it operates at the implicit level. Members are unable to measure valence while participating in a meeting. To use solution valence effectively a group would require a valence coder to announce when a solution has reached the adoption threshold. The group could then explicitly raise the procedural question of whether enough alternatives had been generated for evaluation to begin.

However, valence coding will not become standard practice in most groups, so groups should follow procedures that hold them at the problem-defining or solution-generating stage long enough to allow many options to be considered before they are evaluated.

Groups should also build positive valence for all alternatives suggested, since that would have both a preventive and a constructive function. On the one hand it prevents the early rejection of ill-formed, but possibly very effective, ideas. Only a small number of negative valence points are needed to block solutions from ever being adopted. We should avoid degrading any possible solution without first considering its potential benefits. Such exploration, by adding positive valence to the alternative, places it in potential conflict with other possible solutions treated similarly. Such opposition, in turn, sets the stage for defining the problem more completely and accurately, which often results in creative solutions, or at least more adequate ones.

EXPLICITNESS

The importance of making things explicit cannot be overemphasized. The two principal advantages of explicitness are to enhance understanding among members and to focus their energies on the same set of issues. Both of these advantages contribute to the group's ability to manage its own activities, rather than being victim of implicit mechanisms of control, such as solution valence.

The use of explicit procedures to promote understanding requires a recognition that language and communication are fragile phenomena. We all tend to err in projecting our own interpretations onto others, whether we are sending messages or receiving them. We assume that what we say conveys our entire meaning and intent to the other person. Reinforcing that belief is the same error made by the receiver, who assumes that we meant what he/she believes. Our "solution-minded" or action tendencies then cause us both to agree that we understand each other. "You get it?" "Yeah, sure." If we check the accuracy of our communication by asking the other person what he/she intends to do, we often find that an entirely different, sometimes even opposing, interpretation has been put on the message. Thus, we should actively seek feedback from other people when we are attempting to convey a message.

Such checking-out procedures are especially important at the end of each decision made by a group. They tend to help ensure that the decision will be implemented in the form intended, and the members will be motivated by knowing that they are expected to abide by the decision in particular ways. For example, if Charlie is supposed to supply the group with certain information at the next meeting, it is useful to have Charlie tell the group what information he will have and when it will be ready for the group. In so checking out, Charlie may verify his commitment or reveal his misunderstanding of the commitment he made, and then make a more realistic one. Even the latter is beneficial to the group, since the other members will not act on the basis of false expectations about what Charlie will do.

The willingness of leaders and members both to ask and to entertain questions of clarification at any point in the group meeting is a vital attitude. People are often reluctant to ask such questions for fear of looking dumb or foolish. "If everyone else is discussing the problem so vigorously, there must be something wrong with me if I don't understand what they're talking about." So the clarifying question is not asked.

Leaders often reinforce such self-doubts and inhibit the asking of such questions by responding sarcastically, rather than valuing the interest in the problem evidenced by the questioner. As Maier (1963) so often noted, leaders in organizations should limit their use of power by focusing on facilitating the group's processes. Abusing the members by denying their right to question or to disagree is usually self-defeating (Maier and Hoffman 1965).

Explicitly checking for the members' opinions and feelings toward the end of the meeting is also necessary for ensuring true consensus. The implicit valence-adoption phenomenon is confirmed by the activity of the control phase (see Chapter 6). At that stage members are often reluctant to express their doubts about the decision for fear of deviating from the apparent consensus. As shown in Chapters 8-10, such consensus may be an illusion arising from the dominance of those who favor the high-valence solution. The dominant members assume that others are silent because they, too, see the "obvious" virtues of the decision. The silent members, hearing no other opposition, assume they are all in agreement. By setting a period of checking for consensus—or possibly for opposition—a procedure is legitimized for members to express doubts. Merely asking, "Does everyone agree?" or even "Are there any objections?" as one gathers up papers does not perform this function. Asking for explicit statements about the advantages and, especially, the disadvantages seen in a solution that is about to be adopted, helps the members feel secure in voicing their doubts and opposition. Often these doubts are merely unreasonable fears about events that are improbable, or manifestations of tension about new demands on that person. Reassurances can be given at that point. On the other hand, legitimate objections can also be recognized even at that late stage, objections that may not have been voiced or heard clearly before the group sensed its ability to solve the problem (Maier and Hoffman 1960b). The group may still decide to adopt the dominant solution, but everyone will be alerted to the potential risks.

TIMING AND SEQUENCE

I referred earlier to the need to nurture unusual or poorly formulated ideas so they may be considered by the group, and to avoid their early rejections. Correspondingly, a group should be willing to entertain the possibility of "moving back" in the sequence of problem stages at almost any time. Insights may occur at any time, but often good ideas come late in the discussion, as a member finally solves the doubt he/she had throughout. An openness to such "interference" with getting the problem solved—that is, making a decision—may prevent the wrong decision and facilitate the invention of a better solution. One of the dangers of seeing the problem-solving process as a series of stages that occur in regular order is that the stages become a fixed requirement on the group. By being explicit about which stage the group is in, the group can also decide explicitly to change stages or not, depending on other factors. The question of whether to change stages raises procedural issues to the explicit level for discussion.

TASK PROCEDURES

As noted in Figure 13.4 of the hierarchical model, there have been many procedural inventions designed to be used explicitly to prevent premature movement from one stage to the next. Although there is no way of avoiding the ultimate operation of the valence-adoption relationship, such procedures help it to be grounded in a more factual basis. Brainstorming (Osborn 1947) can be used at any stage of the process to provide more alternatives, not just at the solution-generating stage. Separating the generating function from the evaluative function (Maier 1963) prevents the group from moving prematurely to the next stage by quickly accumulating valence for any single alternative.

Many of the task procedures require skills to apply them. Merely reading this chapter is insufficient to teach people how to implement the recommendations. Both individually and collectively the members of groups must practice the behaviors involved, so that they become habitual parts of their repertoires. Most people are unused to thinking creatively, so they find the rules of brainstorming unsettling. They are embarrassed in their first efforts to contribute an "off-the-wall" idea. But, after practice, members become used to hearing wild ideas, recognizing that poor ideas may lead to good ones.

The same is true of most other procedures. People often become discouraged after using them once, even successfully. They feel awkward or silly, since the behaviors are neither habitual nor generally accepted.

NORMS

To adopt such procedures as part of a group's problem-solving practices, however, requires the members to recognize that the group functions at levels other than the manifest task level. Procedural and maintenance problems have to be solved by the group, and are equally legitimate problems to be discussed. Few groups accept such legitimacy. Many deny it by having norms that preclude the discussion of feelings, relationships among members, the procedures the group is following, or even whether the problem the leader brought in is the correct one. Without a norm to discuss such norms, maintenance problems may be ignored or denied or solved through personal power or subterfuge. As noted in Chapter 12, decision rules can be adopted in a group to limit the leader's abuse of power, because the decision rules become normative and any member can invoke them. Rather than resolving conflicts by the resort to power, the group is better able to resolve them creatively.

The damaging effects that problems at the maintenance level have on the task effectiveness of the group usually are not explicitly recognized by organizational groups (Argyris and Schön 1974). Executives and managers learn to live with problems of that sort, that is, to work around them in some way. Groups that adopt norms that legitimate dealing with their maintenance problems are more likely to capitalize on their members' resources.

In this chapter I have attempted to highlight some of the ways in which the valence studies are relevant to the functioning of problem-solving groups. It was intended as a guide to those possible applications, not a definitive treatment of them. The latter would be premature, in light of the early stages of this research. Nevertheless, they are consistent with other methods that have been suggested for improving group problem solving, and the hierarchical model seems to provide coherence to the variety of approaches and methods already available. Our research on the hierarchical model should provide more evidence concerning its validity and more guides to its application.

APPENDIX A

PROBLEMS

ASSEMBLY PROBLEM

You have been called in as a consultant to a company manufacturing automobiles. Their problem stems from the following situation. Seven men, working in a circle, assemble a carburetor. The casting enters the circle at one point, and each person adds his pieces and pushes the unit to the next worker, who adds his elements. When the unit leaves the circle, it is a completed carburetor. This work arrangement for the subassembly station is diagrammed in the figure.

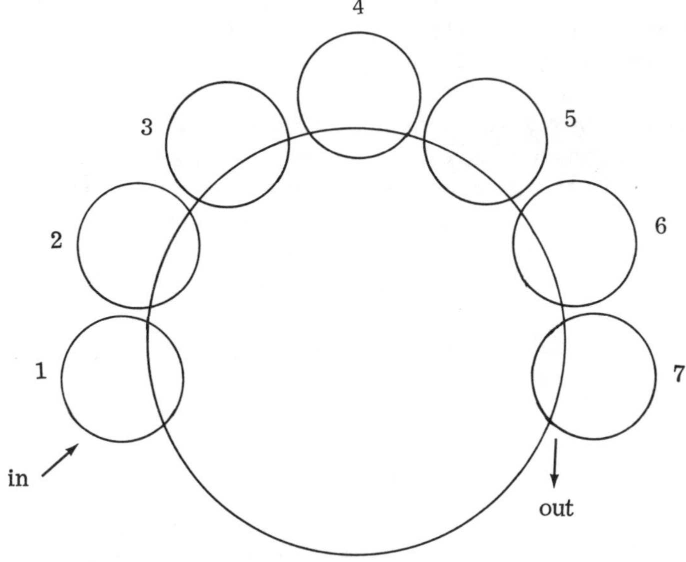

The assembly work is simple and requires a minimum of training for each step. The aptitude requirement is primarily good finger dexterity. The materials for each assembly position are located in bins which are kept supplied by material handlers. Thus, each worker has his essential material at his elbow. The job has been analyzed by time-and-motion experts so that the positions are of equal difficulty. Pay is based on hourly rates.

There are four such subassembly stations in this company, each supervised by a foreman. The total factory production is dependent upon receiving the required number of carburetors from these four stations. The factory needs 300 parts per day from the four stations combined to maintain regular operations. The production is now so low that the factory production as a whole had to slow down. The daily production of the four stations at present is 85, 80, 60, and 50 units. The lowest-producing station had previously produced 60 units, but shortly before you were called in for consultation, the foreman of that station had expressed his dissatisfaction with production by reprimanding the group. Following the reprimand, production fell to 50 units per day.

In observing the stations in operation, you have noticed that the work tends to pile up at one or two positions, where the workers seem somewhat slower than the rest of the group. The pileups are especially apparent in the two low-production stations, although they occur in different positions in the two stations. Despite continuous use of the best personnel selection procedures for a number of years, fairly substantial differences still exist between the best and the poorest workers in each station. Thus, even though the jobs are equally difficult, material accumulates at the position of the least-able worker in the station. Foremen on nonproduction jobs are not willing to accept slow workers as transfers.

The company management has asked for your recommendation on how to make the stations as productive as possible. On the basis of what you now know, describe on the report form provided the action your group agrees is the best for the company to take.

PERSONNEL SELECTION PROBLEM

Group Number _____

INSTRUCTIONS FOR GROUP TASK

The vice-president of marketing in a rapidly expanding division of your company has requested that you individuals, as members of the corporate personnel department, meet as a group and recommend a candidate for his approval from available résumés. The position he is anxious to fill is the newly established job of assistant market planning manager. The person who is selected will be expected to assist in the development and implementation of plans for the marketing of established products in previously unexposed areas throughout North America. Experience with the product line is not necessary, but ingenuity, foresight, and marketing capabilities are essential. The candidate, if effective at this job, will be promoted to a position of even greater responsibility within two years. After familiarizing yourselves with the possible candidates, please meet as a group and select the one applicant who appears to be most suitable.

Sidney Godep
1422 Harpson Drive
Rochester, New York
(716) MA 4-1231

Born: 1928
Married - 5 children
5'10", 170 pounds

Job Experience:

September 1964 to present — Eastman Kodak Company — Rochester, New York

Worked for General Manager of Audio-Visual Products Division. I conducted market research into ways the company can develop and increase its penetration into the vocational education market for audio-visual hardware and software. Work entailed travel and contact with government officials and included written and personal presentation of recommendations.

1954 to 1964 — Eastman Kodak Company

Assistant Product Manager—assisted in the planning and marketing of instamatic cameras in the Northeastern United States.

1952 to 1954 — Sales Trainee for Eastman Kodak — Rochester, New York & Albany, New York

Education:

1958-1954 — Duke University — Durham, N.C.
B.S. in Business Administration
Financed by G.I. Bill

Military Background:

1945-1947

Commissioned an Ensign in the U.S. Navy and qualified as a Navy Diver and Explosive Ordnance Disposal team leader. Assigned to Western Pacific.

Interest: Scoutsmaster, Little League coach, member of Rochester Chamber of Commerce

References furnished on request.

David Kroll	Born 4/17/42
1914 St. Louis Parkway	Single
Minneapolis, Minnesota	5'11", 185 lbs.
(612) 935-1892	

Work Experience:

January 1972 to Present	Parke, Davis, & Co.	Minneapolis

As a Market Research Analyst conducted marketing studies for new and existing products.

During this period developed an EDP simulation model for profitability based on the product life cycle for pacemakers, a product sales forecasting model, and USA and worldwide indices of performance (system still used today).

February 1971 to December 1971	Andel Company Manufacture and sale of fire protection, chemicals, and refrigeration equipment	Indianapolis, Ind.

Market Research Analyst, Chemical Division—Agricultural and Industrial Chemicals. Functions involved conducting mail and field surveys for all products as well as sales forecasting. A detailed market definition was completed for all products.

March 1970 to January 1971	Maytag Co.	Newton, Iowa

As Market Research Analyst was responsible for sales analysis, quotas, and forecasting. Completed a statistical analysis showing the rate of dealer attrition in the U.S.

February 1969 to February 1970	General Electric Co. Housewares Division	Bridgeport, Conn.

General Management Training Program with six months spent assisting in market surveys.

December 1967 to February 1969	Maidenform Corp. Salesman	New Haven, Conn.

Sold maidenform womens wear to stores in assigned district.

Education

1965 to 1967	Boston University	Boston

MBA with concentration in finance.

1961 to 1965 Georgetown University Washington, D.C.

B.A. with a major in political science.

Summer Employment:

1965 to 1966

Salesman for Standard Oil of California in service stations.

1961 to 1965

Salesman in men's clothing store in Washington, D.C.

Military Status:

Deferred, 1Y

Interests:

Hunting, playing cards

References furnished on request

Roger O'Brien
218 Lanimore Lane
Philadelphia, Pa. 19118
(215) AD 3-1162

Born: 5/27/39
Married - 3 children
6', 175 lbs.

Job Experience

November 1970 to Present Colgate-Palmolive Co. Philadelphia

Marketing Staff Assistant at Colgate-Palmolive Company in the Colgate Dental Cream product group. Developed and evaluated premium offers; designed and conducted market tests, and regional and district sales analyses. Also responsible for formulating counter-marketing plan against competitive new product entry.

1966-1970 Colgate Palmolive Co.

Salesman for Colgate-Palmolive Company. Made sales calls on chain headquarters, cooperative jobbers, and individual independent and chain retail stores, selling both new and established products. Special assignment was shelf positioning and new product distribution in chain stores in addition to regular sales duties.

Military Status

1963-1965

United States Navy. Commissioned as Ensign after attending Navy Officers Candidate School. Assigned to U.S.S. WASHTENAW CTY.

(LST-1166). Initial duties were Gunnery Officer and a division of ten men. Later advanced to Lieutenant Junior Grade and put in charge of Deck Division. Duties were administration and training of forty men, supervision of all cargo loading and storage, maintenance of the ship's hull, boats, and cargo spaces, and Special Sea Detail Officer of the Deck. Presently, inactive reserve.

Education Experience

1958-1962 Temple University Philadelphia
B.S. in Business Administration

Debating team, Fraternity business manager.

Interests

Sailing, snowmobiling, horseback riding.

Howard Winston
260 East Chestnut
Chicago, Illinois
(312) DE 7-0299

Born 10/7/32
Single
6'2", 190 lbs.

Job Experience:

June 1972 to Present Quaker Oats Chicago, Ill.

Marketing Analyst engaged in expansion of pet foods into foreign markets.

July 1970 to May 1972 Libby, McNeil, Libby Chicago, Ill.

Junior product manager serving as liaison with advertising agencies in the establishment of a coordinated media strategy.

1966 to 1970 Sears, Roebuck and Co. Chicago, Ill.

Marketing Research Analyst concerned with determining growth directions for catalogue sales.

1963 to 1966 Green Giant Corp. Bloomington, Minn.

Marketing Researcher—made projections of canned goods sales to restaurants, airlines, caterers, and other direct users.

1962 to 1963 Whitehall Laboratories

Assistant mid-west product manager for Dristan tablets, Psorex, and Preparation H.

1960 to 1962 Chesebrough-Ponds, Inc.

Marketing trainee assigned to Vaseline hair tonic division as assistant liaison with the Colgate Palmolive distributors.

1957 to 1960 Pfizer and Company
Pharmaceuticals and Chemicals

As a member of the J. B. Roerig sales division, my responsibilities were calling on physicians, hospitals, and pharmacies in the promotion and sales of Roerig products.

Education

1951-1955 University of Michigan Ann Arbor, Mich.
B.S. in Business Administration

Military Status

Physical deferment

Interests

Travel, stock car racing, wine collecting

Walter Tinneman Born 4/1/39
1492 Arbor Lane Single
Kansas City, Mo. 5'9", 165 lbs.

Job Experience

November 1970 to Present Hallmark Cards, Inc. Kansas City

Market Research Analyst. Conducted studies of consumer brand attitudes in relation to candles, greeting card promotions, and party items. Other projects included studies of consumer reactions to Hallmark Hall of Fame, analyses of Christmas gift wrap market, and development of forecasting methods for various product categories. Supervised up to six persons on a project basis.

February 1968 to October 1970 General American Life Insurance Company St. Louis, Mo.

Employed as an actuary. Member of management team engaged in Variable Annuity product development and subsequent registration with the S.E.C. Registered representative of the National Association of Securities Dealers. Designed computerized sales proposal system for the Pension and Variable Annuity Department. Experience in Systems Analysis and Computer Programming.

April 1965 to January 1968 Xerox Corporation Rochester, New York

General Accounting Operations: Acting accountant for Division's Portable Appliance Department (estimated sales volume $40 million). Responsible for the preparation and accuracy of all financial statements, classified sales reports, product complaint statistics, and Department's current account reconciliation with Corporate Accounting headquarters operations in Schenectady, New York.

December 1963 to March 1965	Xerox Corporation	Rochester, New York

Business Information Systems: Designed, programmed and debugged an out-of-warranty accounting system for Division's Product Service Department with an initial cost savings of 200 man-hours per month, on the G.E. 400 series computer.

Education

1961-1963	Stanford University MBA with major concentration in Accounting and Finance	Palo Alto, Calif.
1957-1961	Wharton School of Finance and Commerce	University of Pennsylvania

Majored in Accounting and Computer Science

Military Status

1Y (deferred)

Interests

Writing short stories, hockey, cycling

Reference furnished upon request.

CHANGE OF WORK PROCEDURES

GENERAL INFORMATION

In a company manufacturing subassemblies for the automobile industry, the assembly work is done by small groups of employees. Several of these groups are under the supervision of a foreman, Thompson. In one of these groups Jackson, Stevenson, and Walters work together assembling fuel pumps.

This operation is divided into three jobs or positions, called position 1, position 2, and position 3. Supplies for each position are located next to the bench where the man works. The men work side by side and can help each other if they wish. Since all the jobs are simple and fairly similar, these three employees exchange positions on the line every now and then. This trading of positions was developed by the men themselves. It creates no financial problem because the crew is paid by a group piece rate. In this way the three members share the production pay equally.

Presently each of you will be asked to be one of the following: Thompson, Jackson, Walters, or Stevenson. Today, Thompson, the foreman, has asked Jackson, Walters, and Stevenson to meet with him in his office. He said he wanted to talk about "something."

ROLE FOR "THOMPSON," FOREMAN

You are the foreman in a shop and supervise the work of about 20 men. Most of the jobs are piece-rate jobs, and some of the men work in teams and are paid on a team piece-rate basis. In one of the teams, Jackson, Walters, and Stevenson work together. Each of them does one of the operations for an hour and then they exchange, so that all men perform each of the operations at different times. The men themselves decided to operate that way, and you have never given the plan any thought.

Lately, Jim Clark, the methods man, has been around and studied conditions in your shop. He timed Jackson, Walters, and Stevenson on each of the operations and came up with the following facts:

Time for Operation

	Position 1	Position 2	Position 3	Total
Jackson	3 min.	4 min.	4.5 min.	11.5 min.
Walters	3.5 min.	3.5 min.	3 min.	10 min.
Stevenson	5 min.	3.5 min.	4.5 min.	13 min.
				34.5 min.

He observed that with the people rotating, the average time for all three operations would be one-third of the total time of 11.5 minutes per complete unit. If, however, Jackson worked in position 1, Stevenson in position 2, and Walters in position 3, the time would be 9.5 minutes, a reduction of over 17 percent. Such a reduction in time would amount to a saving of more than 80 minutes. In other words, the lost production would be about the same as that which would occur if the workers loafed for 80 minutes in an eight-hour day. If the time were used for productive effort, production would be increased more than 20 percent.

This made pretty good sense to you, so you have decided to take up the problem with the crew. You feel that they should go along with any change in operation that is made.

ROLE FOR "JACKSON"

You are one of three people on an assembly operation. Walters and Stevenson are your teammates, and you enjoy working with them. You get paid on a team basis, and you are making wages that are entirely satisfactory. Stevenson isn't quite as fast as Walters and you, but when you feel Stevenson is holding things up too much, each of you helps out.

The work is very monotonous. The saving thing about it is that every hour you all change positions. In this way you get to do all three operations. You are best on position 1, so when you get in that spot, you turn out some extra work and thus make the job easier for Stevenson, who follows you in that position.

You have been on this job for two years and have never run out of work. Apparently your group can make pretty good pay without running yourselves out of a job. Lately, however, the company has had some of its methods experts hanging around. It looks like the company is trying to work out some speed-up methods. If they make these jobs any more simple, you won't be able to stand the monotony. Thompson, your foreman, is a decent person and has never criticized your team's work.

ROLE FOR "WALTERS"

You work with Jackson and Stevenson on a job that requires three separate operations. Each of you works on each of the three operations by rotating positions once each hour. This makes the work more interesting, and you can always help out the others by running the job ahead in case one of you doesn't feel so good. It's all right to help out, because you get paid on a team piece-rate basis. You could actually earn more if Stevenson was a faster worker, but Stevenson is a good friend whom you would rather have in the group than someone else who might do a little bit more.

You find all three positions about equally desirable. They are all simple and purely routine. The monotony doesn't bother you much because you can talk, daydream, and change your pace. By working slowly for a while and then fast, you can sort of set your pace to music you hum to yourself. Jackson and Stevenson like the idea of changing jobs and, even though Stevenson is slow on some positions, the changing around has its good points. You feel you get to a stopping place every time you change positions, and this kind of takes the place of a rest pause.

Lately some kind of efficiency expert has been hanging around. He stands some distance away with a stopwatch in his hand. The company could get more for its money if it put some of these guys to work. You say to yourself, "I'd like to see one of these guys try and tell me how to do this job. I'd sure give him an earful." If Thompson, your foreman, doesn't get him out of the shop pretty soon, you're going to tell him what you think of his dragging in company spies.

ROLE FOR "STEVENSON"

You work with Jackson and Walters on an assembly job and get paid on a team piece-rate basis. The three of you work very well together and make a pretty good wage. Jackson and Walters like to make a little more than you think is necessary, but you go along with them and work as hard as you can, so as to keep production up where they want it. They are good people and often help you out if you fall behind, so you feel it is only fair to try and go along with the pace they set.

Thw three of you exchange positions every hour. In this way you get to work all positions. You like position 2 the best because it is easier. When you get in position 3, you can't keep up and then you feel Thompson, the foreman, watching you. Sometimes Walters and Jackson slow down when you are in position 3, and then the foreman seems satisfied.

Lately the methods man has been hanging around watching the job. You wonder what he is up to. Can't they leave guys alone who are doing all right?

HORSE-TRADING PROBLEM

A man bought a horse for $60, sold it for $70, bought it back again for $80, and then sold it for $90. How much money did the man make in the horse business? (Check one)

_____ He lost $10
_____ He broke even
_____ He made $10
_____ He made $20
_____ He made $30

BRACELET PROBLEM

An unknown woman bought a bracelet for $15 and gave in payment a check for $25. The dealer went to a neighboring store and cashed the check. The woman received $10 change, took her bracelet, and disappeared. The check bounced and the dealer had to make it good. The bracelet cost the dealer $11. How much money did he lose altogether?

TRAFFIC PROBLEM

Date ______________________ Name ________________________

Group No. ____________________

Mr. Johnson receives a traffic ticket for parking for 10 minutes in a no-parking zone in downtown Boston. For some reason he fails to mail in a check for the $2 fine until one day after the 21 days allowed. The clerk of the court, following the regulations, returns the check and informs the man that he will shortly receive a summons to appear in court.

Mr. Johnson then writes a letter to the judge stating that it would work a great hardship on him to miss half a day's work, since he would lose pay; also, his employer would be very displeased because this is an extremely busy season and he needs all his employees. Since his wife has just had a child, it is important that he not lose money or jeopardize his job. For those reasons and because the crime was minor and his fine was only a day late, Mr. Johnson requests that the judge accept his check and not require a court appearance.

What would you do if you were the judge? Why?

________ I would refuse his check and require him to appear in court.

________ I would not require him to appear in court, but would impose an additional fine.

________ I would accept his check.

CHEATING PROBLEM

Date ______________________ Name ________________________

Group No. ____________________

Your friend, whom you have known for over three years, with whom you have double-dated, and of whom you are quite proud, has a poor math aptitude and is having a difficult time in mastering the math in a course in which you and he are enrolled. Before the final, he has been bogged down in a time-consuming social science paper, taking all of his spare time.

Before the final he has asked you to slip him your first blue book after you begin your second, so that he can utilize this last chance to pass the course. He needs a passing grade in order to be admitted to Physics 1 in his senior year, so that he can complete his premedical requirements in time for graduation. At this time you haven't committed yourself.

The test is in the process of being given, you have just finished your first blue book, the proctor has left the room, and your buddy, sitting beside you, looks at you expectantly. What would you do? Why?

_____ I would pass him the blue book.

_____ I would let him look at the blue book while it remained on my desk.

_____ I would let him look at a limited number of answers.

_____ I would not permit him to look at the blue book.

_____ I would threaten to tell the proctor that he was trying to cheat.

_____ I would tell the proctor.

APPENDIX B

VALENCE CODING MANUALS

MANUAL FOR CODING VALENCE ON THE ASSEMBLY PROBLEM

The purpose of the present coding system is to provide a record, based on observations of the group problem-solving process, of the types of statements made by the members in association with various types of possible solutions to the problem under consideration. The form of record sheet employed and the method of coding are intended to yield a picture of the chronological sequence of acts, although no accurate estimate of the actual time involved is possible.

It should be emphasized that at this stage of development, only statements bearing on specific solutions are of concern to the coder. The observations do not include, at this time, statements attempting to define the problem, encouraging total participation, asking for opinions, and so on, which may be important for problem solving. Many qualitative distinctions that might be made with respect to the statements that are coded are also ignored at this point. For example, while all statements justifying the solution proposed are coded, whether the justifications are based on facts in the problem or on the personal biases or prejudices of the speaker is not distinguished.

THE CODING FORM

The coding form has listed down the left-hand side the possible solutions to the problem to be solved. (In cases where an unknown problem is to be solved, spaces are left for the coder to write in solutions proposed or discussed by the group.) Coders will write in, in the space marked "Other," solutions discussed by the group that are not included among those listed. Only statements that refer specifically to the solutions listed or added by the coder are coded in the boxes to the right. Codes are entered on the row corresponding to the solution listed on the left, to indicate that the statement referred to that solution.

The vertical lines divide the page into statement units such that the first statement made with respect to any solution is recorded in the first column on the left and succeeding statements are recorded in successive columns to the right. A new column is used each time any one of the following events occurs:

1. A new person makes a codable statement.
2. The same person makes a codable statement referring to a different solution.
3. The same person makes a statement that is codable differently from the statement just coded.

Each entry in a cell of the coding sheet is composed of two parts: (1) a number representing the group member speaking and (2) a letter indicating the type of statement made. Each member is assigned a number at the beginning of the meeting, which all coders use to designate their contributions to the discussion. The letters used to record the statements made are described in the next section.

STATEMENT CODES

There are two general sets of statements to be coded. One set is generally supportive of the proposed solution and designed to promote its adoption by the group. These include statements of the solution (S), justifications of its value (J), statements of general agreement with it (A), attempts to gain agreement with the solution from other members or to have them adopt the solution (V), questions designed to have the person who proposed the solution describe it in more detail (Q), and so on. A parallel set of statements is generally critical of the solution and designed to prevent its adoption by the group. Each of the above categories of statements has a critical form and is coded with the same symbol followed by a prime notation (such as S^1).

What follows is a description of each of the code categories in more detailed form, with examples of statements that would be coded in each category.

Code S all statements of complete or partial descriptions of solutions, additions of details, or elaborations of the character of the solution. S statements answer the question "What is to be done?" Examples: "We ought to pay the men according to how much they produce." Coded S under the solution "Piece-rate (incentives)." "Let's put the slowest man in team C into team D." Coded S (d), under the solution "Transfer slow worker." The (d) refers to team D in response to the question "Where?" on the solution description.

Code J all statements that describe the possible benefits of a solution, draw analogies between the solution and other solutions or situations, or indicate aspects of the problem that the solution will overcome. J statements answer the question "Why will the solution work?" Examples: "Putting Joe in team D would raise their productivity." Code J under the solution "Transfer slow worker." "A pep talk would encourage slow workers to work harder." Code J under the solution "Foreman use positive motivation."

Code A all statements that express agreement that the solution should be adopted, that indicate the solution is good or is acceptable to the person speaking. These statements differ from J statements in that they contain no content to justify the positive feelings of the speaker. The expression "Uh huh" should be coded A only if it clearly expresses assent. Most such expressions should not be coded, since they merely give the speaker clearance to continue speaking by indicating understanding of what is being said. A statements answer the question "Is the person in favor of the solution?" but contain no reasons for the person's acceptance of the solution. Examples: "That's a great idea!" "I'm willing to go along with that solution."

Code V all statements attempting to gain statements of approval for a solution from another group member or from the group as a whole. Such statements include formal calls for a vote of approval, informal attempts to elicit statements of agreement that the solution is good, demands on the group to adopt the solution. V statements answer the question "Is the speaker attempting to gain support for his solution from another member or members of the group?" Examples: "Jim, don't you think we ought to put the slow man on team D?" Code V under the solution "Transfer slow worker." "How about telling the company that the men should move up one position every two hours?" Code V under the solution "Group rotation."

Code Q all interrogatory statements asking for clarification of the statements of a previous speaker, without any critical implications. These questions usually are requests for more details about how a proposed solution might work, but also may be requests for clarifications of the reasoning behind a solution or behind a criticism of a solution (S^1 or J^1). Any question that does not imply doubt or criticism of the solution is coded in this category. Q statements answer the question "Is the person seeking information concerning the solution?" Examples: "How often would you have the men switch positions?" Code Q under the solution "Group rotation." "Do I understand that if they produce more than 300 units, you would pay them 10 percent more?" Code Q under the solution "Bonus."

Code S^1 all statements of solutions that the speaker indicates are unacceptable to him. These include all rejections of the general solution or of major details or elaborations of the solution. (See below, however, for how to indicate S^1 criticisms of details of a generally acceptable solution.) S^1 statements answer the question "What should not be done?" Examples: "We can't transfer the slowest man in team C." Code S^1 under the solution "Transfer slow worker." "Training the foreman is no good." Code S^1 under the solution "Foreman use positive motivation."

Code J^1 all statements offering reasons for rejecting a solution or details of a solution. (See below, however, for how to indicate J^1 criticisms of details of a generally acceptable solution.) J^1 statements answer the question "Why won't the solution work?" Examples: "Just talking to the slow worker won't help if he's bored with his job." Code J^1 under the solution "Counsel slow worker." "Training the foreman takes too long, and besides it might not work." Code J^1 under the solution "Foreman use positive motivation."

Code A^1 all statements expressing general disagreement with the solution, as long as the critical reaction contains no justification for the feeling. Such statements differ from S^1 statements only in the lack of specific content as to what the object of criticism is. A^1 statements answer the question "Does the person object to the solution?" Examples: "That will never work." "I can't go along with that idea." Code A^1 under the appropriate solution.

Code V^1 all statements attempting to gain statements of rejection of the solution or parts of the solution. Such statements include formal calls for rejecting a solution, attempts to gain expressions of or agreement with criticism of a solution, and demands on the group to reject the solution. V^1 statements answer the question "Is the speaker attempting to elicit criticism or rejection of the solution?" Examples: "We have to avoid criticizing team C, don't you agree, Jim?" Code V^1 under the solution "Reprimand slow worker." "Then we all agree that giving the most productive group a prize will lower production in team C." Code V^1 under the solution "Group competition."

Code Q^1 all interrogative statements that imply doubt about or rejection of the solution. While these questions often ask for details about a solution, they are asked in a critical manner and imply that the obvious answer to the question provides a basis for discarding the solution. Q^1 statements answer the question "Is the person implying doubt or criticism of the solution through a question?" Examples: "Wouldn't introducing an incentive system discourage the poorer workers and reduce productivity?" Code Q^1 under the solution "Piece-rate (incentives)." "How do you know the faster group would accept a slower worker?" Code Q^1 under the solution "Transfer slow worker."

SPECIAL CONVENTIONS

Duration of Statements

A rough determination of the duration of any statement is indicated by drawing a line through successive cells following an entry. Each cell crossed by the line should represent an approximately equal amount of time, that is, if a *J* is coded with a line following it for one cell, it should be equivalent to two *J* remarks. It is recognized that the type of judgment required here is extremely difficult and open to error, so do the best job you can.

In using this notation for the duration of a statement, the convention has also been adopted of indicating agreements (*A*) or disagreements (A^1), which are usually of the "Uh huh" variety, above the line at their point of occurrence, if they do not interrupt the principal speaker, for example, 1J ___2A___. Since our analysis assumes a certain degree of accuracy in the coder's placing of such *A* and A^1 statements, it is important to make such placements so as to reflect their occurrence in time as nearly as possible. A definite interruption stops the line and the new statement is then recorded.

Solution Details

Frequently a group will discuss alternative solutions to a problem that differ from each other only in some minor detail, so that both would normally be coded under the same category. For example, one member might suggest that an incentive be paid to each group member for each unit the group produces beyond 75, while another might suggest that an incentive system be based on any amount in excess of a 10 percent increase in production over the current rate. Both of these would be coded under the solution "Piece-rate (incentives)," but they should be distinguished from each other. Criticisms of one alternative should be separated from criticisms of the other.

The method of distinguishing among alternatives is to divide the solution row horizontally and code one alternative in the top half of the row and the other in the bottom half. Each should be labeled in some clear notation so they can be distinguished and so the coder can be certain for which solution he/she is recording the statements made. If, as sometimes occurs, three alternatives within a solution category are being considered, the row should be divided in thirds, with appropriate labeling and coding.

Combined Solutions

Frequently a group will discuss a solution that combines two or more of the categories in the list, such as to move the slow worker to position 1 on team D, which combines the solutions "Transfer slow worker" and "Put slow worker first." Indicate that the combination is being discussed by connecting the two elements in a bracket; use only one of the two possible rows to code; and, on that row, indicate the combination solution being discussed, for example, coding on the solution row for "Transfer slow worker," write "1D." Another example: "Pay teams on a piece-rate basis and give them a 10 percent bonus for all production over 75 units." This solution combines the solutions "Piece-rate" and "Bonus." Code on the "Piece-rate" row and write "bonus over 75" to the left of the coding.

It is vital that you indicate combinations accurately, since in our analysis we will treat the data as if you had coded both categories at the same time.

CODER________ GROUP NO.______ PROBLEM________ DATE______ PAGE NO.___

Fast workers help slow
Match jobs, ability (make jobs easier)
Group rotation
Combine groups by position
Use conveyer belt (speed up parts)
Retire slow worker
Fire slow worker
Transfer slow worker (where?)
Hire, transfer in, additional help
Promote slow worker
Exchange foreman (which?)
Fire foreman (which?)
Foreman use positive motivation
Counsel slow worker
Train slow worker
Reprimand slow worker
Put slow worker 1st
Put slow worker last
Put slow worker other ______
Group competition
Bonus
Piece-rate (incentives)
Fringe benefits (specify)
Improve selection procedures
Other

MANUAL FOR CODING CRITERIA ON THE PERSONNEL SELECTION PROBLEM

The present coding system was developed in order to better understand the individual and group norm-forming process in problem-solving discussions. Two objectives will be fulfilled: (1) individual and group norms that underlie solution arguments will be enumerated through an analysis of verbal statements; (2) a record of the norm-formation process through time will be made, although no accurate estimate of the actual time involved is possible.

At this stage of development, all statements made by group participants will be of interest, and most will be coded. Again, it must be emphasized that we are interested in the justifications that group members use in supporting or rejecting task solutions represented by statements that they make.

The coding form has various norms associated with task solutions listed down the left-hand side. The vertical lines divide the page into statement units such that the first statement made with respect to any solution is recorded in the first column on the left and succeeding statements are recorded in successive columns to the right.

A new column is used each time a new person makes a codable statement or the same person starts a new sentence.

Each cell entry is composed of two parts: (1) a number representing the group member who made the statement; (2) a plus or a minus representing support or rejection of a particular norm. Please see the following norm definitions for better understanding of individual norm coding. Remember that one sentence made by a participant may support more than one norm. This will be represented by an appropriate plus or minus in the relevant norm category within the vertical line of cells.

NORM CATEGORIES

1. Has diversity of job experience
2. Has stability of employment
3. Has had depth in past jobs
4. Has had many jobs—other
5. Has an MBA
6. Has a business-marketing undergrad major
7. College attended was "good"
8. Is a younger age
9. Has marital stability
10. Single and would like to, or could, travel on new job

11. Is willing to move and not too established
12. Has a sales-advertising background
13. Has a quantitative background in school or previous jobs
14. Has worked with established product
15. Has management experience
16. Has research experience
17. Has planning experience
18. Has implementing experience
19. Has staff experience
20. Has experience in market entry
21. Has marketing experience—general
22. Has worked with good company
23. Has been promoted
24. Has a military background
25. Is friendly
26. Is a risk taker, is aggressive and outgoing in outside interests

GENERAL NOTES

1. A minus in any category should not be used as a criterion in selecting a candidate.
2. Do not code references to ingenuity, foresight, or marketing capabilities.
3. If "uh-huh" is interpreted as not definitely agreeing with the last speaker's point, code as a question mark (?).
4. Do not code when it is unclear how the criterion is to be used, such as "We can look at age also."
5. Do not code when someone asks about what information is on résumés, such as "Is the age here?"
6. Code agreements as agreeing with the last single valence coded, unless the agreement is clearly referring to more.
7. Do not code statements read directly from résumé, unless a criterion is clearly being supposed.
8. Candidate-justification statements that refer to criteria will be coded as such.
9. Do not code references to "personality," such as "A personality that would indicate ingenuity in marketing or something."
10. Do not code interruptions unless they are clear.
11. Code leading questions, but don't code point-of-information questions.
12. Do not code general mention of company's name.

HAS DIVERSITY OF JOB EXPERIENCE

A plus means that having diverse (variety of functions within a job or jobs) job experience is a criterion for selection; it can also refer to having a balanced set of job experiences, having a range of jobs, having worked with a variety of products. This criterion can also suggest a broad outlook on a job. It is also a means for justifying a candidate with this background.

A minus means that having a diversity of job experience should not be a criterion for selection.

Examples:

> "The only problem is that he hasn't had as much experience as the other people." (+)

> "This guy's been around. He's had a lot of good experience with quite a few companies." (++)

> "I think as broad an exposure as he could have had to marketing techniques might be a more important factor." (+)

STABILITY OF EMPLOYMENT

A plus means that having a stable employment history (having been with a company a length of time implies loyalty) is a criterion for selection. It is also a means for justifying a candidate with this background.

A minus means that having an unstable employment history is a criterion for selection. It is also a means of justifying a candidate with this background.

Examples:

> "He's had five jobs in only five years. What a job hopper." (++)

> "I would be worried that you would get him all trained, and then he'd leave us like the others." (++)

> "I say that besides Sidney Godep, Howard Winston was quite stable because he remained four years, for instance, at Sears." (+)

HAS HAD DEPTH IN PAST JOBS

A plus means that having depth (a good expertise in a job dimension) in past jobs is a criterion for selection. It is also a means for justifying a candidate with this background.

A minus means that a lack of depth should be a criterion for selections, or that having a lack of depth is a means of justifying a candidate with this background.

Example:

"He has a lot of concentrated experience." (+)

HAS HAD MANY JOBS

This category refers to all comments made about the number of past jobs that are unable to be coded into the previous three categories: diversity of job experience, stability of employment, and depth in past jobs.

A plus means that having many jobs in the past is a criterion for selection. It is also a means for justifying a candidate with this background.

A minus means that having few jobs in the past should be a criterion for selection. It is also a means for justifying a candidate with this background.

Examples:

"He's held too many jobs." (-)

"The number of jobs shouldn't be a criterion." (-)

HAS AN MBA

A plus means that having an MBA is a criterion for selection. It is also a means for justifying a candidate with this background.

A minus means that not having an MBA should be a criterion. Not having an MBA is also a means for justifying a candidate with this background.

Examples:

"Well this guy's got his MBA, that's a plus." (+)

"I don't think education makes much difference." (-)

"This guy has a good education." (+)

HAS A BUSINESS-MARKETING UNDERGRAD MAJOR

A plus means that having a business-marketing undergrad major is a criterion for selection. It is also a means for justifying a candidate with this background.

A minus means that having an undergrad major other than business-marketing should be used as a criterion. Having an undergrad major other than business-marketing is also a means for justifying a candidate with this background.

Examples:

"He's had some good marketing experience in school." (+)

"He's only a finance major, and we need marketing." (++)

COLLEGE ATTENDED WAS "GOOD"

A plus means that attending a "good" school is a criterion for selection. It is also a means for justifying a candidate with this background.

A minus means that having attended an "average" school should be used as a criterion. Having attended an "average" school is also a means for justifying a candidate with this background.

Examples:

"Look at this: Stanford, Wharton, good schools." (+)

"I think the Stanford man is our candidate." (+)

IS A YOUNGER AGE

A plus means that being a younger age is a criterion for selection. It is also a means for justifying a candidate with this background.

A minus means that being an older age is a criterion for selection. Being an older age is also a means for justifying a candidate with this background.

Examples:

"I was thinking, I'm wondering if the 34 is better than the 45." (+)

"Godep is pretty old; he's an old man." (+)

HAS MARITAL STABILITY

A plus means that being married implies a stability criterion. It is also a means for justifying a candidate with this background.

A minus means that being married implies an instability criterion. Being married with an implication of instability is also a means for justifying a candidate with this background.

Examples:

"Married, three children. He's got a lot of job stability." (++)

"I think the married guys are more settled down. They'll tend to stay with us." (++)

SINGLE AND WOULD LIKE TO, OR COULD, TRAVEL ON NEW JOB

A plus means that being single, with an implication of wanting to travel or the ability to travel on the job, is a criterion. It is also a means for justifying a candidate with this background.

A minus means that being single, with an implication that travel is not required, is a criterion. It is also a means for justifying a candidate with this background.

Examples:

"A single guy is going to be able to handle this job better because he would be able to travel around." (+)

"A single guy isn't going to be tied down; he would enjoy traveling." (++)

IS WILLING TO MOVE

A plus means that the candidate can travel and would not be too established in job or community. It may also imply that the candidate has a limited outlook on life or his job. It is also a means for rejecting candidates who lack this requirement.

A minus means that the willingness to move shouldn't be a criterion.

Examples:

"Godep is too tied down with five kids." (+)

"This guy has spent all his time in Philadelphia. He won't want to move." (++)

HAS A SALES BACKGROUND

A plus means that having a sales background or an advertising background is a criterion for selection; this implies a person with communication and persuasion skills. Also, the candidate has behavioral science characteristics in his background. It is also a means for justifying a candidate with this background.

A minus means that not having a sales background should be a criterion. Not having a sales background is also a means for justifying a candidate with this background.

Examples:

> "He's done a lot of good selling. Look here, self-positioning." (++)
>
> "Here's a guy that's going to be out with the people. He's also good at talking on his feet, persuasive, I mean." (++)
>
> "Here's some good advertising experience." (+)

HAS A QUANTITATIVE BACKGROUND IN SCHOOL OR PREVIOUS JOBS

A plus means that having a quantitative background (numbers-oriented, statistics-oriented, accounting-oriented, computer-oriented, systems-oriented) is a criterion for selection; the criterion can also suggest that a person's job or school background is too technical. It is also a means for justifying a candidate with this background.

A minus means that having a qualitative or behavioral background should be a criterion. Having a qualitative or behavioral background is also a means for justifying a candidate with this background.

Examples:

> "One thing favorable, I think, is his major thing is, he's done a lot of forecasting, computer work, and that." (++)
>
> "He's a numbers man. All he does is produce the numbers and someone else actually uses them. I don't like that." (---)
>
> "I don't think that accounting would come into it a bit." (-)
>
> "Well, he's done a lot of statistical work in Indiana." (+)
>
> "Now this guy here, this Winston guy, all he's done is analyze." (-)

HAS WORKED WITH ESTABLISHED PRODUCT

A plus means that having worked with an established product is a criterion for selection. It is also a means for justifying a candidate with that background.

A minus means that having experience with a new product should be a criterion. Having experience with a new product is also a means for justifying a candidate with this background.

Examples:

> "Well, he worked with an established product at Kodak, didn't he?" (+)

> "I think that we're dealing with a product already around, you know, one that we don't have to introduce." (++)

HAS MANAGEMENT EXPERIENCE

A plus means that having management experience that may imply responsibility, coordination, and so on should be a criterion for selection. It is also a means for justifying a candidate with this background.

A minus means that having management experience should not be a criterion for selection.

Examples:

> "You gotta get a guy that's original, a guy that can put a plan into action and manage it." (+++)

> "I think line experience would be good. Somebody that actually went out and did something." (++)

> "Well, he's gonna be in charge, number 1, it sounds like it's all up to him." (++)

HAS STAFF EXPERIENCE

A plus means that having staff experience, such as marketing analyst or planning manager, should be a criterion for selection. It is also a means for justifying a candidate with this background.

A minus means that having staff experience should not be a criterion for selection.

Examples:

"He's just an office-type guy." (-)

"He has only assisted other people." (-)

HAS EXPERIENCE IN MARKET ENTRY

A plus means that having prior job experience in introducing a product or market plan to an area should be a criterion. It is also a means for justifying a candidate with this background.

A minus means that having experience in market entry should not be a criterion for selection.

Examples:

"He seems to have had some experience doing, or marketing some products like pet foods into foreign markets." (+)

"I think that taking a product into a new area or market is important." (+)

"He's up there, and he penetrated the market." (+)

"He's also been into a foreign market." (+)

HAS MARKETING EXPERIENCE

A plus means that having general marketing experience is a criterion for selection. It is also a means for justifying a candidate with this background.

A minus means that having experience other than marketing should be a criterion. Having experience in areas other than marketing is also a means for justifying a candidate with this background.

Examples:

"This guy has a good marketing background." (+)

"I think we need to look at someone who has had some type of experience in marketing." (+)

HAS RESEARCH EXPERIENCE

A plus means that having research experience, including any experience referred to as "research analyst" or "analyst," should be a criterion for selection. It is also a means for justifying a candidate with this background.

A minus means that having research experience should not be a criterion for selection.

Examples:

"Until his latest job he had very little contact with any kind of good market research." (+)

"He's only a research analyst. Done that his whole life." (--)

HAS BEEN PROMOTED

A plus means that being promoted should be a criterion for selection. It is also a means for justifying a candidate with this background.

A minus means that not having been promoted should be a criterion for selection. Not having been promoted is also a means for justifying a candidate with this background.

(1) Includes demotions

(2) Satisfactory performance and moving up

Examples:

"He's just making lateral transfers." (+)

"Each of his jobs has been a step up. He's getting somewhere." (++)

"I think it's definitely against this Winston that he's gotten nowhere in a 10-year span." (+)

HAS A MILITARY BACKGROUND

A plus means that having a military background is a criterion for selection. It is also a means for justifying a candidate with this background.

A minus means that not having a military background should be used as a criterion. Not having a military background is also a means for justifying a candidate with this background.

Examples:

"You know, it seems like he's had a lot of responsibility in the Navy." (+)

"I don't know how important military experience is these days." (-)

"He's a big managing man, if you look at his military status." (+)

IS FRIENDLY

A plus means that being friendly may suggest a people orientation or a good personality, and it should be a criterion for selection. It is also a means for justifying a candidate with this background.

A minus means that being friendly should not be a criterion for selection.

Examples:

"He seems to be a friendly-type person, one who could get along with people." (++)

"He likes being around people." (+)

"Was he very social-oriented?" (+)

IS A RISK TAKER, IS AGGRESSIVE AND OUTGOING IN OUTSIDE INTERESTS

A plus means that having active outside interests implies an aggressive and risk-taking criterion. It is also a means for justifying a candidate with this background.

A minus means that having inactive outside interests implies a conservative criterion. It is also a means for justifying a candidate with this background.

Examples:

"I think we should look at their extracurricular activities, because we don't want somebody who only writes short stories." (+)

"This guy looks active—see, stock car racing, traveling." (+++)

"Sailing, snow-mobiling. So he's always moving around. He's always mastering these things." (++++)

HAS PLANNING EXPERIENCE

A plus means that having planning experience or experience in designing plans should be a criterion for selection. It is also a means for justifying a candidate with this background.

A minus means that having planning experience should not be a criterion for selection.

(1) Refers to "development of products" also.

Examples:

"This job requires some type of planning ability." (+)

"Planning or forecasting is important." (+)

"I feel that Tinneman isn't so good at planning." (+)

HAS IMPLEMENTING EXPERIENCE

A plus means that having implementing experience in any phase of business (putting a plan into action, and so on) should be a criterion for selection. It is also a means for justifying a candidate with that background.

A minus means that having implementing experience should not be a criterion for selection.

Examples:

"O'Brien has actually put a plan into action, he's done something." (++)

"The candidate should be able to implement a marketing proposal." (+)

HAS WORKED WITH GOOD COMPANY

A plus means that having worked with a good company, that is, a company with a good reputation, is a criterion for selection. It is also a means for justifying a candidate with this background.

A minus means that having worked for a good company should not be a criterion for selection.

Examples:

"Kodak has a pretty good training program." (+)

"Obviously, if you're a marketing man with Colgate, it might weigh a little bit more than if you're a marketing man at XYZ Company or someplace." (+)

BIBLIOGRAPHY

Anderson, H. H. 1959. "Creativity in Perspective." In Creativity and Its Cultivation, edited by H. H. Anderson. New York: Harpers.

Argyris, C., and D. Schön. 1974. Theory in Practice. San Francisco: Jossey-Bass.

Bales, R. F. 1970. Personality and Interpersonal Behavior. New York: Holt, Rinehart.

______. 1953. "The Equilibrium Problem in Small Groups." In Working Papers in the Theory of Action, edited by T. Parsons, R. F. Bales, and E. A. Shils, pp. 111-61. New York: Free Press.

______. 1950. Interaction Process Analysis: A Method for the Study of Small Groups. Reading, Mass.: Addison-Wesley.

Bales, R. F., and F. L. Strodtbeck. 1951. "Phases in Group Problem Solving." Journal of Abnormal and Social Psychology 46: 485-95.

Bales, R. F., T. Mills, and M. Rosenborough. 1951. "Channels of Communication in Small Groups." American Sociological Review 16: 461-68.

Barnlund, D. C., and F. S. Haiman. 1960. The Dynamics of Discussion. Boston: Houghton Mifflin.

Bartlett, F. 1958. Thinking. New York: Basic Books.

Bass, B. 1961. "Some Aspects of Attempted, Successful, and Effective Leadership." Journal of Applied Psychology 45: 120-22.

Bennett, E. 1955. "Discussion, Decision, Commitment and Consensus in 'Group Decision.'" Human Relations 8: 251-74.

Berger, J., B. P. Cohen, and M. Zelditch, Jr. 1972. "Status Characteristics and Social Interaction." American Sociological Review 37: 241-55.

Berger, J., T. Conner, and M. Fisek. 1974. Expectation States Theory: A Theoretical Research Program. Cambridge, Mass.: Winthrop.

Berkowitz, L. 1956. "Personality and Group Position." Sociometry 19: 210-22.

Bion, W. R. 1959. Experiences in Groups. New York: Basic Books.

Blake, R. R., and Jane S. Mouton. 1961. Group Dynamics—Key to Decision Making. Houston: Gulf.

Block, M. W. 1974. "Member Commitment to Group Decisions: A Study of Individual and Group Determinants." Ph.D. dissertation, University of Chicago.

Bouchard, T. J. 1972. "Training, Motivation, and Personality as Determinants of the Effectiveness of Brainstorming Groups and Individuals." Journal of Applied Psychology 56: 324-31.

Bower, J. L. 1963. "Group Decision Making: An Experimental Study." Ph.D. dissertation, Harvard Business School.

Brehm, J. W. 1966. A Theory of Psychological Reactance. New York: Academic Press.

Bruner, J. A. 1957. "On Perceptual Readiness." Psychological Review 64: 123-52.

Burke, R. J., N. R. F. Maier, and L. R. Hoffman. 1966. "Functions of Hints in Individual Problem-Solving." American Journal of Psychology 79: 389-99.

Carey, Gloria J. 1958. "Sex Differences in Problem-Solving Performance as a Function of Attitude Differences." Journal of Abnormal Social Psychology 56: 256-60.

Chapple, E. D. 1940. "Measuring Human Relations: An Introduction to the Study of the Interaction of Individuals." Genetic Psychological Monographs 22: 1-47.

Coch, L., and J. R. P. French, Jr. 1948. "Overcoming Resistance to Change." Human Relations 1: 512-32.

Cyert, R. M., W. R. Dill, and J. G. March. 1958. "The Role of Expectations in Business Decision Making." Administration Science Quarterly 3: 307-40.

Dalkey, N. C. 1969. The Delphi Method: An Experimental Study of Group Opinion. Santa Monica, Calif.: RAND.

Davis, J. H. 1973. "Group Decision and Social Interaction: A Theory of Social Decision Schemes." Psychological Review 80: 97-125.

Deutsch, M., and H. Gerard. 1955. "A Study of Normative and Informational Social Influence upon Individual Judgement." Journal of Abnormal and Social Psychology 51: 629-36.

Duncan, C. P. 1959. "Recent Research on Human Problem Solving." Psychological Bulletin 56: 397-429.

Duncan, S., Jr., and D. W. Fiske. 1977. Face-to-Face Interaction Research, Methods and Theory. Hillsdale, N.J.: Erlbaum.

Duncker, K. 1945. "On Problem Solving." Psychological Monographs 58, no. 5 (whole no. 270).

Falk, G. 1978. "An Examination of Some Normative Effects on Unanimity and Majority Rules on the Quality of Solutions in Problem Solving Groups with Unequal Power." Ph.D. dissertation, University of Chicago.

Festinger, L. 1957. A Theory of Cognitive Dissonance. Evanston, Ill.: Row-Peterson.

______. 1954. "A Theory of Social Comparison Processes." Human Relations 7: 117-40.

Fisek, M., and R. Ofshe. 1970. "The Process of Status Evolution." Sociometry 33: 327-46.

Fisher, B. A. 1974. Small Group Decision-Making: Communication and the Group Process. New York: McGraw-Hill.

Flavell, J. H., A. Cooper, and R. H. Loiselle. 1958. "Effect of the Number of Pre-Utilization Functions on Functional Fixedness in Problem Solving." Psychological Reports 4: 343-50.

French, J. R. P., Jr., J. Israel, and D. As. 1966. "Participation and the Appraisal System." Human Relations 19: 3-20.

______. 1960. "An Experiment on Participation in a Norwegian Factory: Interpersonal Dimensions of Decision-Making." Human Relations 13: 3-19.

French, J. R. P., Jr., and B. Raven. 1959. "The Bases of Social Power." In Studies in Social Power, edited by D. Cartwright, pp. 150-67. Ann Arbor: Institute for Social Research, University of Michigan.

Goffman, E. 1974. Frame Analysis. New York: Harper and Row.

Greiner, L. 1967. "Patterns of Organizational Change." Harvard Business Review May-June: 119-30.

Hackman, J. R. 1975. "Group Influences on Individuals in Organizations." In Handbook of Industrial and Organizational Psychology, edited by M. D. Dunnette. Chicago: Rand-McNally.

Hackman, J. R., and C. W. Morris. 1975. "Group Tasks, Group Interaction Process and Group Performance Effectiveness." In Advances in Experimental Social Psychology, edited by L. Berkowitz, vol. 8. New York: Academic Press.

Hall, J., and W. H. Watson. 1970. "The Effects of a Normative Intervention on Group Decision-making Performance." Human Relations 23: 299-317.

Hare, A. P. 1978. Handbook of Small Group Research. 2nd ed. New York: Free Press.

Hemphill, J. K., and C. M. Westie. 1950. "The Measurement of Group Dimensions." Journal of Psychology 29: 325-42.

Heyns, R. W., and R. Lippitt. 1954. "Systematic Observational Techniques." In Handbook of Social Psychology, edited by G. Lindzey, pp. 370-44. Reading, Mass.: Addison-Wesley.

Hoffman, L. R. 1965. "Group Problem Solving." In Advances in Experimental Social Psychology, edited by L. Berkowitz, vol. 2, pp. 99-132. New York: Academic Press.

______. 1959. "Homogeneity of Member Personality and Its Effect on Group Problem-Solving." Journal of Abnormal and Social Psychology 58: 27-32.

Hoffman, L. R., R. J. Burke, and N. R. F. Maier. 1965. "Participation, Influence, and Satisfaction among Members of Problem-Solving Groups." Psychological Reports 16: 661-67.

______. 1963. "Does Training with Differential Reinforcement on Similar Problems Help in Solving a New Problem?" Psychological Reports 13: 147-54.

Hoffman, L. R., E. Harburg, and N. R. F. Maier. 1962. "Differences and Disagreement as Factors in Creative Group Problem Solving." Journal of Abnormal and Social Psychology 64: 206-14.

Hoffman, L. R., and N. R. F. Maier. 1966. "Social Factors Influencing Problem Solving in Women." Journal of Personality and Social Psychology 4: 382-90.

______. 1961a. "Quality and Acceptance of Problem Solutions by Members of Homogeneous and Heterogeneous Groups." Journal of Abnormal and Social Psychology 62: 401-07.

______. 1961b. "Sex Differences, Sex Composition, and Group Problem Solving." Journal of Abnormal and Social Psychology 63: 453-56.

______. 1959. "The Use of Group Decision to Resolve a Problem of Fairness." Personnel Psychology 12: 545-59.

Hollander, E. P. 1978. Leadership Dynamics. New York: Free Press.

Holloman, C. R., and H. W. Hendrick. 1972. "Adequacy of Group Decisions as a Function of the Decision Making Process." Academy of Management Journal 15: 175-84.

Humpal, J. J., and L. R. Hoffman. 1979. "Normative Conflict in a Business Setting." Paper given at Eastern Psychological Association, Philadelphia, April.

Jackson, J. M. 1960. "Structural Characteristics of Norms." In National Society for the Study of Education, The Dynamics of Instructional Groups. Chicago: University of Chicago Press.

______. 1959. "Reference Group Processes in a Formal Organization." Sociometry 22: 307-27.

______, and H. D. Saltzstein. 1958. "The Effect of Person-Group Relationships on Conformity Processes." Journal of Abnormal and Social Psychology 57: 17-24.

Janis, I. 1972. Victims of Groupthink. Boston: Houghton Mifflin.

Janis, I. L., and L. Mann. 1977. Decision Making. New York: Free Press.

Jones, M. H. 1957. Executive Decision Making. Homewood, Ill.: Irwin.

Kadane, J., and G. Lewis. 1969. "The Distribution of Participation in Group Discussions: An Empirical and Theoretical Reappraisal." American Sociological Review 34: 710-22.

Katz, D., and R. Kahn. 1978. The Social Psychology of Organizations. 2nd ed. New York: Wiley.

Lewin, K. 1947. "Frontiers in Group Dynamics: Concept, Method, and Reality in Social Science, Social Equilibria and Social Change." Human Relations 1: 3-42.

______. 1935. A Dynamic Theory of Personality. New York: McGraw-Hill.

Likert, R. 1967. The Human Organization: Its Management and Value. New York: McGraw-Hill.

Lorge, I., D. Fox, J. Davitz, and M. Brenner. 1958. "A Survey of Studies Contrasting the Quality of Group Performance and Individual Performance, 1920-1957." Psychological Bulletin 55: 337-72.

Luchins, A. S. 1942. "Mechanization in Problem Solving—the Effect of Einstellung." Psychological Monographs 54: no 6 (whole no. 248).

Luft, J. 1969. Of Human Interaction. 1969. Palo Alto, Calif.: National Press Books.

Maier, N. R. F. 1970. Problem-Solving and Creativity. Belmont, Calif.: Wadsworth.

______. 1963. Problem-Solving Discussions and Conferences: Leadership Methods and Skills. New York: McGraw Hill.

______. 1960. "Maier's Law." American Psychologist 15: 208-12.

______. 1958. The Appraisal Interview: Objectives, Methods and Skills. New York: Wiley.

______. 1953. "An Experimental Test of the Effect of Training on Discussion Leadership." Human Relations 6: 161-73.

______. 1952. Principles of Human Relations. New York: Wiley.

______. 1933. "An Aspect of Human Reasoning." British Journal of Psychology (general section) 24: 144-55.

______. 1931. "Reasoning in Humans. II. The Solution of a Problem and Its Appearance in Consciousness." Journal of Comparative Psychology 12: 181-94.

______. 1930. "Reasoning in Humans. I. On Direction." Journal of Comparative Psychology 10: 115-43.

______, and L. R. Hoffman. 1965. "Acceptance and Quality of Solutions as Related to Leaders' Attitudes toward Disagreement in Group Problem-Solving." Journal of Applied Behavioral Science 1: 373-85.

______. 1961. "Organization and Creative Problem Solving." Journal of Applied Psychology 45: 277-80.

______. 1960a. "Using Trained 'Developmental' Discussion Leaders to Improve Further the Quality of Group Decisions." Journal of Applied Psychology 44: 247-51.

______. 1960b. "Quality of First and Second Solutions in Group Problem Solving." Journal of Applied Psychology 44: 278-83.

Maier, N. R. F., and A. R. Solem. 1962. "Improving Solutions by Turning Choice Situations into Problems." Personnel Psychology 15: 151-57.

______. 1952. "The Contribution of a Discussion Leader to the Quality of Group Thinking: The Effective Use of Minority Opinions." Human Relations 5: 277-88.

______, and A. Maier. 1957. Supervisory and Executive Development. New York: Wiley.

Maltzman, I., W. Bogartz, and L. Breger. 1958. "A Procedure for Increasing Word Association Originality and Its Transfer Effects." Journal of Experimental Psychology 56: 392-98.

Maltzman, I., L. O. Brooks, W. Bogartz, and S. S. Summers. 1958. "The Facilitation of Problem-Solving by Prior Exposure to Uncommon Responses." Journal of Experimental Psychology 56: 399-406.

Maltzman, I., S. Simon, D. Raskin, and R. Licht. 1960. "Experimental Studies in the Training of Originality." Psychological Monographs 74: no. 6 (whole no. 493).

Mann, R. D. 1961. "Dimensions of Individual Performance in Small Groups under Task and Social-Emotional Conditions." Journal of Abnormal and Social Psychology 62: 674-82.

______. 1959. "A Review of the Relationships between Personality and Performance in Small Groups." Psychological Bulletin 56: 241-70.

March, J. G. 1956. "Influence Measurement in Experimental and Semi-Experimental Groups." Sociometry: 260-71.

Marquis, D. G., H. Guetzkow, and R. W. Heyns. 1951. "A Social Psychological Study of the Decision-Making Conference. In Groups, Leadership and Men, edited by H. Guetzkow, pp. 55-67. Pittsburgh: Carnegie Press.

Miller, G. A. 1956. "The Magical Number Seven, Plus or Minus Two." Psychological Review 63: 81-97.

Milton, G. A. 1958. "Five Studies of the Relation between Sex-Role Identification and Achievement in Problem Solving." Technical Report no. 3. New Haven: Departments of Industrial Administration and Psychology, Yale University.

Newell, A., and H. A. Simon. 1972. Human Problem Solving. Englewood Cliffs, N.J.: Prentice-Hall.

Orne, M. T. 1962. "On the Social Psychology of the Psychological Experiment: With Particular Reference to Demand Characteristics and Their Implications." American Psychologist 17: 776-83.

Osborn, A. F. 1957. Applied Imagination. Rev. ed. New York: Scribner's.

Osgood, C. E., G. J. Suci, and P. H. Tannenbaum. 1957. The Measurement of Meaning. Urbana: University of Illinois Press.

Peak, H. 1958. "Psychological Structure and Psychological Activity." Psychological Review 65: 325-47.

______, ed. 1955. "Attitude and Motivation in M. R. Jones." In Nebraska Symposium on Motivation, 1955. Lincoln: University of Nebraska Press.

Pepinsky, P., J. K. Hemphill, and R. N. Shevitz. 1958. "Attempts to Lead, Group Productivity, and Morale under Conditions of Acceptance and Rejection." Journal of Abnormal and Social Psychology 57: 47-54.

Reynolds, P. 1971. "Comment on 'The Distribution of Participation in Group Discussions' as Related to Group Size." American Sociological Review 36: 704-06.

Riecken, H. W. 1958. "The Effect of Talkativeness on Ability to Influence Group Solutions of Problems." Sociometry 21: 309-21.

Rokeach, M. 1960. The Open and Closed Mind. New York: Basic Books.

Rosenberg, M. J. 1969. "The Conditions and Consequences of Evaluation Apprehension." In Artifact in Behavioral Research, edited by R. Rosenthal and R. L. Rosnow, pp. 279-349. New York: Academic Press.

______. 1960. "An Analysis of Affective-Cognitive Consistency." In M. J. Rosenberg, C. I. Hovland, W. J. McGuire, R. P. Abelson, and J. W. Brehm, Attitude Organization and Change: An Analysis of Consistency among Attitude Components, pp. 15-64. New Haven: Yale University Press.

Schachter, S. 1951. "Deviation, Rejection, and Communication." Journal of Abnormal and Social Psychology 46: 190-207.

Schachter, S., N. Ellertson, D. McBride, and D. Gregory. 1951. "An Experimental Study of Cohesiveness and Productivity." Human Relations 4: 229-38.

Schanck, R. L. 1932. "A Study of a Community and Its Groups and Institutions Conceived of as Behavior of Individuals." Psychological Monographs 43 (2).

Schutz, W. C. 1958. Firo: A Three Dimensional Theory of Interpersonal Behavior. New York: Rinehart.

Seashore, S. 1954. Group Cohesiveness in the Industrial Work Group. Ann Arbor: Institute for Social Research.

Shaw, D. M. 1960. "Size of Share in Task and Motivation in Work Groups." Sociometry 23: 203-08.

Sherif, M., and C. W. Sherif. 1969. Social Psychology. New York: Harper and Row.

Simon, H. A. 1956. "Rational Choice and the Structure of the Environment." Psychological Review 63: 129-38.

______. 1955. "A Behavioral Model of Rational Choice." Quarterly Journal of Economics 69: 174-84.

Simpson, G. G. 1960. "The World into Which Darwin Led Us." Science 131: 966-74.

Stein, R. T., L. R. Hoffman, S. J. Cooley, and R. W. Pearse. 1979. "Leadership Valence: Modeling and Measuring the Process of Emergent Leadership." In Crosscurrents in Leadership, edited by J. G. Hunt and L. L. Larson, Leadership Symposium Series, vol. 5. Carbondale: Southern Illinois University Press.

Steiner, I. D. 1972. Group Processes and Productivity. New York: Academic Press.

Stephan, F., and E. Mishler. 1952. "The Distribution of Participation in Small Groups: An Exponential Approximation." American Sociological Review 17: 598-608.

Stevens, S. S. 1951. "Mathematics, Measurement, and Psychophysics." In Handbook of Experimental Psychology, edited by S. S. Stevens, pp. 1-49. New York: Wiley.

Strodtbeck, F. L. 1951. "Husband-Wife Interaction over Revealed Differences." American Sociological Review 16: 468-73.

Thibaut, J. W., and H. H. Kelley. 1961. The Social Psychology of Groups. New York: Wiley.

Thomas, E. J., and C. F. Fink. 1961. "Models of Group Problem Solving." Journal of Abnormal and Social Psychology 68: 53-63.

Thompson, J., and A. Tuden. 1959. "Strategies, Structures, and Processes of Organizational Decisions." In Comparative Studies in Administration, edited by J. D. Thompson et al., pp. 195-216. Pittsburgh: University of Pittsburgh Press.

Torrance, E. P. 1955. "Some Consequences of Power Differences on Decision Making in Permanent and Temporary Three-Man Groups." In Small Groups: Studies in Social Interaction, edited by A. P. Hare, E. F. Borgatta, and R. F. Bales, pp. 482-92. New York: Knopf.

Tuckman, B. W. 1965. "Developmental Sequence in Small Groups." Psychological Bulletin 63: 384-99.

Vroom, V. H. 1960. Some Personality Determinants of the Effects of Participation. Englewood Cliffs, N.J.: Prentice-Hall.

Vroom, V. H., and P. W. Yetton. 1973. Leadership and Decision-Making. Pittsburgh: University of Pittsburgh Press.

Wertheimer, M. 1945. Productive Thinking. New York: Harper.

Willard, D., and F. L. Strodtbeck. 1972. "Latency of Verbal Response and Participation in Small Groups." Sociometry 35: 161-75.

Wright, P., and F. Barbour. 1977. "Phased Decision Strategies: Sequels to an Initial Screening." In Tims Studies in the Managerial Sciences, vol. 6, pp. 91-109. North Holland.

NAME INDEX

SUBJECT INDEX

BIOGRAPHICAL SKETCHES

L. RICHARD HOFFMAN is professor of psychology in the Graduate School of Business and in the Committee on Social and Organizational Psychology of the University of Chicago. He received his Ph.D. degree in industrial/organizational psychology from the University of Michigan, where he later taught and directed the I/O Program.

His publications include coauthorship of _Automation and the Worker_ (1960) and of _Superior-Subordinate Communication in Management_ (1961). In addition he has written numerous articles reporting research on automation, organizational structure, individual problem solving, interviewing, training, organization, leadership, and group problem solving.

Dr. Hoffman has consulted with a number of companies on problems of selection, training, management, employee morale, and consumer preferences. He also has spoken to many industrial and government executive groups on the application of psychology to organizational functioning.

His current research interests are centered on the elaboration of the hierarchical model of group problem solving described in this book. The model is designed to move the study of decision-making groups from laboratory settings to organizational contexts, where the character of the problems to be solved is typically more ambiguous and the solutions of more importance to the group members.

MYRON BLOCK received his Ph.D. from the Graduate School of Business of the University of Chicago in 1974. Following a period of teaching at Northwestern University's Graduate School of Management, he has consulted on a variety of organizational problems and is currently manager of organizational development for the American Bar Association.

GARY BOND received his Ph.D. in social psychology from the University of Chicago in 1975. His dissertation on norms in therapy groups served as prelude to his current role as project director on the analysis of self-help groups. He is assistant professor in Northwestern University's Medical School.

RONALD BURKE is professor in York University's Faculty of Administrative Studies. After receiving his Ph.D. in industrial/organizational psychology from the University of Michigan, he taught at the universities of Minnesota and British Columbia before taking his present position. He has published extensively on topics including individual problem solving, superior-subordinate relations, and helping relationships and stress in organizations.

MOLLY MOONEY CLARK is a Ph.D. candidate in the Behavioral Science Department of the University of Chicago.

GARY COLEITE was a graduate student in psychology at the University of Michigan at the time he conducted the study reported here.

GIDEON FALK is assistant professor in the College of Business Administration of the University of Illinois at Chicago Circle after several years of teaching at Governors State University. His interests in decision making in organizations led him to his dissertation on the effects of decision rules on group problem solving, which he did in the Graduate School of Business at the University of Chicago.

KENNETH FRIEND left the Graduate School of Business of the University of Chicago to become assistant professor of organizational behavior at Clarkson College's School of Management. His research interests, besides group problem solving, include coalition formation and the reduction of work-related stress. He received his Ph.D. in psychology from Carnegie-Mellon University.

NORMAN R. F. MAIER was one of America's outstanding psychologists for almost half a century. His contributions to the fields of neuropsychology, comparative psychology, learning, problem solving, and frustration had earned him an international reputation (including the AAAS Distinguished Science Award in 1939) before he began his work in social and industrial/organizational psychology, on which he spent most of his last 30 years. His numerous books reflect this diversity of interests and competence: *Problem-Solving Discussions and Conferences*, *Psychology of Industrial Organizations*, *The Appraisal Interview*, *Principles of Comparative Psychology* (with T. C. Schneirla), *Frustration: The Study of Behavior without a Goal*.

RORY O'DAY is professor of social work at Dalhousie University, where he is studying the role of the therapist in group therapy. After receiving his Ph.D. in psychology from the University of Michigan, he taught at the universities of British Columbia and Waterloo.

DATE DUE